LONESOME LUKE'S LIVELY LIFE

HAL ROACH, HAROLD LLOYD AND THE ROLIN FILM CO.

STEVE MASSA

Split Reel
Culpeper, Virginia
2025

Lonesome Luke's Lively Life:
Hal Roach, Harold Lloyd and the Rolin Film Co.

© 2025 Steve Massa.

All Rights Reserved.

All photographs courtesy of Suzanne Lloyd and Richard Simonton Jr. unless otherwise noted.

Published in the United States by:

Split Reel
P.O. Box 946
Culpeper, VA 22701
split-reel.com
info@split-reel.com

Cover design by Marlene Weisman

ISBN 978-1-964384-04-7 (Paperback)
ISBN 978-1-964384-05-4 (Hardcover)

To Serge Bromberg,

the "silent film Sherlock Holmes," whose boundless enthusiasm, amazing finds,

and unlimited generosity have made an indelible mark on film preservation of

both the 20th and 21st Centuries. I'm lucky and proud to have him as a colleague,

and even more so as a friend.

Harold investigates suspicious looking ankles in 1916's *Luke Locates the Loot.*

TABLE OF CONTENTS

Harold co-ordinates the musical disabilities of Charles Stevenson, Billy Fay, Dee Lampton, Snub Pollard and Earl Mohan in 1916's *Luke Pipes the Pippins*.

FOREWORD BY
SUZANNE LLOYD

Harold and Bebe receive Bud Jamison's blessing in *Luke Wins Ye Ladye Faire* (1916).

My name is Suzanne Lloyd and I'm Harold Lloyd's granddaughter (and also the granddaughter of Mildred Davis, Harold's leading lady and lovely wife).

I have had the privilege and great pleasure to represent my grandfather's films for fifty years. I love introducing him to new audiences all over the world. Harold can light up a screen and take you on a wonderful heartfelt journey that most people will enjoy, and hopefully become fans of his treasured films.

Harold made over two hundred films during his career – starting in 1913 as an extra, and then the next year with the humble one-reelers detailed in this book. Entering the motion picture industry on the bottom rung he persevered and learned, and like his character in 1923's *Safety Last* climbed to the top of the Hollywood hierarchy.

Steve Massa has taken a very deep study on what really made Harold …Harold Lloyd. In these earliest films, Harold learned all aspects of the film industry. His brief time at the Mack Sennett studio taught him comedy production - how a studio ran at a quick pace. Being an actor he learned how to work a camera to his advantage. At the same time, he learned production of movies, how to work with distributors and theatre owners, and what sold audiences to come back and see him again on the silver screen. His early one-reelers led to two-reelers, then three-reelers, and finally features – silent and sound.

Another important element of his early success was a beautiful young actress who had been in films for Selig, Pathé, and Vitagraph – Bebe Daniels, who by the way was Harold's first young love. Of course, her mother came along as an actress and a costumer at the Rolin company. Harold was always looking for complete collaboration with his team and crew at the studio. This was a major point I believe in his success.

Harold would be proud that his legacy lives on. As his special Academy Award said he was indeed a "master comedian," and his glorious body of work helped define motion picture comedy.

MEMORIES OF HAROLD
BY RICHARD SIMONTON, JR.

Bebe Daniels, Harold, and Mae White have dramatic reactions to Dee Lampton's honky
bulb horn in *Luke's Society Mix-Up* (1916).

Harold Lloyd was unknown to my generation. When I tried to discuss his movies with my friends, they returned blank stares and changed the subject. But I was raised with an advantage: Harold and my father were best friends and met for lunch once a week when not traveling, and they traveled a lot. In late September, 1964, I went to New York with my father when Harold happened to be there, too, also with business meetings to attend. But Harold took a day off and met me at Radio City Music Hall to see *Mary Poppins*, the Disney film that had just opened, and no one ever enjoyed it more than he did. I divided my attention between watching the screen and Harold's delighted face.

On that same trip, Harold was a guest on *The Tonight Show* and I was in the audience. Buddy Hackett was brilliantly funny as the main guest. An actress named Ina Balin was also a guest, but Buddy continued to provide the entertainment. At one point, Ms. Balin's long skirt fell open displaying very appealing crossed legs, but Buddy kept going until the distraction proved too much and he said, "Put those away." That was the biggest laugh of the evening. When Harold came out, he told her she could keep them there, that it was just fine. No, it wasn't funny, but Harold soon won the admiration of all, without the need of words.

Johnny Carson welcomed Harold to the show with only a few minutes remaining, and no idea of what to talk about, so they showed three minutes of film--a preview of *Harold Lloyd's Funny Side of Life*-- which was all Harold could find in New York to bring on short notice. Well, the audience loved it, Johnny was blown away, and Buddy respectfully kept his mouth shut. Seeing Harold in action was all it took to win them as fans. The show ended as Johnny got a promise that Harold would come back soon which, sadly, never happened, and the episode does not exist.

Several years before that New York trip, we had begun running Harold's movies in our home theatre in North Hollywood, with live accompaniment by Gaylord Carter on our Wurlitzer pipe organ, as was the standard for film music in the 1920s. In fact, Harold had recommended Gaylord to Sid Grauman for his Million Dollar Theatre on Broadway in Los Angeles in 1926. Harold offered us *Safety Last!* and *The Freshman* to show, but my father insisted on *The Kid Brother*. Always *The Kid Brother*, and to Harold that film had been a disappointment. But after a few showings, with standing ovations for Harold at each, he began to appreciate it. Some film scholars consider it one of the most perfectly-constructed silent movies of all, and I think so, too.

Harold was particularly fond of *Grandma's Boy*, and insisted it was his first feature, because it is the first in five reels. It became a huge success, and a milestone on his journey from the Lonesome Luke films starting in 1915, and overlapping with what he called his "Glass Character" films in 1917. I asked Harold if Glass implied anything more, but he replied that it simply meant Glasses, which is the way most people say it anyway.

We used to sit and talk to Harold in his dressing room early mornings, with him in his bathrobe, sitting in his green chair, and with us sitting on the floor handing him "stills" from his movies to discuss and reminisce about. "Us" were Rich Correll and Dave Nowell, who were maintaining his film collection, airing out the nitrate fumes and discarding any decomposition, while I was there raiding his vast photo collection. I would take a handful of 8x10 negatives to print, then return the following week to hand them one at a time to Harold. His life had been so full, that he could not always remember everyone's names, particularly in the early Lonesome Luke photos, and the things he recalled were often as if glimpses into past lives. It feels like that to me now.

Harold's granddaughter, Suzanne, when not in school, was listening to Harold with us or helping to wind nitrate film to air it, and much of his present fame and acclaim, and our opportunities to see his films on discs or in theaters, can be traced to her efforts to save and promote them, her lifetime of dedication. And now there's her Official Harold Lloyd Facebook page, with photos every day.

In conclusion, I wonder whether any other movie star's career could possibly be as fully documented as Harold's, with credit to his proud and devoted father, Foxy, who filled scrapbooks with Harold's movie photos and ads from his earliest films. And I am deeply grateful to Steve Massa for this thoroughly researched and fascinating travel guide to that exciting time when a film completed in a week meant $50 in Harold's pocket.

INTRODUCTION AND ACKNOWLEDGEMENTS

Luke's in over his head as usual in *Giving Them Fits* (1915).

This is a book that Harold Lloyd would not have enjoyed. Being a perfectionist, he went out of his way to not talk about and dismiss his *Lonesome Luke* films. Or as he said in his autobiography *An American Comedy* – "I do not like to recall it, and I am sorry that it is necessary to exhume it for this autopsy."

When you see the *Luke* shorts today (not an easy task) you see Harold in the process of learning how to be funny. Back in 1989 I first saw Kevin Brownlow and David Gill's documentary *Harold Lloyd: The Third Genius*, and was puzzled by this statement from producer Hal Roach:

> Harold Lloyd was not a comedian.... but he was the best actor
> to act the part of a comedian of any person I ever saw.

When Roach began producing independent films in 1914, Harold was the first person he hired, and as the company needed a lead comedian he became one by default. Having focused on and trained to be a dramatic performer, Harold suddenly had to shift gears and become a comic. I think this is what Roach meant when he said that Lloyd wasn't a comedian – he had to play the comedian in their first films. But with amazing determination he set out to become skilled and learn all that he could, and ended up as one of the greatest comedy creators of the silent era.

In the teens there were a ton of little fly-by-night independent companies which organized, cranked out a few shorts, and folded in record time. The Rolin Company could have been one of them, but unlike the many others, Roach, Lloyd and company did something right. This book is an exploration to see why they thrived, and eventually became film comedy institutions.

The importance of Lonesome Luke's success can't be minimized – without it the fledgling Rolin Studio wouldn't have survived, and without it not only would there be no mature Harold Lloyd films, but also no Our Gang, Charley Chase, Max Davidson, or Laurel & Hardy. We'd be left with an immeasurable hole in the comedy films of the 1920s, 1930s and 1940s.

This book really began in 1979. At that point I hadn't seen many of the Lloyd films – I think only *I'm On My Way* (1919) and *Haunted Spooks* (1920) in the versions put out by Blackhawk Films. Already being a silent comedy nut, I had seen plenty of Chaplin, Keaton, and Laurel & Hardy, but Harold's films weren't really around. I had even seen more Larry Semon comedies.

This changed when I found out that a New Jersey PBS station was showing the half an hour series *Harold Lloyd's World of Comedy* (the same title used for Lloyd's 1962 compilation feature and Edward Cahn's 1964 book on Harold). Once a week, one of the twenty-six episodes would air, and since most New Yorkers still didn't have cable, I would spend the half hour before the program adjusting and fiddling with my TV's rabbit ear antennas to get the least snowy image possible.

Each episode would consist of a condensed short, bolstered by clips from other shorts and features. There was no information given about the films, as Henry Corden's Pete Smith-like narration was made up of exclamations like "Uh-oh. Look Out Harold!" The show opened with the bouncy title song *Hooray for Harold Lloyd*, which still lives in the back of the heads of many silent comedy buffs.

While perhaps not the archival way to see Harold's films – they worked. Although unidentified, I was able to figure out which shorts were shown thanks to the synopsis provided in Adam Reilly's *Harold Lloyd: The King of Daredevil Comedy*. Harold's personality and comedy came across strongly, and not only had me looking forward to the next week's episode, but made me more than ready to see the features when they really began circulating again in the 1980s.

An Eastern Westerner (1920) was one of the great shorts that I saw for the first time on TV's *Harold Lloyd's World of Comedy*.

The next twenty years saw me catch up on the Lloyd films, and come to appreciate his skills as a comedy creator and constructionist. But the *Lonesome Luke* comedies were still elusive. Outside of well-worn prints of *Luke's Movie Muddle* and *Luke Joins the Navy* (both 1916) there was little available. In 2009 Ben Model, Ron Magliozzi and I embarked on programming a regular series of silent comedies at New York's The Museum of Modern Art. With the title of *Cruel and Unusual Comedy* we used MoMA's vast collection of films to illustrate the unruly, unpretentious, and anarchic aspects of the genre. Luckily MoMA has a lot of early Lloyd in their holdings, so we were able to program and screen *Just Nuts* (1915), *Luke and the Bang-Tails*, *Luke's Shattered Sleep* (both 1916), *Lonesome Luke on Tin Can Alley*, and *Lonesome Luke's Wild Women* (both 1917).

Since then, thanks to other archival sources, I've been able to catch up with *Tinkering with Trouble*, *Peculiar Patient Pranks* (both 1915), *Luke, the Candy Cut-Up*, *Luke Does the Midway* (both 1916), *Lonesome Luke's Lively Life*,

Lonesome Luke, Messenger, and *Clubs are Trump* (all 1917). There's a handful of others scattered at various archives, but it comes to about twenty-one known survivors out of the sixty-seven made.

Very little serious examination has been given to Harold and Hal's earliest days in the movies. Usually the same few points are touched on as the writers rush to get to the point where Harold puts on his first pair of horn rims. Part of this comes from the fact that the pair of them weren't backward looking people – even late in life they were thinking ahead, talking of their current projects and what their next would be. Practically all of the very first films are missing, and we don't even have a complete list of titles. But there is quite a bit of info out there, and my idea for this book was to gather up as much of it as possible before the passage of time makes certain links even more cloudy and obscure.

As a janitor Luke has gotten shown the door in a scan from the only known surviving copy of *Tinkering with Trouble* (1915). *Courtesy of Peter Bagrov.*

Also important was to give a picture and feeling of what early Hollywood was like - to show what the two fledglings were up against, which makes their rise up the cinematic ladder more stunning. Besides the particulars on Harold and Hal, background is given on the life and difficulties of being a Hollywood extra, the catch-as-catch-can style of making comedy shorts, and the dangers and pitfalls of dealing with shady independent distributors like Sawyer, Inc. and the United Film Service. Portraits are drawn of important collaborators such as Dwight Whiting, Pathé, Fred Newmeyer, Gilbert Pratt and James A. Crosby, in addition to the numerous supporting players. Some such as Bud Jamison, James T. Kelly, and Gus Leonard became dependable regulars in the general fabric of the silent comedy universe. Others, which include A. H. Frahlich, May Cloy, Winna Brown, Ben Corday, Nina Speight, and Fred Jefferson have been forgotten. Many are being profiled here for the first time.

One Rolin performer has remained frustratingly elusive:

> Rose Mendel has been engaged to play character parts.
>
> *Motion Picture News*, January 1, 1916

In this scene from *Luke Pipes the Pippins* (1916) could the woman on the right of Gene Marsh and Harold be the elusive Rose Mendel?

Mendel was a vaudeville performer who was busy in burlesque musical shows such as *Man from Mars*, which toured San Francisco and the West Coast theatre circuits. She was the wife and stage partner of Jules Mendel, a German dialect comic who became a regular supporting player in the Hal Roach shorts of the 1920s. Never able to find an image of her, I suspect that she's the long and lanky character actress that appears prominently in photos for titles like *Luke and the Rural Roughnecks* and *Luke Pipes the Pippins* (both 1916). Like the actress in the photos, Ms. Mendel's name disappears from the theatrical trade papers in the late Teens. Rose seems to have dropped out of show business, and was replaced in the stage act, and as Mrs. Mendel, by Teddy La Due.

There are so many people to thank – so many good friends and colleagues who love silent comedy and have shared information and films over the years – that it's hard to know where to begin.

First, I'd like to thank Suzanne Lloyd and Richard Simonton Jr. for all their generosity and encouragement. Their insights and memories of Harold, full of love and admiration, gave me a strong link to his strength of character and determination. They also made Harold's incredible collection of photographs available to me. Unless otherwise noted, this accounts for the majority of images included. Revealing and evocative, they were my initial inspiration, and tell so much of the story on their own. I only hope my prose can do a little justice to their clarity and beauty. I'm honored to have had Suzanne and Richard's trust in me to tell the amazing story of Harold and Hal's beginning in the film industry.

For encouragement, guidance, and inspiration I'm indebted to Serge Bromberg, Kevin Brownlow, Sam Gill, Elif Rongen-Kaynakci, Dave Kehr, Mike Mashon, Ben Model, Rob Stone and Brent Walker. The generosity of Robert Arkus, Michael Aus, Peter Bagrov, John Bengston, Christopher Bird, Serge Bromberg, Bruce Calvert, David Denton, Rob Farr, Jorge Finkielman, Sam Gill, Dave Glass, Michael J. Hayde, Dave Lord Heath, Junko Iio, Elif Rongen-Kaynakci, Dave Kehr, Jim Kerkhoff, Crystal Kui, James Layton, Ron Magliozzi, Mike Mashon, Bruno Mestdagh, Glenn Mitchell, Ben Model, Tom Reeder, Uli Ruedel, Rob Stone, Ashley Swinnerton, Jack Taylor, Frank Thompson, Brent Walker, Richard Ward and Jay Weissberg for sharing information, films, photos, and other materials has been overwhelming and impossible to ever repay.

Special thanks goes to Rob Stone for not only publishing this book, but for access to his research in the Hal Roach Production Files at USC. Likewise that of Rob Farr, Joe Moore, and Richard Ward. I'm also indebted to the authors who have written about Lloyd and Roach in the past – Wesley W. Stout, William Cahn, William K. Everson, Richard Schickel, Adam Reilly, Tom Dardis, Annette D'Agostino Lloyd, John Bengston, Richard M. Roberts, Jeffrey Vance, Suzanne Lloyd, Craig Calman, and of course Harold himself in his honest and detailed 1928 autobiography *An American Comedy*.

It would have been impossible for me to have done this project without the collaboration of two extremely talented people – Robert Arkus and Marlene Weisman. Rob's critical input was overseeing the transferring and tweaking of this book's images, just as he's done on my previous books. His superb eye, great ideas, and untiring work made this volume possible. As she did on *Slapstick Divas*, *Rediscovering Roscoe* and *Lame Brains and Lunatics 2*, Marlene designed and executed this wonderful cover. I couldn't wait to see what she would come up with as her images are always striking – harkening back to the silent era, but at the same time modern and edgy. The results, as always, were fantastic.

During the shooting of *Hoot Mon* (1919), Hal Roach, Stan Laurel and company welcome Pathé Board of Directors members Fred Quimby (center holding straw hat) and Paul Brunet (center with moustache). *Courtesy of Serge Bromberg.*

In addition to everyone mentioned above there are the friends, fellow researchers, and film lovers Mike Abadi, Mana Allen, Norbert Aping, Lisa Bradbury, Neil Brand, Geoff Brown, David Callahan, Michael Campino,

Philip Carli, Thomas Christensen, Rachel Del Gaudio, Kim Deitch, Dennis Doros, David Eickemeyer, Shane Fleming, Valario Greco, Bob Greenberg, Lisa Stein Haven, Mike Hawks, Geraldine Hawkins, Mark Heller, Tommy Hicks, Nelson Hughes, Pamela Hutchinson, Mark Johnson, Rob King, Robert James Kiss, Richard Koszarski, Ron Magliozzi, Leonard Maltin, Jon Mirsalis, Molly Model, Joe Moore, Jenny Paxon, Jack Roth, Cynthia Rowell, Steve Rydzewski, Jeni Rymer, Frank Scheide, Lynanne Schweighhofer, Zoran Sinobad, Randy Skretvedt, Larry Smith, Melinda Solan, Yair Solan, Tommy Stathes, David Stenn, Cathy Suroweic, Karl Tiedemann, Lee Tsiantis, Ed Watz, George Willeman, Peter Williamson, Steve Winer, Matt Vogul, and Steve Zalusky.

Sadly no longer here to receive my thanks are Robert S. Birchard, Eileen Bowser, William K. Everson, Donna Hill, Ron Hutchinson, Cole Johnson, Jay Leyda, Madeline Matz, Michael Schlesinger, Rick Sheckman, David Shepard, Linda Shah, Charles Silver, Marilyn Slater, Bill Weber, David Wyatt, and Joseph Yranski, but I'm still benefiting from their influence and am grateful to have known them. With each new book this list unfortunately gets longer.

As far as archives, libraries, and research facilities I must first thank my colleagues in the Billy Rose Theatre Division at the New York Public Library for the Performing Arts at Lincoln Center, especially Jeremy MeGraw, Charlie Morrow, and Doug Reside. I also want to give thanks to:

Roach Studio party circa 1918. Among the attendees are (back to front) Frank Lloyd, Harold Lloyd, Charley Chase, Gus Leonard, Mae Laurel, Sammy Brooks, Snub Pollard, Stan Laurel, James Parrott, Dee Lampton, Beatrice La Plante, Dorothy Vernon, Helen Gilmore, Marie Mosquini, Bebe Daniels, Ethel Teare, Estelle Harrison, and Harry Burns.

The Museum of Modern Art: Dave Kehr, James Layton, Ron Magliozzi, Rajendra Roy, Cara Shatzman, Josh Siegel, Ashley Swinnerton, Katie Trainor, and Peter Williamson. The Library of Congress: Mike Mashon, Lynanne Schweighofer, Zoran Sinobad, Rob Stone, and George Willeman. EYE Filmmuseum, Netherlands: Catherine Corman, Rixt Jonkman, Elif Rongen-Kaynakci, Marlene Labst, Mark Paul Meyer, Dorette Schootemeijer, and Frederique Urlings. George Eastman Museum: Anthony L'Abbate, Peter Bagrov, Jared Case, and Nancy Kaufman. Royal Film Archive of Belgium – CINEMATEK: Bruno Mestdagh. UCLA Film and Television Archive: Allison Francis, Meg de Waal.

Thank you to Rob Stone, Split Reel, Michael J. Hayde, and the Al Joy Fan Club (East Coast chapter) for the opportunity to make this volume a reality.

My most important thank you goes to my very patient family – my wife Susan Selig, and my son and daughter-in-law David Massa and Grace Huntley, who have always put up with and supported my silent comedy obsession. Without their love and encouragement this study wouldn't have been possible.

Harold listens to the piano as Jim Mason fiddles, and Robert Z. Leonard broods in the foreground in the Rex short *When Fate Disposes* (1914). *Courtesy of Robert James Kiss.*

This book is made possible through the generous support
of the following Kickstarter backers:

Erik Andersson, Rob Arkus, Dan Atwell, Benita Auge, Michael Aus, Pete
Bainbridge, Matthew Michael Barry, Andreas Baum, Bianca Baynum, Andreas
Benz, Terry Berman, Deborah Birkey, Shane Bliss, Brian R. Boisvert, Wilson J.
Bowlby, Brett Bradford, Bruce Calvert, Kyle & Candace Borcz, Michael Richard
Catlin, Richard & Karla Chamberlain, Eric Cohen, Frank Commins, Kenneth
Cone, C. James Cook, Volker Cremers, Jerome A. Dennis, David Denton, Ben
Dutton, Curtis B. Edmundson, David Eickemeyer, Simon Falk, The Fritz Family,
William Ferry, Frank Flood, Colin Foster, Nile Joseph Fraschetti, Ray Frieders, S
Frost, Michiel Geurtse, Joe Gillis, Dave Glass, Samantha Glasser, Kari Glödstaf,
Barbara Goldman, Ana Igareta Gómez, Rowby Goren (Rowby.com), David
Greenberg, Tim Greer, Lisa Stein Haven, P. David Hawksworth, Asher and Hazel,
H Hewitt, Steven Higgins, Jeff Hinkelman, Harry Hoppe (Laurel & Hardy Archive),
Damien HUON, Junko Iio, Fred W Johnson, Warren Johnson, Daniel W. Jolley,
John Michael Jones, Gideon Jones-Davies, Linda Keenan, Jennifer Keenan, Jim
Kerkhoff, Larry Sean Kinder, Kirk S. King, Jason Kinsey, René Klammer, Tetiana
Kocherhan, Robert Krajeski, Brad Kurtzberg, Ronald Larimore, Dr. Robert Lawlor,
Peter W.Y. Lee, Robert Lipton, Kerr Lockhart, Elizabeth Lynch, Kally
Mavromatis, Agnes B McFadden, don't list me, James Michielli, Stewart Milakovic,
Ben Model, Daniel Mollise, Shawn D. Moore, Joe Moore, Irv Mouallem, Paul R.
Murphy, Jeffrey "Duckie" Nelson, John R Nelson, Darren Nemeth, Rocco Nigro,
Steven Nordhougen, R Ogden, Karen Owen, Geoffrey Palmer, Ron Pesch, R
Michael Pyle, Alexander Rannie, Thomas Reeder, Jim Reid, Kevin Rollason,
Steven E. Rowe, Jay Rozgonyi, Benjamin Ruder, Uli Ruedel, David W. Sanderson,
Julienette Sararose, Suzanne Scherrer, Florian Schiffmann, Mike Schott, George B
Schramm III, Susan Selig, Ivan G. Shreve, Jr., Scott Montgomery Sidner, Robert
Siwczyk, Robert E. Slaven, Karen Snow, Ron Spayde, Denise Stacks, Jakob
Stegelmann, Martin Stein & Scott Saxon, Thomas Stemper, Matthew Stieg, Thomas
A. Stillabower, John R. 'Doc' Strange, Tony Susnick, Stan Taffel, Troy M. Taylor,
Hilary Taylor, Jack Taylor, Todd D. Terpening, David Thoburn, Frank Thompson,
Ronald Tremblay, Mitch Trimboli, Paul & Laura Trinies, Tim Tucker, Arcadian
Vanguard, Paul Volpe, Harold L. Wallin, Richard Lewis Ward, Walter Wardrop,
Richard Warner, George Ross Watt, Edward Watz, Jeremy D Weinstein, Elizabeth
Weitzman, Brian J Williams, Jan L. Willis, Troy Willis, Lance Wilson, Ben Wink,
Lawrence Wolff, Stephen M Wolterstorff, Steve Zalusky.

Actor Jim Mason started as an extra with Harold and Hal. From his scrapbook comes this cover from the November 18, 1913 *Universal Weekly* that shows Hal (standing back right with a big mustache) and Harold (back left) in the 1913 Bison film *The Raid of the Human Tigers*. Courtesy of Robert James Kiss.

Archives Key:
ACAD: Academy Film Archive, Los Angeles
ARG: Fundacion Cinemateca Argentina, Buenos Aires
BFI: British Film Institute/National Archive, London
BOLOG: Cinetca di Bologna, Bologna, Italy
BRUS: Cinematheque Royale de Belgique/Cinematek, Brussels
CNC: Centre National de Cinema et de L'image Animee, Paris
ESM: Filmoteca Espanola, Madrid
EYE: EYE Filmmuseum, Amsterdam
FRIU: Cineteca de Friuli, Gemona
FPA: Film Preservation Associates, Paris (formerly Lobster Films)
FRANC: Cinematheque Francaise/Musee de Cinema, Paris
GEM: Film Department/George Eastman Museum, Rochester, New York
GOS: Gosfilmofond, Moscow
LOC: Moving Image Section/Library of Congress, Washington, DC
MoMA : The Museum of Modern Art Department of Film, New York
NAZ : Fondazione Centro Sperimentale di Cinematografia – Cineteca
Nazionale, Rome
OTT: National Film, Television and Sound Archives, Ottawa
UCLA: UCLA Film and Television Archive, Los Angeles

CHAPTER ONE:
LUKE
WARMS UP

If you remember the early days in the picture business, you will know that Hal Roach practically made Lloyd and Lloyd practically made Hal Roach.

Motion Picture Magazine, May 1927

Hal and Harold share a laugh during the making of *Get Out and Get Under* (1920).

This is the story of two young men who were determined to find success in the early American film industry. While not entirely sure at first in exactly what capacity their success would lie, through sheer will power and single-minded determination they found opportunities that enabled their natural talents to thrive. There are many people who had substantial movie success in the Teens and 1920s – Morris Schlank, Wallace Worsley, Reginald Barker – who are totally forgotten today, but Hal Roach and Harold Lloyd defied the odds to produce important bodies of work that are still viewed and appreciated.

As one of the great partnerships in film history, they both entered the industry at the bottom rung but became major Hollywood forces by the 1920s, and along the way made a huge mark on screen comedy.

Hal Roach was born first on January 14, 1892 in Elmira, New York. His birth name was Harry Eugene Roach, which he legally changed to Hal Roach in the 1920s. Compared to his fellow Hollywood moguls he was something of an everyman. Adolph Zukor, William Fox, Samuel Goldwyn, and Louis B. Mayer had all been successful merchants who switched from selling furs, gloves, and even junk to a new product: movies. Hal, on the other hand, went to the college of hard knocks.

By his own admission a poor student, Hal shuffled around to various schools until he dropped out at sixteen. On the advice of his father, he went to Seattle to visit family, but while there took a job to work on the railroad in Alaska. This started the teenager on a variety of jobs in wide-ranging places. What brought him to Los Angeles was a position as a salesman for a new line of trucks with pneumatic tires. Even in L.A. he moved around to different jobs – one for a company laying pipe had him on horseback all the time, so as a kid from the East he outfitted himself with a full western get-up – boots, bandanas, Stetson hat, etc.

Hal Roach looking very western circa 1914.
Author's collection.

The above came in handy when he spotted an ad in a L.A. paper for a film company that wanted men in western costume. The instructions were to be in front of the post office the next day at 7 a.m. At that time, a good amount of film recruitment was done on the city's street corners. Future screenwriter and director Grover Jones, who came to Hollywood at the same time, remembered:

> I used to stand at the corner of Hollywood Boulevard and Cahuenga – that was the casting office in these early days. Everybody stood there. In those days Hollywood was rather

colorful because nobody took off his makeup at night, and everybody walked up and down the streets at night dressed like Napoleon, and did their business. And we used to wait to get a call at the corner there, and when we got the call we would grab a sand wagon and go to Universal which was the popular studio at the time.

National Labor Relations Board testimony, October 1937
(courtesy of *Story by Grover Jones*, Split Reel, 2024)

Universal City outdoor stage around the time that Hal and Harold began there. The gentleman pointing in the center is producer/director Al Christie.

Hal said three hundred people showed up that next morning, from which about seventeen were picked – including him. He was then taken to the Universal lot for one of their Bison Film productions:

I arrived on the set – it was a saloon scene. I'd spent a couple of years in Seattle, where they had gambling and roulette, so I walked over to watch them and they're rolling the ball and the wheel in the same direction! Knowing nothing about pictures, I butted in and said, "That's wrong – the ball goes one way, the wheel goes the other." A man – who I didn't know was the director – asked me what I knew about roulette. I said, "Well, what do you want to know about it?" He says, "You're too young to be the croupier, but you sit here and tell this guy what to do." So I sat there and told him.

At 3 p.m., somebody came up to me and says "Be here at 8 o'clock in the morning – you're an actor now." I says. "What does it pay?" He says, "Five dollars a day." Well, I was making $65 a month in construction so five dollars a day for working 8 to 4 was a helluva good salary in those days. Right away, I said I would be there at 8 a.m. It took the rest of the week to finish the picture – that was in the days when you only had sunshine for lighting. I said, "Hell, this is the racket for me!"

Screen Actor, Winter 1987

Quickly becoming serious about the business, he worked hard and even practiced shooting films with people like Frank Borzage;the idea being that they would be ready if an opportunity arose.

Universal also had a ranch – a group of cowboys and a bunkhouse really – and they got $35 a week, a place to sleep and meals. So I moved out there, not for the $35, but for the experience. I went there to learn because they worked you every day.

After work, we used a cigar box and a tripod as a camera and we'd take turns directing and writing and acting. After dinner, until dark, we played "making motion pictures." There were about 60 to 70 of those guys, and practically all of them became of some importance in the picture business.

Screen Actor, Winter 1987

Harold Clayton Lloyd was born on April 20, 1893 in Burchard, Nebraska, to a family that was maritally and financially unstable – with frequent moves dictated by his father's search for steady employment. From his mother Harold and his older brother Gaylord inherited a love of the theatre. Gaylord was working as a prop master and stage hand at their local opera house in Beatrice, Nebraska, and got Harold his first walk-on part. After this appearance he did everything he could to become an actor. While still a teenager, he found a theatrical mentor in the person of John Lane Connor. Over the next few years Harold acted for Connor, was a student in Connor's School of Expression, and became a general assistant in his stock company.

By 1912 his parents had divorced and Harold was living with his father when they had an unexpected windfall – a settlement from a buggy accident brought them $3,000 – quite a sum at the time. His father (Foxy) wanted to use the money to locate back East, but Harold wanted to go to San Diego, California so he could rejoin Connor's theatre company. A coin was tossed, and Harold won.

Harold (fourth from left) in the San Diego High School production of *Going Some*.
Courtesy of the Academy of Motion Picture Arts and Sciences.

In San Diego Foxy bought a pool hall and a lunch counter, and Harold finished high school while he studied with Connor. Thanks to Connor, he had his first job in motion pictures. In 1912 the Edison Company came to Long Beach for a season, and when they needed extras for the short *The Old Monk's Tale* (1913) they enlisted from Connor's school, so Harold made his film debut as a Yaqui Indian. Not impressed with pictures Harold looked for stage work and had some small parts for the well-known Morosco Stock Company in Los Angeles. When stage opportunities dried up, Foxy suggested the movies – "'Course that isn't the stage, but it's acting and you might learn to like it." Harold sort of held his nose and tried the movies to make money.

There may be some tougher things than trying to break into motion pictures. I suppose there are. But I haven't come across them. Of all the sheer discouraging, heart-breaking games in the world, that's it. Nobody knows you. Nobody will pay any attention to you. If they do, they'll give you a cold look as much to say, "Now what could you do?"

Photoplay, June 1924

He contacted the Edison people in Balboa, and got some more work from them:

> The swellest thing about that was the free lunch they used to serve on location. I can remember it yet. A great big table, spread in a tent, and hot food piled all over it. Gee, nothing before or since ever tasted so good, and I did justice to it.

Photoplay, June 1924

Foxy and Harold (center) circa 1913, possibly behind the scenes at Universal. *Courtesy of the Academy of Motion Picture Arts and Sciences.*

Since Universal had many companies working at once, he then turned his attention to them. Applying for extra work he had no luck, but while hanging around he noticed that at noon a crowd of actors and extras drifted out in make-up to eat at a nearby lunch counter. The gatekeeper passed them out and back in again without question. The next day Harold brought his make-up kit, and when the group went to lunch he put on a make-up, mingled as one of them, and passed through the gate with them unchallenged:

I got no work – hardly expected to get it – but I did learn useful things about studio routine, meet older heads among the extras, learn the names of directors and assistant directors and after a time begin to register on their memories as a regular. On the way out I made a point to speak to the gatemen, and on future entrances, if he looked the least suspicious I would say, carelessly, "With Smalley" – Philips Smalley being one of the directors.

An American Comedy, 1928

Eventually he began to make connections and got work (in addition to gathering material for future comedies like 1918's *Hey There*). After a few months, Universal opened a large new studio, and Harold found himself attached to director J. Farrell MacDonald's unit that was making pictures starring J. Warren Kerrigan.

Hal Roach is visible on the left as director J. Farrell MacDonald addresses the company of 1914's *Samson.*

Now that Hal and Harold were each in Hollywood and working as extras, it was just a matter of time before their paths crossed. Both remembered that they met on one of the Kerrigan pictures directed by MacDonald. According to Harold "We became very fast friends." Cast as thugs, Roach was given a small bit of business to do, but not being an actor or having any performing experience he couldn't do it to the satisfaction of MacDonald. Harold was then given the business and did it smoothly. Harold remembered:

Hal thought "Damn.......," but funnily enough, this was what really started our partnership. He had a kind of respect for my histrionic art, if you'd call it that!

The Parade's Gone By, 1968

This may have been *Rory O' the Bogs* (1913). Other known titles that they appeared in together are *The Raid of the Human Tigers* (1913), *Samson*, and *Damon and Pythias* (both 1914). Hal was indeed impressed with Harold as they worked together on films for Universal, as decades later he told a reporter:

"On every one of those pictures," he said, "I was watching him all the way through, seeing the way he played even lesser parts with great finesse."

New York Times, January 23, 1992

In his autobiography Harold succinctly laid out the realities and different strata of "picture work a'la 1914":

Extras waiting in an early studio holding pen. The tall, white-haired gentleman in the center with the beard is D.L. "Daddy" Franck, a bit player who turns up in Chaplin's. *A Dog's Life* (1918) and other comedies. *Courtesy of Jorge Finkielman.*

Other than leads there were four grades of picture actors. The highest made up the stock company – that is, supporting players regularly employed. Next below ranked the guaranty people – extras at the regular three dollars a day, but assured of a minimum of four or five days' work a week and given group dressing rooms. Just extras, my own classification, formed the third group, cooling their heels from eight until mid-afternoon in the bull pen. No casting window ever admitted until late in the day that no work was in prospect – a device that cost the studio nothing and assured a supply of extras if a director suddenly called for them. At two or three o'clock, when it was too late to try other studios, the word was passed from the window:

"Nothing to-day folks; but be sure to be here in the morning."
Below us were only the mob extras, recruited when needed by want ads and paid one dollar a day, luncheon and car fare. They were almost exclusively hobos and an unfragrant lot, pictures not yet having attracted the curiosity seekers.

The pair did well at Universal and worked themselves up to five dollars a day. But, when the studio decided that they would pay no more than three dollars, Hal and Harold struck and had to look for work elsewhere. To try to make more of an impression Harold had portraits taken of himself in widely varying make-ups, and took them around with him to show the different casting directors. Some of them perused the photos, but still didn't give him any work. While Harold and Hal were trying hard to maintain their three dollars a day, they ended up working together on some L. Frank Baum Oz features such as *The Patchwork Girl of Oz* (1914). They were playing Gillikens, Munchkins, Hottentots and whatever else was needed, when out of the blue:

Roach surprised me – though "surprise" is a faint word for it – one day by announcing that he had gotten hold of several thousand dollars with which he intended making pictures on his own. He would be the director and I could be the first brick to his company at the usual three dollars a day. A few days later he rented a corner in the Bradbury Mansion as an office, with the use of a stage in the back yard, and Hal Roach was a producer.

An American Comedy, 1928

Two make-up studies from what Harold referred to as "The Lloyd Portrait Gallery."

The accepted and often recounted story of how Hal Roach "had gotten hold of several thousand dollars" is that he received an inheritance in 1914 that enabled him to fund his own film unit. No other details are given – no word on who left him the money, how they died, or what the amount of the bequeathment was, etc., etc. Turns out that the basic outline of the story is true, but there's a lot more meat and details on the bones. Hal essentially married a rich widow. British Hal Roach maven Dave Lord Heath discovered this, doggedly did all the research, and succinctly laid it out on his invaluable Roach website *Another Nice Mess*.

The founder of the said money was Frederick E. Woodbury, a civil engineer who hit it big in the mining industry. Woodbury was married to a woman named Helen Grant Duncan, but by 1910 they were separated with Frederick living in Milwaukee and Helen in Los Angeles. When Frederick was killed in a January 1914 mining accident, Hellen was still his wife and only heir, so she inherited the kaboodle. In July of 1914 the Rolin Film Corp. was incorporated, and in October 1914 Helen and Hal Roach were married, so it appears that Hellen gave Hal the money but with wedding strings attached. She was forty-seven, and Hal was twenty-two.

One probable reason that this marriage has flown under the radar for so long is that the marriage license is in Hal's real and legal name of Harry Eugene Roach (with his profession listed as Motion Picture Manufacturer).

This is the exact same name and profession on his June 5, 1917 World War I draft registration card. The pair was only married a couple of years as Helen died of bronchial pneumonia on May 4, 1916. Hal was her heir and the administrator of her estate, and on September 29, 1916 he married the actress Marguerite Nichols (usually referred to as "the first Mrs. Hal Roach"). Helen is buried in Glendale, Ca.'s Forest Lawn Memorial Park as Helen G. Roach.

The Hal Roach – Helen Woodbury marriage certificate from October 19, 1914.
Author's collection.

So, on July 23, 1914, Roach, with Dan Linthicum and I.H. Nance, formed the Rolin Film Company. Nance is a mysterious figure, and since there was a mandate that a minimum of three corporate officers were necessary for legal incorporation, he may have been drafted just to fulfill that need.

Dan Linthicum had also been mysterious until Craig Calman filled in the details in his 2014 book *100 Years of Brodies with Hal Roach*. Hal's silent business partner Daniel Anthony Linthicum was born in Arkansas in 1878, and had been a bank president in New Mexico and Texas, before settling in Los Angeles in the early teens as President of The Linthicum Chemical Company. In addition to supplying funds, he played a lead in their unreleased comedy *Two Bum Heroes*. Linthicum wasn't involved in the unit for very long, according to film historian Brent Walker:

Dan Linthicum was supposed to put up half the money, so Roach named him in "Rolin" in advance. However, he never came through with the dough, so Roach ended up taking on Dwight Whiting as his partner, but the company was already named with "lin" in the name.

After having been bought out by Roach very early, he moved around quite a bit working for various concerns, eventually becoming President of Red Anchor Dock and Steamship Company before his death in 1952.

Dwight Whiting, the mysterious Dan Linthicum, and Hal Roach proudly touting Rolin and their short-lived association with Sawyer, Inc. *Author's collection.*

Like so many early company names like Kalem and Essanay - "Ro" came from Roach, and "lin" from Linthicum to make Rolin. Luckily, Nance didn't seem to care or they would have ended up with something like The Ro-nan-lin Film Co. By August 17th Nance was replaced by Dwight Whiting (see Chapter Two, *Luke Lugs Luggage*, page 91), and the incorporation was announced in the trade publications a few months later:

> The most recent organization to begin operations in Los Angeles is the Rolin Film Company, composed of H.E. Roach, president and general manager; Dwight Whiting, vice-president; and D.A. Linthicum, secretary and treasurer; incorporated under the laws of California, with a capital of $10,000 all of which has been paid in.
>
> *Motion Picture News*, October 17, 1914

At the time of this announcement, Rolin had what looked like (on paper anyway) a great deal with Sawyer, Incorporated, a distribution chain for independent films that billed itself as the "World's Greatest Film Mart":

> The company has contracts with Sawyer, Inc., of New York for release of comedies, and recently filmed a one-reel "A Barber for a Day," which is a laughmaking burlesque on a correspondence school woman barber.

> **Will Be Agents for Sawyer**

> The directing was in charge of H.E. Roach, formerly with the Universal and Pathé companies. In addition to making comedies the company will act as western agents for Sawyer in the purchase of films manufactured by companies not having a regular release.

> Among the members of the producing companies are Harold Lloyd, Gene Marsh, Martha Mattox and James T. Kelly. The company has rented offices at the Los Angeles Film Corporation Studio, 406 Court St.

> *Motion Picture News*, October 17, 1914

Harold (center) with James T. Kelly and Mark Jones on the left, in what might be the early Rolin tramp comedy *A Dusty Romance*.

Unfortunately, the arrangement with Sawyer went south very quickly. Although set up with much fanfare, Sawyer did poorly and was out of business by March of 1915. They took finished films from Rolin, but never paid them. The Roach Studio payroll ledgers, which are in the collection of the University of Southern California, have "Swiped by Sawyer" written in Hal's hand in the margins of the listings for some of the first Rolin productions.

The company also tried the United Film Service, which was an arm of Warners Features, Inc., an early effort of Warner Brothers. United distributed comedies by independent outfits such as Luna, Starlight, and Superba, and dramas from Premier and Empress. Again Rolin was ripped off, with only *Willie Runs the Park* (1915) actually seeing the light of day through United. As late as the 1980s Hal was saying that Warner Bros. still owed him money.

According to the February 1, 1922 issue of *American Cinematographer*, the cameraman for the new unit was Fred W. Jackman:

> He photographed Harold Lloyd's first comedy and twenty more following, Hal Roach directing.

Jackman moved on to Keystone where he was one of their top cameramen for many years, but he would return in the 1920s to shoot and direct pictures for Roach. In a 1950 *American Cinematographer* there's a photo of Roach and Jackman telling Mack Sennett that when they made their first picture it was with negative "borrowed" from the Sennett lot.

At this late date it's hard to know exactly how many fledgling shorts there were, as several in the Rolin records are just listed as "untitled." Some of the known titles include *A Self Made Nut*, *Opium Fire*, *A Shine for a Dime*, and *A Barber for a Day*. The latter two may have eventually seen the light of day in 1915 through Pathé as *Pete the Pedal Polisher* and *Close-Cropped Clippings*. Photos from *Pete the Pedal Polisher* have Harold operating a shoeshine stand, complete with complications from James T. Kelly and Gene Marsh. *A Barber for a Day* was previewed by the *Motion Picture News* as "a laughmaking burlesque on a correspondence school woman barber." Stills from *Close Cropped Clippings* show Harold, Gene Marsh, and James T. Kelly in a chaotic scene with lady barbers in a shop, and the January 1, 1915 *Motography* described:

> **Close Cropped Clippings** – Pathé – Punctual Pete needs an assistant for his shaving shop. Gertie, almost a soubrette, learns of this and rushes home, where she masters the technique of the

ABOVE: Harold is doing more than polishing shoes in *A Shine for a Dime/Pete the Pedal Polisher* (1914/1915). BELOW: Martha Mattox wields a pair of shears as James T. Kelly (sitting right) gets the treatment from Gene Marsh (center) and Harold in the early *A Barber for a Day/Close-Cropped Clippings* (1914/1915).

tonsorial art via an instruction book. She applies for the job and is hired. From this point on the fun is furnished by her experiments upon the comical characters who stroll into the shop. Finally she catches sight of a bank roll of a "live one" and, after securing it, makes her getaway.

It could be that Sawyer sold these two to Pathé with the original titles changed, or perhaps Rolin did. Since Sawyer stiffed the company on them, Rolin would have had it within their rights to try to get them out through someone else. The early short subjects market was like the Wild West – retitling and double dipping weren't unusual. Warners plainly did this with some Al St John two-reelers. Lobby cards exist for the 1920 productions *Ship Ahoy* and *Trouble* where the titles have been changed to *Fired Again* and *The Paper Hangers*.

Martha Mattox watches as Harold is strangled in *The Fall of Lady Sampson*.

One title that's been bandied about as an early Rolin short is *The Hungry Actors*. Some sources say that it was even released through Universal, but there's no trace of it in the Universal release schedules. Photos survive from *The Sampson*, one of the first crop of shorts that depicts a low-rent theatrical troupe touring the tank towns. Harold seems to be the company manager with a big handle bar mustache, and Martha Mattox is clearly the strong woman of the title. Because of the subject matter it's possible that *The*

Hungry Actors was another name for *The Fall of Lady Sampson* (due to the lack of information on these early productions there's room for a certain amount of "supposin'" but I've tried to keep it to where there's some kind of evidence or logic).

Making these various one-shot items, Harold was searching:

> For my comedy stuff, I was always trying new characters. I invented any number of weird make-ups, and we tried them out, reaching for just the right one.
>
> *Photoplay*, June 1924

While trying to get these individual shorts distributed, the unit tried its hand at a comedy series. Willie Work was the unoriginal name given to the main character, played by Harold. At least three shorts with Willie were filmed in October of 1914 – *Troubles of the Work Family, Willie Runs the Park,* and *Willie Works Buys a Harem:*

> The Work Family, including Willie, Helen and May, the children, are soon to appear in comedies. A series is now being made by the Rolin Film Company, releasing through Sawyer, Inc. at the Court Street studio, under the direction of H.E. Roach. Harold Lloyd is the leading comedian, playing the part of Willie.
>
> *Motion Picture News*, November 14, 1914

> Hal Roach, at the Rolin Film Company studio, is making the third of the Work Family comedy series. In this "Willie Work Buys a Harem." The comedies are released through Sawyer, Inc.
>
> *Motion Picture News*, November 21, 1914

Of the above three mentioned it appears that only the middle one was ever released – through United on January 2, 1915:

> **Willie Runs the Park** (United-Warner-Rolin) February – There is a distinct atmosphere of vulgarity about this film, which is inexcusable.
>
> *Moving Picture World*, February 6, 1915

The only known surviving image of Willie Work is a photo from *Willie Runs the Park*, and it matches Harold's description of him:

> I experimented with dress and make-up and about the fifth picture settled on a character we christened Willie Work. The

name wrongly suggests a tramp; it was, instead, a hash of different low-comedy get-ups, with a much-padded coat, a battered silk hat, and a cat's whisker mustache as its distinguishing marks.

An American Comedy, 1928

The only known surviving photo of Harold as Willie Work in *Willie Runs the Park* (1915). Harold's on the left, with an unidentified person in blackface and cop James T. Kelly.

Although the trades mention three official Willie Work shorts, Harold said that there were more:

> In another Willie Work picture Roach thought up the droll idea of putting me to bed with a skunk. The polecat's first line of defense had been removed and Roach told me that he had read somewhere that a skunk so treated makes a perfect pet, as playful, affectionate and gentle as a kitten. Evidently the skunk had not read the article, for he bit me and not in affection.
>
> *An American Comedy*, 1928

This looks to be the following unreleased film that Dwight Whiting described in a 1918 letter:

"A Smell There Was" – Lloyd plays the lead in this and it deals with the troubles of a traveling man with three pet skunks which get loose in a residence. Slapstick.

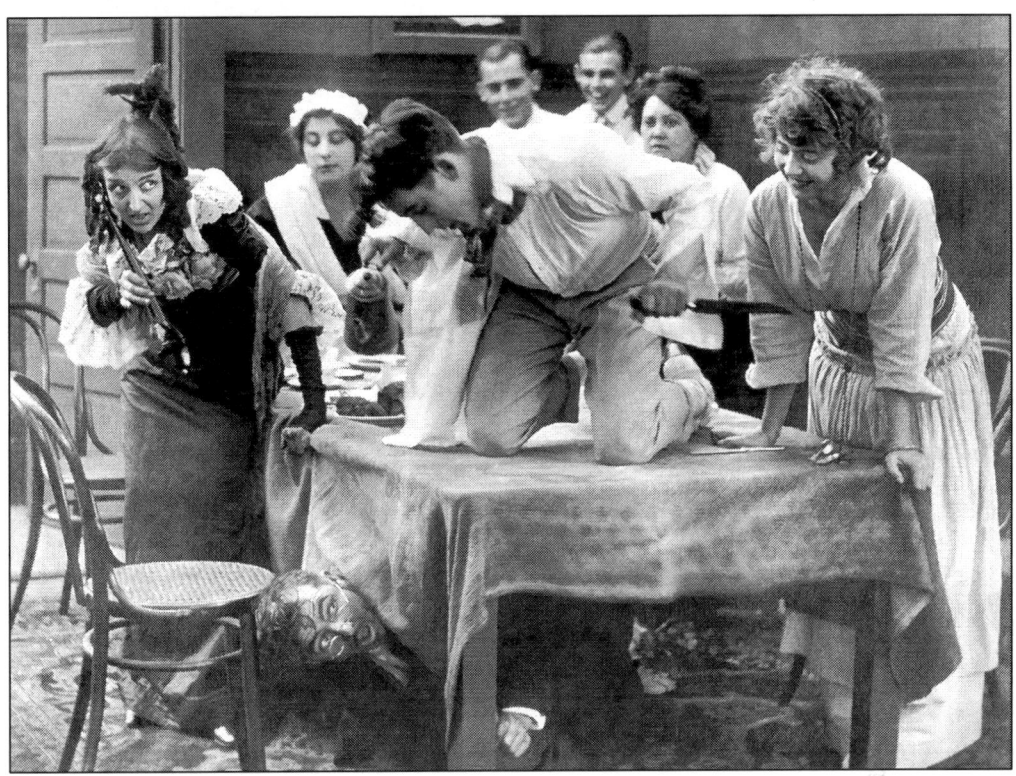

Harold's actions on the table give Martha Mattox, Mark Jones, Agnes Steele, and Jane Novak a good idea of *Why the Boarders Left* (1915).

Other unreleased items mentioned in Whiting's letter include *A Dusty Romance*, a tramp story with Harold in the lead. There were also four pictures without Harold – *A Duke for A Day*, *Two Bum Heroes* (Dick Rossin & Danny Linthicum), *Powder Monkie* (George Whiting), and *A Daubbo*. The unreleased items were sold off to a group named Motion Pictures Specialties Corporation.

One that did see the light of day through them was *Why the Boarders Left* (1915). MinA Comedies (short for Made in America) was a series of one-reel comedies released through the General Film Program starting at the end of 1914 and running throughout 1915. Its chief director was Milton H. Fahrney, and it turned out shorts with Harry La Pearl, Amy Jerome, George Ovey, Goldie Colwell, "Smiling" Bill Parsons, and even a young Constance Talmadge. But like most smaller outfits, it picked up an occasional stray short to fill up their release schedule. It's uncertain if Harold was in the production, as the lead was listed as an unknown comic named George Duncan, who received some good notices:

The very peculiar antics of an erratic hotel proprietor make very amusing situations in the MinA release of September 30, "Why the Boarders Left." George Duncan, who takes the leading part is a new figure on the screen but his work is marked with originality and he possesses a line of comic caperings that are all his own.

Moving Picture World, October 2, 1915

Why the Boarders Left (MinA) Sept. 30 – Hotel life from a burlesque point of view is shown in this one-reel picture. Speed has been the watchword of the producer, but he has not forgotten the necessity of humor as well. The young man who plays the hotel clerk is a clever comedian and is given good support by the rest of the cast.

Moving Picture World, October 16, 1915

Since there are no previous or subsequent traces of Mr. Duncan, it's possible that he's a renamed Harold. Often when a company would pick up a film from another unit they would change all the names to disguise its origins. There are also a few early unidentified Rolin photos of what appears to be hijinks in a boarding house, with Harold front and center as the main disturber. These might be from the film, but of course, it's only a possibility. We'll never know for sure unless the film itself resurfaces.

Why the Boarders Left was still a bit of a bitter blow for Rolin, as they received no credit on its release. But the company had a modicum of success with Universal when they sold them a couple of dramas. The three known titles are: *From Italy's Shores* (May 19, 1915), *Into the Light* (June 17, 1915), and *The Greater Courage* (October 21, 1915). Missing today, they were simple and straightforward melodramas, directed by Hal, which starred Roy Stewart and Jane Novak with Harold in support.

From Italy's Shores (Laemmle):

On arriving in America, the Italian and his wife are separated. Through a blow on the head the foreigner is rendered unsound in the mind. His wife becomes a singer of no little repute. As time passes her husband is employed as a gardener, and at a lawn party he sees his wife singing. The sight of her restores his mind and all ends happily.

ABOVE: *From Italy's Shores* (1915) finds Harold as a thug (left) setting his sights on Jane Novak and Roy Stewart (right). BELOW: Harold displaying his make-up skill as Jane Novak's elderly voice teacher in *From Italy's Shores* (1915).

This was made for Universal by the Rolin company, with Roy Stewart playing the Italian. He and the other principals give pleasing performances. The picture is very good as regards photography and the scenes and settings are most appropriate, especially the garden party. The story is of the variety which will please those who care for subjects that sacrifice logic and realism to procure heart-interest and sympathetic presentation. It is not a picture to project before an intelligent audience.

Motion Picture News, May 22, 1915

Thanks to surviving photos we can see that Harold did double-duty – playing a thug as well as the wife's elderly voice teacher.

Into the Light (1915) has Harold (left) making a last-minute confession to clear Roy Stewart (center).

Into the Light had Stewart as a burglar who has a change of heart when the leading lady doesn't turn him over to the police. He becomes a parson in a small village, but is falsely accused of robbery and murder. At the last minute the real criminal gives himself up, so Stewart is exonerated and re-united with the leading lady:

A familiar story, but produced in an impressionistic style lending it attractiveness. The players interpret the action almost totally by bodily actions, seldom moving their lips or changing the expression of their faces. The moral of the production is decidedly worthy, it being to remain true to religion no matter what occurs.

Motion Picture News, June 19, 1915

The last of the trio was *The Greater Courage*, and this time the focus was on Jane Novak's character – a woman with a criminal brother goes out West and marries a hardy miner for protection. The brother changes his ways, makes good, and arrives out West and redeems himself. According to the October 9, 1915 *Moving Picture World*:

> The interest is well sustained and the vigor of the scenes in the western mining camp reflect credit on the cast.

The production was summed up as "An out-of-the-ordinary western drama that will please the multitude." It's not definite exactly when these three shorts were sold to Universal, but by the time they were released Roach and company were already busy at work for Pathé on their *Lonesome Luke* series.

At the time these dramas were made, a comedy titled *Just Nuts,* was also shot. It's not known if this was offered to Universal along with the dramas, but it would eventually come out through Pathé. New York's Museum of Modern Art, George Eastman Museum, the BFI, and other archives have prints, which makes this the earliest surviving Hal Roach film. As the only look at the fledgling Rolin product the closest thing it resembles is an L-Ko Comedy. The first half of this one-reeler is set in a park with Harold assuming the Billie Ritchie role as he bothers people there. He even looks like Ritchie with a cane, baggy pants, moth-eaten mustache, jacket buttoned high on his chest, and a scowl on his face.

This incarnation is different from Harold's earlier Willie Work. In fact, it's Roy Stewart as Harold's tramp friend who wears the battered top hat, padded coat, and mustache of *Willie Runs the Park* (1915). So, Harold isn't Willie Work, and isn't yet Lonesome Luke either. No name is given to this character – he's introduced via title card as "a poor, misguided nut."

After the hi-jinks in the park, the action climaxes in a busy nightspot/cabaret where Harold hits, kicks, and sticks forks into various customers and wait staff, while he tries to avoid a cop patrolling outside. He eventually loses the girl to the cop, and the whole thing ends in a big restaurant brawl. Besides the three leads, two recognizable supporting players are Gaylord Lloyd and little Gus Alexander. Gaylord was of course Harold's older brother (see Chapter Two, *Luke's Double*, page 114), and was always ready to do whatever was needed for Harold's films.

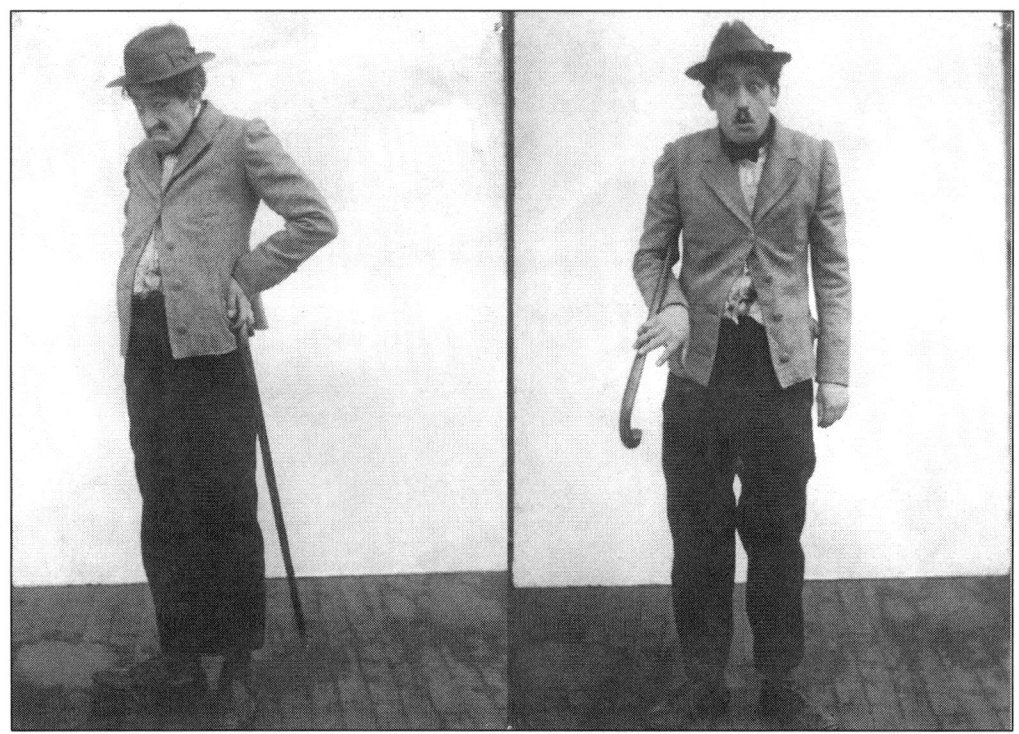

Two studies of Harold's Billie Ritchie-ish character in *Just Nuts* (1915).

It's a bit of a surprise to see Gus Alexander turn up as the little waiter in this tyro production as he had been appearing in Al Christie's Nestor comedies since 1911. Co-starring as Jeff in Nestor's *Mutt and Jeff Comedies* like *Mutt and Jeff Join the Opera* (1911), he was very busy in films until 1919. Later he based himself on the East Coast, and appeared in Broadway shows as well as independently made New York films.

The token of Harold's affection (and obsession) is Jane Novak. Before joining the Rolin unit, Novak entered films in 1913 at Vitagraph, appearing alongside her aunt Anna Shaefer. She seems to have been with Rolin very early, as she can be seen in a photo from *Pete the Pedal Polisher/A Shine for a Dime*, and was one of the first, if not the very first leading lady for the company. After her work there the rest of her career was spent in dramas, and included productions for Universal, Fox, Ince, William S. Hart, Maurice Tourneur, and Paramount such as *Behind the Door* (1919), *Three Word Brand* (1921), *Lazybones* (1925), and *Redskin* (1929).

The California-born Roy Stewart, having previously worked for the Amex Company under director Joseph de Grasse and at Masterpiece with Max Figman, was Rolin's most seasoned performer. He played the leads in the dramas – Harold in the comedies. A problem arose when Harold found out that Stewart was getting $10 a day, while he was only getting $5. When Harold confronted Roach about this, Hal told Harold that Stewart wouldn't work for less and that he couldn't pay both of them that amount – so he should just be patient. Harold's response was to walk.

Harold's early Rolin co-stars Jane Novak and Roy Stewart. *Author's collection.*

Without his star comedian, Roach tried Dick Rossin (or Rawson) and George Whiting, but after a few films like *Powder Monkie*, Rolin Films went into suspended animation. Both Hal and Harold got rebound work almost immediately:

> Hal Roach, formerly director for the Rolin Film Company has been made director of the second Essanay comedy company and is finishing his first subject. The principals of the company are Marjorie Reieger, Bud Jamison, Jack Cherry and Harry Pollard.
>
> *Motion Picture News*, May 22, 1915

At this moment, Essanay had the services of the biggest movie star in the world - Charlie Chaplin. He was the studio's first comedy company, and Roach became the second unit referred to:

> We [Rolin] made a few comedies and four two-reel dramas, and our money was exhausted. Our money didn't come back from New York and I went to work for Essanay with Charlie Chaplin. Chaplin had at that time about six English

comedians who were cast for his pictures. I took the people he was not using and made one-reelers with them; each week I made a one-reeler.

The Silent Picture, #6 Spring 1970

Chaplin's regular support included Bud Jamison, Margie Rieger, James T. Kelly, Ed Armstrong, Jack Pollard, Dee Lampton, and Harry Pollard (soon to become "Snub"), so they made up the casts of Hal's 1915 shorts like *Street Fakers*, *Tale of a Tire*, *Mustaches and Bombs*, and *Off for a Boat Ride*. Definitely five, but possibly eight, comedies were made by Hal during his brief tenure with Essanay.

Bud Jamison and Margie Rieger in the Hal Roach-directed
Mustaches and Bombs (1915). *Author's collection.*

Off for a Boat Ride (Essanay) Sept. 30 – Unadulterated farce of the liveliest description is the only ingredient of this one-reel photoplay. It is built after the latest and most approved plans for works of its class, and is given every advantage by the playing of James T. Kelly, Ann Ivers, Margie Reiger, Jack Pollard and Bud Jamison.

Moving Picture World, October 16, 1915

While Roach was busy with this series, Harold got a toehold at Mack Sennett's Keystone Studio:

They tried me out as an Italian fruit-vendor. I surprised the director with an unexpectedly good make-up, but he was only mildly interested in whether I looked like an Italian peddler or a Norwegian fisherman. The action called for a motorcycle to rip through my fruit cart and for me to take a comedy fall in the midst of the fruit. Could I fall or was I just an upright actor was the question. Keystone comedies were a series of falls and Keystoners fell as no one has since Adam or Niagara.

The cart was a break away, built in two sections. It burst asunder as the motorcycle charged through. The fruit erupted and I leaped into the air and came down on the back of my neck among oranges and bananas to the critical approval of the director. I was one of them.

An American Comedy, 1928

Love, Loot and Crash (1915) survives, so Harold's Keystone baptism of fire can still be viewed today. During the months of April and May he kept busy playing a selection of callow youths, ministers and cooks in entries such as *Their Social Splash*, *Miss Fatty's Seaside Lovers*, *Her Painted Hero*, and *A Submarine Pirate* (all 1915). His best part was a sizeable role as an innocent young man accused of stealing a necklace in *Court House Crooks* (1915).

Although Rolin's temporary shut down and the rift between Hal and Harold were emotionally painful, the time spent apart was professionally beneficial for them. At Keystone Harold worked with and rubbed elbows with veteran comics like Ford Sterling, Roscoe Arbuckle, and Syd Chaplin, while he honed his stunting skills. Getting accepted as one of them had to have boosted his confidence as a slapstick performer. For Hal, it was also an opportunity to expand his comic capacities, and introduced him to players such as Pollard, Jamison, Kelly and Lampton whom he would soon bring to

Rolin. He also hooked up with Thomas J. Crizer, a former cowboy at Essanay's Niles branch. Crizer had become an editor on the studio's *Snakeville Comedies*, and worked on, as well as appeared in, Hal's one-reelers. Before long, he would join Rolin to edit the *Lonesome Luke* shorts, and would remain Roach's editor and production manager until 1926.

Joe Bordeaux, Harold, and Edgar Kennedy on the lookout for an heiress or two in a frame scan from *Miss Fatty's Seaside Lovers* (1915). *Courtesy of the Library of Congress.*

What brought Roach and Lloyd back together and reactivated the dormant Rolin unit was a contract to turn out a steady series of shorts for Pathé. During the pause in Rolin's production Dwight Whiting had continued putting out feelers for distribution, and had been talking with Pathé. Movie mythology says that Rolin initially connected with Pathé when the distribution company picked up their one-reeler *Just Nuts* and released it on April 19, 1915. Making a solid connection with a distributor like Pathé was akin to finding the Holy Grail to a tiny outfit like Rolin.

Having started in 1896 in Paris, Pathé Frères was the largest and best-known of the French film studios. With their famous rooster logo, they turned out many actualities, historical re-enactments, and trick films, but their comedy output was prodigious - made by the fathers of film comedy such as Max Linder, Andre Deed, Charles Prince, and director Romeo Bosetti. Pathé's main strength was their distribution, which included Central Europe, Asia, the Americas, and Africa. The Linder and Prince comedies made in France were popular around the world, and the company produced their own comedies in America, as well as picked up films made by small independents such as Robbins, Hartigan, Eclectic, Mayo, All Comedy Films, Inc., the Esperanto Film Manufacturing Co., Balboa Amusement Producing Co., Mittenthal, and finally Rolin.

Pathé's famous rooster logo.

The story goes that Pathé told Roach that if he could round up *Just Nuts'* three leads – Harold, Roy Stewart and Jane Novak – they wanted more films. Only Harold was available, but that was enough. The truth is that Pathé had released at least three Rolin shorts before *Just Nuts* – *Pete the Pedal Polisher*, *Close-Cropped Clippings* (both on January 30, 1915), and *Beyond His Fondest Hopes* (February 1, 1915).

As mentioned before, the first two look like they were the very early productions *A Shine for a Dime* and *A Barber for a Day*, which seem to have been shopped around after originally being stolen by Sawyer. *Beyond His Fondest Hopes* is about a newsboy who gets chauffeured for misadventures at the beach with a wealthy friend, and may be the early production that Harold described in his autobiography as:

> Roach had an idea that there would be novelty and money in
> kid pictures – a conviction which he vindicated eventually with the
> Our Gang comedies. He hired two boys and built his first picture,
> a one-reel comedy, about their boisterous day at the beach. I was
> the adult lead – the chauffeur who chaperoned them and bore the
> brunt of their boyish mischief, the little dears.

In a 1986 interview Roach remembered that Rolin's first contact with Pathé was an indirect one:

> The comedies we sent to a company in New York that turned out to be Warner Brothers, though they weren't using that name then. We never heard from them again. A few months later, one of those comedies showed up at a theatre in Los Angeles owned by the Pathé company. So we called Pathé, you know: "What's going on?" Pathé says, "We've been trying to find out who made that film. Audiences love it. We want you to make more of 'em." But Warners wouldn't tell Pathé who made the film, because Warners hadn't paid us. I never got paid to this day!

It's possible that Pathé's interest didn't come from just one of the films, but the quality of a few of them together. Also, since Harold was in all four of these first Rolin/Pathé releases, his charisma and screen presence was no doubt a determining factor in their decision to contract for a steady stream of films. The alliance with so big a distribution organization boosted the little Rolin to a new level.

CHAPTER TWO:

LONESOME LUKE'S
PHILM-OGRAPHY

SNAP! **CRASH! WOW!!**

Then Comes the Laugh!

All this spells | ROLIN PICTURES
COMEDY

Released Exclusively through Pathe Exchange, Inc.

Direction, Hal E. Roach

It Does the Trick!

ROLIN FILM CO., 907 Brockman Bldg., Los Angeles, Cal.

D. WHITING, Manager

October 2, 1915 ad for the Rolin-Pathé product.

After numerous ups and downs for almost a year, Roach and company finally got a firm footing in the film industry with their new Pathé contract and were off and running making a series with the brand name *Phun Philms* with Harold as the star:

Rolin Making Pictures In Los Angeles For Pathé

The Rolin Film Company, which has not been producing for the past four or five weeks, is again active, now working at the commercial studio of the Los Angeles Film Corporation, 406 Court Street, where the studio is making a series of comedies entitled "Lonesome Luke" from stories and scenarios by Tad, the cartoonist, well known for his pictures entitled "Indoor Sports," "Silk Hat Harry" and others.

The direction of these pictures is under Hal Roach, president of the company, and the principal players are Harold O. Lloyd, Eleanor Whitney, Gene Marsh, T. Kelly, and Clyde Whitney. These pictures are being made for, and will be released by Pathé.

Motion Picture News, July 10, 1915

Since Willie Work and the character from *Just Nuts* hadn't started any fires, Hal and Harold decided that they needed a new star character. Harold elaborated:

Chaplin was going great guns, his success was such that unless you wore funny clothes and otherwise aped him you were not a comedian. Exhibitors who could not get the original demanded imitations – and were given them in numbers from brazen counterfeits to coy skirtings about the Chaplin manner. Had I had the glass character then, and had I been allowed to try it out, I have no doubt that it would have sold on its merits, but these are two large ifs. On the one hand, I had only vague yearnings to do something different; on the other hand, the distributors and exhibitors would hear of no departure from the Chaplin track.

I told Roach that I had something that was an improvement on Willie Work, at least. When he saw it he approved. Later it was tagged with the name of Lonesome Luke. For it my father had found a worn pair of Number 12AA last shoes in a repair shop on Los Angeles Street, where they had been left for resoling by an Englishman on his uppers. Dad asked the cobbler if he though five dollars would compensate the owner. The cobbler was sure of it – five dollars bought a good pair of shoes. In a haberdashery dad found a black-and-white vertical-striped shirt and bought out the stock. The coat of a woman's tailored suit, a pair of very tight and short trousers, a vest too short, a cut-down collar, a cut-down hat and two dots of a mustache completed the original version of Lonesome Luke. The cunning thought behind all this, you will observe, was to reverse the Chaplin outfit. All his clothes were too large, mine all too small. My shoes were funny but different; my mustache funny but different.

Nevertheless, the idea was pretty imitative and was recognized as such by audiences, though I painstakingly avoided copying the well-known Chaplin mannerisms.

Harold mops up for Rolin and Pathé.
Courtesy of the Academy of Motion Picture Arts and Sciences.

Rolin inherited the name Lonesome Luke from Pathé, as they had contracted for five scenarios by the cartoonist Thomas Aloysius Dorgan. A comic strip artist who signed his work as "Tad," he specialized in sports cartoons, and created the popular character Judge Rummy. Dorgan is credited with popularizing expressions like "the cat's meow," "dumbbell," "for crying out loud," and even "Twenty-three skidoo." With other comic strip makers like George McManus and Winsor McCay being tapped for movies, Pathé felt that Dorgan was a good bet and contracted for five scripts. He was later involved in Judge Rummy and Silk Hat Harry cartoons for William Randolph Hearst's International Film Service, but his association with Pathé was short-lived, leaving them with the Luke name and to mete out his five supplied scenarios.

The first Lonesome Luke short was a non-Rolin production, made by Pathé:

Lonesome Luke – Pathé.

This is a short comedy from the pen of the famous cartoonist Tad. Lonesome Luke, a resident of the village jail, is promised his freedom if he will don a bear skin and dance with a lion at a political function. Luke agrees, but changes his mind when he sees the lion. A long and ludicrous chase follows his escape. On the same reel with *A School of New Guinea*.

Motography, June 12, 1915

The April 30, 1915 issue of *Variety* offered some details about the production:

Tad's Comic Series

The Pathé Company has signed with Tad the "Evening Journal" cartoonist to publish a series of comedy films based on his drawings. The first of the series will be "Lonesome Luke."

Alma Hanlon (Mrs. Walter Kingsley, who is one of the Hanlon family), has been engaged as principal woman for the picture, and Jack Terry (a nephew of Ellen Terry), will be leading man.

E. Mason Hopper has been engaged especially to direct the Tad series.

This split-reeler was finally released as *When the Lion Roared* on June 7, 1915. Other "Tad" scenarios were given to the Starlight Company, who were making films in New Jersey and Yonkers for Pathé release. The "Tad" Starlights were *Once Every Ten Minutes*, *Soaking the Clothes*, and probably *Pressing His Suit* (all 1915). These films have been confused for many years as possible Roach productions, but *Once Every Ten Minutes* survives at the Library of Congress, and its original titles identify it as a Starlight Comedy. The cast includes Walter Hiers and Priscilla Dean. Probably because of the Dorgan scripts Pathé listed them as *Phun Philms*, but the photos from the

Pathé Bulletin for *Soaking the Clothes* and *Pressing His Suit* show the same Starlight actors involved. Rolin had nothing to do with them.

Since the total "Tad" scenarios counted five, this left *Spit-Ball Sadie* for Rolin to inherit, but they kept the moniker "Lonesome Luke."

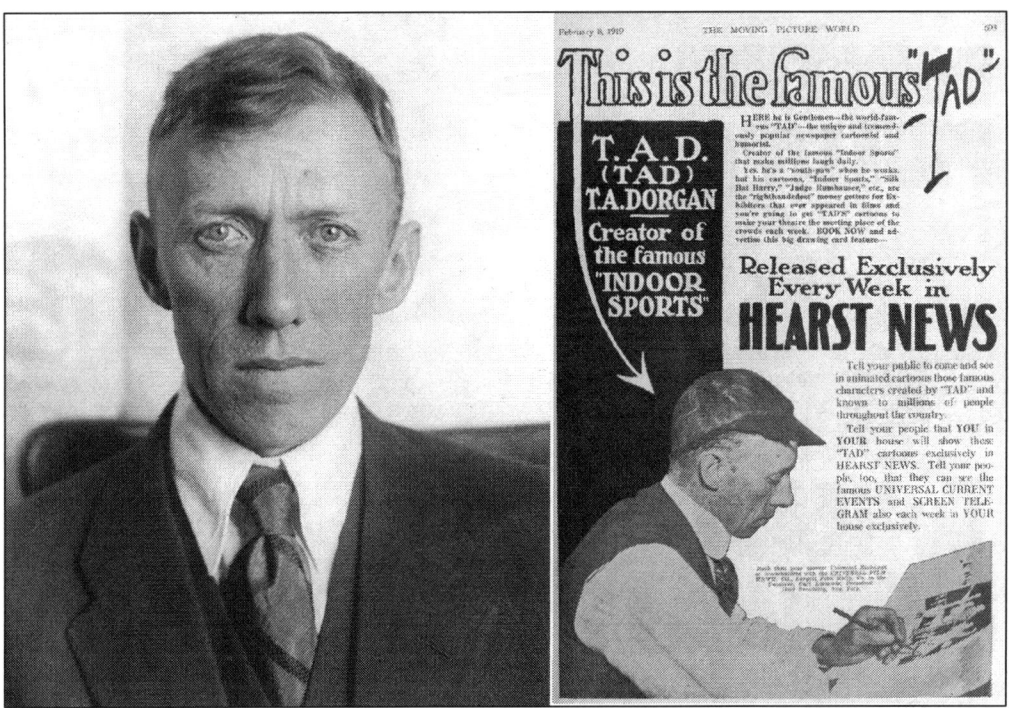

Comic strip artist "Tad" Dorgan and an ad for his International Film Service series.

Spit-Ball Sadie

Released July 26, 1915. A Phunphilm, produced by Hal Roach for the Rolin Film Company. Distributed by Pathé. Directed by Hal Roach. Based on a story by Tad Dorgan. Working title: ***Lonesome Luke – He Becomes a Pitcher***. One reel. (Filmed June 15-19, 1915 & June 25, 1915 for retakes). With Harold Lloyd, Gene Marsh, Blanche White, Jack Spinks.

Two girls' baseball teams are about to play for the championship when the captainess of the favorites learns that Lizzie Pinktee, her pitcher, had hurdled to the Feds. She is disconsolate that her one best bet should have allied herself with the outlaws, but a brave handsome man promises to get Spit-Ball Sadie to do the box work for her that afternoon. Sadie of the moist delivery was none other than himself, so attired as becomes a female, he enters the rifle pit prepared to hurl the game of his life.

The score is a tie up to the ninth, when Spit-Ball Sadie becomes as wild as a left-hander. The manager of the other team runs a pinch hitter into the breach with two down and three on. Sadie aviates just long enough to pass the batter, forcing in the winning run. The twirler is then chased out of the ball park, through the streets and finally lands in a large barrel, where he succumbs in hiding himself from the infuriated females who have learned of his deception. The Peerless Leader of his team saves him, however, by directing the pursuers the wrong way, and tells him coyly that she knew him all the time. (*Moving Picture World*, July 24, 1915).

Harold and the girl's team in *Spit-Ball Sadie* (1915).

With the working out of the Pathé contract Harold left the Keystone Studio and returned to Rolin. On his way out of the Sennett fun factory he made an offer to studio ingénue Dixie Chene. In an August 1, 1967 interview with film historian Sam Gill Ms. Chene reported:

> Harold Lloyd made four or five comedies at Keystone. In fact, it's funny to think about it now, but he asked me to join him when he decided to leave Sennett and go back to his own company as his leading lady; but I said "Oh, no thank you," knowing well that whatever fly-by-night comedy studio he was thinking about, would never offer much competition to the famous and well-established Sennett Keystone studio.

An example of Harold's new star salary.

As Rolin's star, Harold was now getting $50 a week, and at this point the stock company consisted of Gene Marsh and James T. Kelly. One important player was still needed. Harold remembered:

> We lacked a leading woman and the wages paid did not attract a long line of applicants. It used to be a custom with many Los Angeles apartment houses to fit up their basements with pianos and dance floors to give weekly and semi-weekly dances to attract and hold young people. I liked to dance, did so often at these free parties, and knew that there was no lack of pretty girls in the city. I suggested to Roach that we might find a leading woman at such a dance, and we did – a pretty blonde. She left after the first picture.
>
> *An American Comedy*, 1928

The leading lady in question actually does turn up in images for a couple of other shorts like *Terribly Stuck Up* and *A Mix-Up for Maisie*, but is gone by the time Bebe Daniels shows up in *Giving Them Fits*. Unfortunately, Harold didn't remember or mention her name, and like *Spit-Ball Sadie* itself it's been lost to time.

Moving Picture World (July 31, 1915): "A rather enjoyable farce comedy centered about a baseball game in which the female pitcher of the female team that comes to town causes a sensation, and mischievous Luke in an attempt to impersonate the lady, gets what's coming to him."

Motion Picture News (July 31, 1915): "This isn't very funny and some its scenes are slightly repelling. A man dresses up as a woman and pitches for the female nine. His disguise is penetrated and he is forced to run. The actions of the leading man, although not original, are somewhat humorous."

Terribly Stuck Up

Released August 28, 1915. A Phunphilm, produced by Hal Roach for the Rolin Film Company. Distributed by Pathé. Directed by Hal Roach. Working titles: *Terrible Stuck Up* and *Lonesome Luke, He Does His Best and You Can't Blame a Guy For Trying*. One reel. (Filmed June 22-26 & July 3, 1915). With Harold Lloyd, James T. Kelly, Frank J. Coleman, Jack Spinks.

Harold is attacked by a racial stereotype in *Terribly Stuck Up* (1915).

Tanglefoot Tom was born under an unlucky star. He gets into trouble with his landlady and a cop, but covers them both with flypaper and succeeds in making his escape. He takes refuge in a flour barrel in the bakery of his father-in-law-to-be and is passed unnoticed.

Dotty Dough, the sweetheart, thinks Tom is the ideal of her dreams as handed down by her favorite authors, but goes out with Samson Strong, the village "roughneck" just the same. Tom succeeds in throwing them both in the water as they cross a rather shaky bridge on their travels, and recues the fair one from Mr. Strong's clutches. He and Dotty then stroll to the riverfront and are standing on a wharf, Tom telling what a hero he is, when the cry "woman overboard" is raised. Tanglefoot demurs at going after her, but Samson, who has followed throws him into the deep. He has to be fished out with the aid of bystanders, however. One of the helpers is a peddler who has left his fruit cart alone, and just a Tanglefoot rescues the "woman," who proves to be the leg of a department store dummy, and is safely on the dock once more, the cart starts down the slope and again throws him into the deep, and Dotty is left for Samson. (*Moving Picture World*, September 11, 1915).

Looking for various ways to promote their output, Pathé included a number of their new *Lonesome Luke* comedies in a special exhibitor's guide:

Pathé Films for Children

The Pathé Company has produced a large number of films especially suitable for children. These are listed in convenient form in a booklet which the company will send to an exhibitor upon request.

Motography, June 3, 1916

Terribly Stuck Up was on the list, as well as other 1915 and 1916 Rolins such as *Just Nuts*, *A Mix-Up for Maisie*, *Fresh from the Farm*, *Ragtime Snap Shots*, *Bughouse Bellhops*, *Peculiar Patient Pranks*, *Luke Lugs Luggage*, *Lonesome Luke*, *Circus King*, and *Luke's Double*. Also included were Max Linder, Charles Prince, some of the Starlight *Heinie & Louie* shorts, plus cartoons and scenic films.

On hand as support in this short was silent comedy forgotten foot soldier Frank J. Coleman. Plump and round, with a big bald head, he supported some of the biggest comedians of his day, and although ubiquitous his work went unnoticed by the public. A graduate of vaudeville with the garden City Quartette, and Bennett-Morton Stock Company, Coleman made his first screen appearances in 1915 for L-Ko Comedies and in Rolin shorts like this and *A Mix-Up for Maisie*, but his most important early work was in Charlie Chaplin Essanay comedies such as *A Night in the Show*. He continued with Chaplin, turning up in eleven out of twelve of the comic's Mutual shorts. His time with Chaplin led to stints with Mack Sennett and Fox Sunshine Comedies for titles such as *Sheriff Nell's Tussle*, *Love Loops the Loop*, *A High Diver's Last Kiss*, *Roaring Lions on the Midnight Express* (all 1918), and *His Musical Sneeze* (1919).

Attention from Frank J. Coleman (right) and Phil Dunham (center) make Alice Howell
A Convict's Happy Bride (1920).

From this point on the rotund comic was a fixture in comedies and worked everywhere – at Jack White Comedies, at Reelcraft with Alice Howell, a few of the Henry Lehrman Specials, Century Comedies, and with Larry Semon at Vitagraph. Often an authority figure, and sometimes in drag as a large society matron, Coleman could always be counted on for sterling support and to get his laughs. In 1924 he had a brief return to the Sennett fold when he played the heavy in the early Harry Langdon films *The First 100 Years* and *The Luck of the Foolish*. The last few years of his career were spent back at Fox where he made screen life difficult for Jerry Madden, Ernie Shield, and Lige Conley in numerous *Imperial Comedies* like *Jerry the Giant*, *Honeymoon Hospital* (both 1926), and *Slippery Silks* (1927). Leaving films before the changeover to sound, he remained in Los Angeles until his death in 1948.

Moving Picture World (August 8, 1915): "This is a farce comedy which is very attractive. It presents a rivalry for the hand of the pretty maid of the story, which ends by a fall in the water for all concerned. The picture has been put on with considerable skill."

Motography (September 11, 1915): "Dottie meets Lonesome Luke and believes him to be the ideal of her dreams. Luke considers it best to deal with his rivals at long range; a brick being one of his favorite weapons. His methods prove efficient and ere long he has Dottie all to himself."

A Mix-Up for Maisie*

Released September 6, 1915. A Phunphilm, produced by Hal Roach for the Rolin Film Co. Distributed by Pathé. Directed by Hal Roach. Extant: GOS. Working title: *Lonesome Luke, He Loses Out in a Battle for a Fair Jane*. One reel. (Filmed July 2-3, 7-10, 12 &14, 1915). With Harold Lloyd, James T. Kelly, Gene Marsh, Elsie Greeson, Jack O'Brien, Frank J. Coleman, Jack Spinks.

A frame scan from the only known surviving copy of *A Mix-Up for Maisie* (1915) has a Hollenbeck Park confrontation for Harold and Elsie Greeson. *Courtesy of Peter Bagrov.*

Maisie Orpe is a dispenser of victuals in a second-rate beanery and is the light of the lives of several of the town "swells." But Luke de Fluke, an all-round gay lad; and Shorty Magee, the local tough nut; seem to lead the field in Maisie's blue orbs. This finally causes strained diplomatic relations between the pair, and a duel to the death is arranged. Each contestant writes to his object of his attentions that if she wants to see his rival she must be on hand at dawn the next day. Then both choose the same second. The dawn of the next day sees the two rivals at the appointed place with the one second to attend to both.

The duel starts per schedule, but while they are fighting their hardest they look up and see Maisie going off with the second. This, of course, causes a cessation of hostilities and both look longingly in the direction of the loving couple. Luke's sword catches in the ground and he has to resort to his feet to gain the decision. This gives Shorty the chance he's been looking for and he hurls a bomb at his adversary and blows him up. Luke comes down after a while, however, and they, too, call the contest, through mutual sympathy over the loss of Maisie, who has gone with the second. But later on Shorty lands the "bird," and the way he does it and the anguish of Luke are a fitting climax to this rip-roaring comedy. (Pathé Bulletin, September 3, 1915).

As of this writing *A Mix-Up for Maisie* has the distinction of being the earliest known surviving *Lonesome Luke* short. Residing in the collection of Moscow's Gosfilmofond Archive, it's currently unavailable, but frame scans from the film show that much of it was shot in Hollenbeck Park and its stone pergola (setting for other comedies such as 1915's *Mabel and Fatty's Wash Day*), as well as a supporting cast that includes James T. Kelly, Elsie Greeson, Jack O'Brien, Frank J. Coleman, and comedienne Gene Marsh.

Ms. Marsh is an early, important, and forgotten member of the Rolin Film stock company, having featured roles in fledgling shorts like *Pete the Pedal Polisher* and *Close-Cropped Clippings* (both 1915). Born Gladys Keller, she started performing as a child, singing in amateur theatricals with her father and siblings. By 1913 she was billing herself on stage as Gene Keller Marsh, and began her film career with two-and-a-half years at the Reliance-Majestic Company in shorts such as the Komic Comedy *Dizzy Joe's Career* (1914), and *Down the Hill to Creditville* (1914) with Dorothy Gish.

Briefly going to Keystone, this tall brunette's best-known appearance is as the King's favorite wife who flirts with Charlie Chaplin in *His Prehistoric Past* (1914). Soon switching over to the nascent Rolin unit, she was frequently "Maizie Nut" in the ensemble of the *Luke* comedies. Following shorts such as *Luke, the Candy Cut-Up* and *Luke Foils the Villain*, she left the screen. In 1919 she married vaudevillian Dale Bale, who performed under the stage name Bill Bailey, and traveled with him around the country. During the depression they moved overseas and eventually opened a nightclub, The Coconut Grove, in Singapore, where they both passed away.

Moving Picture World (September 11, 1915): "One of the 'Lonesome Luke' series and very amusing. The rivalry between Luke and another of his kind for the hand of a pretty miss, causes disastrous results for Luke, in his sorrow decides that life holds no further charm for him. The picture is constituted to please almost any audience."

Motography (September 11, 1915): "An amusing slap-stick comedy in which Lonesome Luke and Shorty spare themselves no pain to win the favor of Maisie, the pretty waitress of a 'popular priced' beanery. But their attentions, well meant as they are, only makes trouble for the fair one."

Gene Marsh is stuck on Snub Pollard in *Luke, the Candy Cut-Up* (1916).

Some Baby

Released September 20, 1915. A Phunphilm, produced by Hal Roach for the Rolin Film Company. Distributed by Pathé. Directed by Hal Roach. Working title: *Lonesome Luke – He Minds a Baby*. One reel. (Filmed July 12-17, 19-20, 24 & August 20, 1915). With Harold Lloyd, Elsie Greeson, Gene Marsh, Jack Spinks, Arthur Harrison.

Harold holds Elsie Greeson's lemonade in *Some Baby* (1915).

Luke has a difficult time finding a job. At last he gets a temporary assignment. A man has been asked by his college friend to go meet his friend's little niece at the railroad station, but the man has a big date with Florrie. He pays Luke to pick up the niece, who will be identified by the initials W. M. on her suitcase. Luke can hardly believe his good fortune when the niece turns up as a beautiful young lady. He has been given expense money, which he spends taking her for a soda, for a boat ride, and other amusements, before he takes her to the man's office. Meanwhile, the man has spent a lot of money on Florrie, including buying her a hat. When he arrives at his office, he is disgusted to find that Luke has been able to spend much less entertaining a much prettier girl. (*Moving Picture World*, October 2, 1915).

Amusement parks were a great location for silent comedies – like regular parks they were public and free. One of the initial Keystone releases had Mabel Normand, Ford Sterling, and Mack Sennett frolicking on the spinning

discs and famous Steeplechase in *At Coney Island* (1912), and Roscoe
Arbuckle revisited there in *Fatty at Coney Island* (1917).

Arbuckle, in particular, was fond of using amusement parks, so they
turned up in *A Bath House Beauty*, *Zip the Dodger* (both 1914), *Mabel's Wilful
Way*, *Fatty's Fickle Fall* (both 1915), *A Reckless Romeo* (1917), *The Cook* (1918),
and *Peaceful Oscar* (1927). Comics from the most forgotten to the best-known,
all spent time at the parks – everyone from Marcel Perez in *Oh! What a Day*
(1918) to Charlie Chaplin in the opening of *The Circus* (1928).

Portrait of the early film ingénue Elsie Greeson.

The titular "some baby" was played by Elsie Greeson, a busy movie ingénue who worked all over for outfits such as Kalem, Selig, Majestic, Nestor, Vogue, Tringle, Fox, and even the young Rolin Company. She was with Rolin for three productions –this, *A Mix-Up for Maisie*, and *Fresh from the Farm* (both 1915). Born in St. Louis, Mo., she started her career upon graduating from Los Angeles High School in 1913. Most of her work was done in comedies, such as episodes of Selig's *Chronicles of Bloom Center* series, and Al Christie-produced Nestor shorts with Eddie Lyons and Lee Moran. She even found time to appear in vaudeville with Mr. & Mrs. Carter De Haven. She was married to screenwriter/director Robert A. Dillion, and lived to be one hundred when she passed away in 1995.

Moving Picture World (September 25, 1915): "A farce that insures a good many laughs. The situation is first class and the players are lively and amusing. Pretty good."

Fresh from the Farm

Released October 4, 1915. A Phunphilm, produced by Hal Roach for the Rolin Film Company. Distributed by Pathé. Directed by Hal Roach. Working title: *Lonesome Luke, He Tries a College Course*. One reel. (Filmed July 20-24, 27, 29 & 31, 1915). With Harold Lloyd, James T. Kelly, Gene Marsh, Elsie Greeson, Jack Spinks, Arthur Harrison.

Harold is *Fresh from the Farm* (1915) and has a run-in with the law.

Rube Slivers is a farm boy whose father sends him to college. Rube eagerly chases the female students and has encounters with the president. Rube likes best Dolly Smawl, which makes the others jealous. Rube mixes up a chemical explosion in the chemistry lab. The I Eata Pie fraternity invites Rube to join. During the initiation rites, he is ordered to pose in the place of a cigar store Indian. Dolly comes by with a rival, and Rube hits him on the head with his tomahawk. The police chase Rube. He foils his pursuers by using a box of rotten eggs as gas bombs. (*Moving Picture World,* September 11, 1915).

Luke is not only a farm boy in this early entry but actually goes to college – two unusual roles for our India rubber tramp. Higher learning is not something that Luke generally aspires to, although Harold would later memorably go to college in *The Freshman* (1925). Other slapstick scholars included Buster Keaton, Dorothy Devore, Billy West, Buddy Messinger, Arthur Lake, Alice Ardell, Carter De Haven and even Al St John in titles like *The College Orphan* (1915), *The Scholar* (1918), *A Sorority Mix-Up* (1927), *College* (1927), *Rah, Rah, Rah!* (1928), and *Hot or Cold* (1928). There was also Universal's 1926 to 1929 series *The Collegians*, which was set in college and was big on athletics and hijinks, but weak on laughs.

Luke's farmer father is played by James T. Kelly, a silent comedy veteran and stalwart of the fledgling Rolin Company. Thanks to surviving photos Kelly appears to have been with the organization from its very beginning – appearing with Harold in *Willie Runs the Park, Pete the Pedal Polisher,* and *Close-Cropped Clippings,* as well as the first Luke shorts such as *Terribly Stuck Up, A Mix-Up for Maisie,* and *A Foozle at the Tee Party* (all 1915). Kelly seemed to have always been old, and specialized in playing decrepit bellhops or Irish laborers, which isn't surprising as he was born in Castlebar, Ireland in 1854. Raised in Baltimore, his years in theatre began in 1876 and encompassed the Pete Daly Company and vaudeville, in addition to being the principal comedian at San Francisco's Tivoli Opera House. The Tivoli was something of a glorified beer hall when Kelly starred there in drag as the lead in *The Widow O'Brien* in 1886.

When Kelly began his film career at Essanay in 19143, he was already sixty-one years old. In addition to Chaplin Essanay shorts like *A Night in the Show* (1915), he worked in comedies being directed there by a young Hal Roach with people like Snub Pollard and Bud Jamison. Roach continued to use Kelly when he set up Rolin, and from there he moved to his best-remembered work as part of Charlie Chaplin's Mutual comedies. His last appearance with Charlie was *A Dog's Life* (1918), and from there he became one of the most ubiquitous faces in silent comedy. A regular in Hank Mann

James T. Kelly (center) with Gene Marsh and Harold in
A Shine for a Dime/ Pete the Pedal Polisher (1914/1915).

shorts like *A Gas Attack* and *Broken Bubbles* (both 1920), he also supported Lloyd Hamilton, Snub Pollard, Baby Peggy, Monty Banks, Al St John, and Big Boy, to name just a few. He even returned to work with Harold in *An Eastern Westerner* (1920), *Among Those Present* (1921), *Dr. Jack* (1922), and *Safety Last* (1923). L-Ko, Century Comedies, Jack White Comedies, CBC, Weiss Brothers, and Arrow are only a handful of the outfits he worked for until 1929. He passed away close to the eighty-year mark in 1933.

An early and overlooked on screen and behind the scenes Rolin regular was Arthur Harrison:

> Hal E. Roach, president of the Rolin Film Company, is in charge of direction and is assisted by Arthur Harrison.
> *Motion Picture News*, September 18, 1915

Having been born in 1888, Harrison was very young when he entered the film industry after four years in the Navy. Before joining Rolin in 1915 he had spent six years with outfits such as Universal, Equitable, and the MacNamara Feature Film Company where he had been assistant director for King Baggot, George Loane Tucker, William Robert Daly, and Walter MacNamara. Most recently he had been part of the ensemble at MinA Comedies, and then fulfilled the same function in the *Lonesome Luke* shorts. Rolin ads said "Arthur Harrison as utility," and he maintained his dual role of actor and assistant director in 1915 entries such as *Bughouse Bellhops*, *Great While It Lasted*, *A Foozle at the Tee Party*, and *Lonesome Luke, Social Gangster*. Leaving the organization in 1916, he returned for 1917 shorts such as *Lonesome Luke, Plumber, Stop! Luke! Listen!*, and a few early glass character one-reelers like *Bliss* and *The Flirt*.

Giving Them Fits*

Released November 1, 1915. A Phunphilm, produced by Hal Roach for the Rolin Film Company. Distributed by Pathé. Directed by Hal Roach. Working title: **Lonesome Luke's New Occupation**. Extant: BFI. One reel. (Filmed August 10, 14, 16, 19-21, 23-26, 28, 30, 1915). With Harold Lloyd, Bebe Daniels, Snub Pollard, Gene Marsh, Jack O'Brien.

Luke de Fluke is a clerk in a shoe store. He has no time for male customers as long as females are in the shop. The manager complains, to no avail. Luke gets into trouble, though, with the shoe repairer, Joe. Joe runs to a nearby explosives factory, gets a bomb, and throws it at Luke, making a wreck of the whole store. All the boxes of shoes come tumbling down on Luke, and the last seen of him is his own feet sticking out of the debris. (*Moving Picture World*, November 13, 1915).

This appears to be the first short with Bebe Daniels and Snub Pollard in place as Lloyd's regular co-stars. There is a possibility that one or the other may have been in the previous *Fresh from the Farm*, but as the film is missing and neither appears in surviving photos, it's impossible to verify. They are both in the surviving *Giving Them Fits*, and would continue to appear together as a team for four years - until 1919's *Captain Kidd's Kids*.

> Dwight Whiting announces that Bebe Daniels is to be exclusively featured in forthcoming releases on the Rolin screen offerings.
>
> *Moving Picture World*, November 13, 1915

Virginia Daniels (nicknamed Bebe as an infant) had a fifty-plus year career that encompassed stage, silent and sound films, radio, and television. Having been on stage as a child, and working in films since she was eight for Selig, Pathé, Bison, and Vitagraph, Bebe first made a name for herself in Harold's comedies.

Bebe and Snub have joined Harold as shoe store staff in *Giving Them Fits* (1915).

"I was only fourteen when I got my engagement with Rolin. I shall never forget the day Mr. Whiting, the studio manager, telephoned mother that they were trying out girls to play with Mr. Lloyd, and asked her to send me down. She put my aunt's dress on me. It fitted perfectly and made me look seventeen."

"I was never so uncomfortable and self-conscious in my life," went on Bebe. "But I was anxious to get into picture work again, so my hopes were high until I discovered that the Eastern office of Pathé insisted that they have a blonde girl in the Rolin comedies. I was on the verge of offering to wear a yellow wig, when the manager said they would try me out anyway. They did – and here I am – black hair and all."

Picture-Play, December 1918

Starting as Harold's leading lady in 1915 (at $10 a week), Bebe was never a conventional shrinking and demure heroine – but was instead a feisty tomboy who gave back as good as she got. Bebe and Harold were romantically involved, but after four years she went out on her own to play the "other woman" in Cecil B. DeMille films like *Male and Female* (1919) and *The Affairs of Anatol* (1921), while at the same time starring in breezy comedies for Paramount's subsidiary Realart.

Snub Pollard and Bebe Daniels start their three-year run with Harold.
Courtesy of The Museum of Modern Art.

In 1924 Paramount started putting her in a series of fast paced "modern everywoman" comedies on the order of *The Campus Flirt* (1926) and *A Kiss in a Taxi* (1927). She did well in the change-over to sound in a variety of pictures such as *Rio Rita* (1929), *42nd Street* (1933), and *Counselor-At-Law* (1933), but moved to England with husband Ben Lyon, where they appeared on stage and became radio and television institutions with their hit shows *Hi Gang!* and *Life with the Lyons*. During World War II the Lyons were very involved in the war effort, and after the war President Harry Truman awarded Bebe the Medal of Freedom for her patriotism. Over the years Bebe and her husband remained very close to Harold. Having worked all her life, she retired in 1961 and died ten years later at age seventy.

Still one of the most recognizable faces in silent comedy, Snub Pollard was born Harold Fraser in Australia in 1888 and came to America as part of the child comic opera troupe Pollard's Lilliputians. Making the rounds of California theatre with Ferris Hartman's company, his earliest known film is Rex's *Sally Scraggs: Housemaid* in 1913. Appearing regularly in Essanay films, he turns up in Chaplin's *By the Sea* (1915) and *Police* (1916), and in shorts like *A Countless Count*, *Tale of a Tire*, *The Drug Clerk*, and *Fun at a Ball Game* (all 1915) directed by a young Hal Roach. When Roach got rolling with the *Lonesome Luke* shorts at his own studio, he hired Snub to support Harold.

Working as Lloyd's second banana until 1919, it was when Harold was out of commission after his bomb accident that Pollard was given his own starring one-reel series. With his character of a goofy goon with a Fu Manchu mustache, Snub's series lasted at the Roach lot until the mid-1920s, after which he moved to the independent Weiss Brothers Artclass Pictures. In sound films he plugged away in shorts, features, soundies, and television – even a stint as a sidekick in some low budget oaters. Working right up to his death in 1961, Snub sometimes appeared as himself in films about old Hollywood such as *Man of a Thousand Faces* (1957).

Moving Picture World (November 13, 1915): "This one-reel comedy produced by the Rolin Co., could not be referred to as being very high class. It is a farce comedy into which a remarkable amount of vulgarity has been worked. Toward the end of the reel some very amusing slapstick stuff has been presented, and it is unfortunate that the remainder of the picture is not as free from the objectionable as this portion referred to."

Bughouse Bellhops

Released November 8, 1915. A Phunphilm, produced by Hal Roach for the Rolin Film Company. Distributed by Pathé. Directed by Hal Roach. Working title: ***Hotel Picture***. One reel. (Filmed September 13-18, 25 & November 10, 1915). With Harold Lloyd, Bebe Daniels, Snub Pollard, Earl Mohan, Gene Marsh, Billy Fay, Jack O'Brien, Arthur Harrison.

Lonesome Luke and his accessory Moke Morpheus are discovered in bellhop uniform, blissfully dozing on a bench in the lobby of the Bughouse Hotel. Comes a guest, and the desk clerk rings a bell.

But, in the words of Aristotle, or Ted or someone, "you can ring and you can ring, but the house is boarded up." The clink of a few pieces of silver seems to touch some dormant chord in the boys' subconscious minds, and they immediately get on the job. Moke, after seeing the guest to his room, tries, of course, to hide the fact that a tip would be in order, and because of his modesty flies quickly from the room with the kindly aid of the roomer's leather encased pedal extremities. Luke escorts a girl guest to her room, and is starting quite a flirtation with her, when Moke whose motto is "pass nothing up" approaches them and tells Luke that there is a tall tip awaiting him in the new guest's room. Luke goes, and the guest learns how foolish and wasteful it is to break a perfectly good water pitcher on a bellboy's head. Luke then staggers back to Moke, and sends him with neatness and dispatch through a door and into the lap of a retiring guest.

With the arrival of a roughneck bouncer and his pretty wife, a fascinating free-for-all is started in which Luke, with a fire hose, gallantly stands off the concerted attack of the whole household. (*Moving Picture World*, November 20, 1915).

Bebe and Earl Mohan are aghast to see Snub and Harold fighting over Arthur Harrison's bag in *Bughouse Bellhops* (1915).

Another title for this entry could have been "Battling Bellhops" – which of course was a long tradition in silent slapstick. Fatty Arbuckle & Buster Keaton, Heinie & Louie, and Oliver Hardy & Bobby Ray do plenty of battling between answering bells in shorts like *The Bell Boy* (1918) and *Hop to It!* (1925). As in *Bughouse Bellhops*, the hotel setting is an excuse for the main comic to disrupt the service model of the institution – whether it's Musty Suffer in *The Lightning Bell-Hop* and *Belles and Bells* (both 1916), Billy West in *The Chief Cook* (1917) and *Bright and Early* (1918), Larry Semon as *The Bellhop* (1921) or Douglas MacLean in his feature *Bell Boy 13* (1923).

A cornerstone of the early Rolin Company was Earl Mohan, who as funny regular support sometimes gave Harold a run for his money. Born in Pueblo, Colorado in 1889, Mohan's background was a combination of show business and the fight game. He was a long-time boxer and promoter, but also spent time in vaudeville and with the Sells-Floto Circus. He entered films in 1914, and joined Rolin in late 1915, to play a variety of bumbling cops, irate hotel managers, and frequent drunks. Inebriation was his comic specialty, which he would do often. A fascinating feature of these early appearances is that he frequently wore glassless horn-rimmed spectacles, which eventually ended up on Harold in 1917 and became the basis for his up-and-coming young man persona.

Earl Mohan (right) about to be bonked by Snub Pollard under the guidance of Charles Stevenson (left) in *Luke and the Rural Roughnecks* (1916).

Besides photos, Mohan can still be seen in surviving *Lukes* like *Tinkering with Trouble, Peculiar Patient Pranks* (both 1915), *Luke, the Candy Cut-Up, Luke's Movie Muddle, Luke and the Bang-Tails* (all 1916), and *Lonesome Luke on Tin Can Alley* (1917). At the time of the changeover to Harold's glasses character Mohan was seen in only a few sporadic shorts as he devoted himself to boxing - developing and promoting fighters on the West Coast circuit of California, Oregon, Colorado, etc. Eventually he returned to Hollywood, and his comeback to movies was his hilarious performance as the pesky drunk in Harold's feature *Safety Last* (1923).

This launched him on a busy three-year run on the Roach lot. Not only did he turn up supporting Charley Chase, Will Rogers, and *The Spat Family*, but Roach launched him in his own series. Nine shorts were made with Mohan and little Billy Engle as "Hunky-Dorrey." In entries like *The Bouncer, All Wool*, and *Fast Black* (all 1925) they were inept fighters, tailors and Pullman porters. Sadly, audiences didn't warm up to their adventures, and Mohan left Roach to work elsewhere. Besides shorts like *Love and Lions* (1925) for Fox and Lloyd Hamilton's *Nothing Matters* (1925), he had a brief bit in Keaton's *The General* (1926) and larger supporting roles with Lloyd in *For Heaven's Sake* (1926) and the Fox feature *Love Makes 'Em Wild* (1927).

His last known appearances are quick walk-ons in *Find the King* (1927) and *Behind the Counter* (1928), two of the Edward Everett Horton two-reelers produced by the Harold Lloyd Corporation. Mohan looks terrible – haggard and bleary-eyed, so it's not a surprise that the October 17, 1928 *Variety* reported:

> Earl Mohan, veteran pugilist and film actor, died Oct. 15 at General Hospital, Los Angeles, just a week after the death of his wife.

The official cause of death was "General paresis" with bronchopneumonia as a contributing factor. General paresis is an arcane term for the mental deterioration occurring in advanced stages of syphilis. Mohan wasn't alone; other comics who died of it include Buster Keaton regular Big Joe Roberts and Chaplin supporting player Paddy McGuire. Only thirty-nine at the time of his death, Mohan never achieved the recognition he deserved for his comic talents.

Motion Picture News (November 13, 1915): "Luke and Moke with jobs as bellboys, nearly put a good hotel out of business. Through his eagerness for tips, Luke is batted around from guest to guest, and Moke is also having trouble, when a newly arrived couple attract their attention. The newcomers look 'easy' until it develops that the man is a professional bouncer."

Tinkering with Trouble*

Released November 17, 1915. A Phunphilm, produced by Hal Roach for the Rolin Film Company. Distributed by Pathé. Directed by Hal Roach. Working title: *Lonesome Luke, He Becomes a Janitor*. Extant: GOS. One reel. (Filmed August 26-28, 30-31, & September 2-4, 10, & October 2, 1915). With Harold Lloyd, Bebe Daniels, Snub Pollard, Phyllis Daniels, Earl Mohan, Frank J. Coleman.

Luke is busier on the phone than with his janitorial duties in this frame scan from 1915's
Tinkering with Trouble. *Courtesy of Peter Bagrov.*

Sour ball Joe gets the "can" for sassing the tenants, Easy Otis supplants him. But the latter does not know an awful lot of the art of "janitoring" and soon gets into many and various jams with the people upstairs. Multifarious are the tasks assigned to him and he knows naught of any of them. Then to cap the climax, the janitor who received his passports comes back to start something. He figures that to change the gas and water pipes would be a good stunt and he does it.

Upstairs, a fair dame wants her gas stove fixed, but when she turns it on, out comes many streams of water. A love-sick lad across the hall contemplates suicide by gas, but he too, gets water instead. And so it goes until the whole place is in an uproar. Then they start for Otis, but he believes discretion is the better part of valor and takes in on the run. (*Moving Picture World*, November 27, 1915).

After *A Mix-Up for Maisie* and *Giving Them Fits*, the third earliest *Lonesome Luke* survivor is *Tinkering with Trouble*. It is also in the collection of the Gosfilmofond Archive, and was publicly screened with *Luke Does the Midway* (1916) in a 2016 archive festival. So far it hasn't circulated otherwise.

Luke and Snub as inept janitors is standard silent comedy material. Whether it was as janitors, plumbers or wall paperers, slapstick comedians from Al St John, Ben Turpin and Bobby Vernon could be counted on to do the worst possible job imaginable. The switching of the gas and water pipes was a usual ingredient, and would continue to serve all the way up to 1940 with the Three Stooges in *A Plumbing We Will Go* and Laurel & Hardy's *Saps at Sea*.

An irascible tenant who's not at all happy about the water and gas switch is played by Phyllis Daniels, Bebe Daniels' character actress mother. After an extensive stage career she entered movies in 1911, working at Bison (she and Bebe both turn up in 1911's surviving *A Range Romance*) and appearing in many Kalem comedies with Ruth Roland and John E. Brennan such as *Ranch Girls on a Rampage* (1912), *The Laundress and the Lady* (1913), and *The Confiscated Count* (1916). There's a possibility that Phyllis worked at Rolin before her daughter, as the character actress in surviving photos from *Spit-Ball Sadie* (1915) resembles her. Bebe is quoted as saying "Mr. Whiting, the studio manager, telephoned mother that they were trying to find girls to play with Mr. Lloyd," suggesting that Phyllis may have already had a working relationship with the unit.

Bebe Daniels' mother Phyllis in the Kalem comedy *The Laundress and the Lady* (1913).

Once Bebe became one of the three leads in the series, Mrs. Daniels continued to turn up at Rolin in occasional shorts such as *Peculiar Patient Pranks* (1915) and *A Sammy in Siberia* (1919). She later became the Keystone wardrobe mistress and did bits in Sennett and Triangle comedies like *Skirt Strategy*, *His Hidden Talent*, *Their Husbands* (all 1917), and *Hide & Seek, Detectives* (1918). Phyllis appeared on and off in pictures for many years, and passed away in London in 1959.

At this time a young woman named Dolly Twist, a friend of general-manager Dwight Whiting's family, began submitting story ideas. It's difficult to say how detailed these "scenarios" were as the company was used to shooting off the cuff, but a number of her ideas were bought for twenty bucks a pop. Besides *Tinkering with Trouble*, other known titles she worked on include 1915's *Giving Them Fits*, *Ragtime Snap Shots*, *A Foozle at the Tee Party*, and *Peculiar Patient Pranks*. Although there's scant information, her association with the company seems to have continued on and off for a couple of years – her story *His Wash Laundry* probably became the July 3, 1916 release *Luke's Washful Waiting*, and she seems to be mentioned when the *Motion Picture News* detailed Rolin's activities in April 28, 1917:

> Dorothy Twist has been placed in charge of the scenario department.

There's no record of her working as Dolly or Dorothy at any other studio, and her involvement with Rolin seems to have ended with Dwight Whiting's exit from the organization in 1918.

The Journal (Meridian, Connecticut, December 17, 1915): "'Tinkering with Trouble' is an excellent comedy that has a laugh for every foot of film."

Natchez Democrat (November 29, 1915): "'Tinkering with Trouble' a Pathé comedy full of clever and eccentric comedy."

Great While It Lasted

Released November 24, 1915. A Phunphilm, produced by Hal Roach for the Rolin Film Company. Distributed by Pathé. Directed by Hal Roach. Working title: **Lonesome Luke, He Falls Into a Fortune and Out**. One reel. (Filmed August 10-14, 21, 23, 25 & September 20, 1915). With Harold Lloyd, Bebe Daniels, Snub Pollard, Gene Marsh, Arthur Harrison.

Byron Bearskin and Hugo Snubb, on the brink of despair, are threatened to put one foot over when they receive a laundry and rent bill for $20.02. Hugo Snubb having broken his last nickel for lollipops, they ache for eats. When lo! – glad tidings – Byron is rich; someone has died that he might live.

With a new shroud, plenty of money, and a new "vally" in the person of Hugo Snubb, and with cards printed to announce his importance, thusly: "Byron Bearskin. Worth $20,000,000.36," he sallies forth to flock with the queens and becomes a social lion. At a garden party a would-be pretender to Bearskin's social position, slits his trousers, forcing him to hie to a near-by body of water, where he must stand until a barrel is procured that he might proceed to home – and bad news. He isn't an heir, and as he finds out from the treatment accorded to him by his landlady, none of the glory of riches attaches to him. (*Moving Picture World*, December 4, 1915).

Harold's gotten an inheritance and all the ladies (including Snub) are vying for a piece of the action in *Great While It Lasted* (1915).

Luke and the Phunphilms were beginning to make an impression with audiences and critics, but it wasn't always the one hoped for. Here's a comment from reviewer Marion Howard in her column *Spokes from the Hub* from the December 25, 1915 issue of *The Moving Picture World*. Ms. Howard happened to catch this short between the Robert B. Mantell feature *The Unfaithful Wife*, and *Mr. Grex of Monte Carlo* with Theodore Roberts:

Harold's in a barrel with Bebe and the crowd in *Great While It Lasted* (1915).

To see some big star I go to the Modern – when I have the price – because it has always been the home of big productions and we are not inflicted with loud music, their organ being just right. So I was surprised the other day to have sandwiched between Mantell and Roberts one of the worst slapstick pictures yet seen, outclassing Chaplin and Dressler. It was called "Great While It Lasted," but it should be amended to "Rot," etc. Still any numbers of persons roared and really thought it a comedy. I claim that there are real comedies minus vulgarity which might better be presented and would cause as much laughter.

Motography (December 4, 1915) "Lonesome Luke comedy in which Luke inherits a fortune from a relation he never heard of. Luke breaks into society. While at a lawn party a jealous acquaintance causes Luke no end of embarrassment. He is not wealthy very long, for it is discovered that he is not the rightful heir."

Ragtime Snap Shots

Released December 1, 1915. A Phunphilm, produced by Hal Roach for the Rolin Film Co. Distributed by Pathé. Directed by Hal Roach. Scenario by Dolly Twist. Working title: ***Lonesome Luke, He Is Some Photographer***. One reel. (Filmed September 22-25, 27-30 & October 1 & 9, 1915). With Harold Lloyd, Bebe Daniels, Snub Pollard, Bud Jamison, Earl Mohan, Billy Fay.

Lucas and Larkin, his running mate, after looking for a job for some time, finally land one in a photographer's shop and immediately start to take possession of the place. They rule supreme in their own inimitable way until a be-spectacled college graduate arrives to have his diploma, and incidentally himself, photographed. He looks rather harmless with his bone-rimmed goggles , but when Lucas and Larkin attempt to take his feet off the table where he has placed them for safekeeping, he shows them a few new ones in the manly art of self-defense. Then Harry Hardguy makes his appearance. He looks more dangerous than the college boy, and makes outlaw the rule that looks are deceiving. He literally cleans out the place, and the last we see of Lucas and Larkin is when they are both making a bee-line for the street and safety. (Moving Picture World, December 4, 1915).

As Billy Fay's assistants Harold and Snub would rather shoot Bebe instead of Bud Jamison in *Ragtime Snap Shots* (1915).

Antics in a photographer's studio is a silent comedy perennial, used by the likes of the Powers Kids in *Having their Picture Took* (1913) and *Smile Please* (1924) with Harry Langdon. Harold would recycle this for his glasses character a couple of years later in *Look Pleasant, Please* (1918), and the Roach crew retooled it for Our Gang in 1933's *Wild Poses*. Photographic problems were also popular. Inept shutterbugs were the subject of two comedies titled *The Cameraman* – one a 1920 short with Billy Franey and the other the much better-known 1928 feature starring Buster Keaton. Our Gang even made their own movie in *Dogs of War* (1923) filled with startling double-exposures and upside-down scenes.

> Hal Roach, director of the Rolin Film Company, is busy this week on another Pathé comedy with his collection of comedians. The lead is in the hands of Harold Lloyd, who is a great fall artist. He is supported by some slapstick men such as Harry Pollard and Bud Jamison, who by the way, was only last week brought into this company from Essanay.
>
> *Moving Picture World*, October 16, 1915

Ragtime Snap Shots appears to be the first *Lonesome Luke* that features Bud Jamison - one of the rocks of early screen comedy - in support. Jamison worked practically everywhere and with every one during the silent and sound years. William Edmund Jamison made his film debut with Charlie Chaplin in *A Night Out* (1915), and worked at Essanay the remainder of that year for Chaplin and in shorts directed by Hal Roach. At the end of 1915 he became a regular in the *Lonesome Lukes* and stayed at Roach to support Harold in his glasses character shorts, as well as Toto and Stan Laurel until 1919.

From there he spent the next twenty-five years all over – working for every unit turning out comedy shorts, in addition to supporting roles in features. Although best remembered in sound for his appearances with The Three Stooges, he worked non-stop until his death in 1944. Sadly, a gangrenous infection that he refused to treat (he was a Christian Scientist) may have led to the heart attack that killed him at age fifty.

Motion Picture News (December 25, 1915): "This is an unusually amusing comedy staged in a photograph gallery. Luke and his partner, attracted by the pretty face of the photographer's clerk, get jobs as assistant photographers, and immediately turn things topsy turvy.

When the Two Dancing Dolls come to be photographed their rivalry becomes intense. Then they become involved with two husky characters who enter the place, and are pursued up chimneys and across roofs. Trick photography has aided considerably in producing situations and actions, and fun is fast throughout."

An amazingly young Bud Jamison.

A Foozle at the Tee Party

Released December 8, 1915. A Phunphilm, produced by Hal Roach for the Rolin Film Company. Distributed by Pathé. Directed by Hal Roach. Story by Dolly Twist. Working title: ***Lonesome Luke – He Tries His Hand at Golf***. One reel. (Filmed July 29, 31, and August 2-4, 7, 9-10, 14, 25 & 30, 1915). With Harold Lloyd, Bebe Daniels, Snub Pollard, James T. Kelly, Billy Fay, Jack O'Brien, Gene Marsh, Phyllis Daniels, Arthur Harrison, Clifford Silsby.

Lonesome Luke wanders near the golf course and is angered when hit by a stray ball from the driver of Lord Smitem. He returns the ball with considerable speed and Smitem, who received it on the head, is "put out" for a time. Luke dons the golfer's clothes and makes his way to the club house, where he meets Letty Lotsocoin. He makes good progress but the time is too short, for Smitem, upon awakening, enlists the aid of the caddies and Luke is not only discredited but suffers physical discomfort as well. (Motography, December 25, 1915).

Harold's *A Foozle at the Tee Party* (1915) that gets taken care of by Billy Fay, Bebe, James T. Kelly, Phyllis Daniels, Jack O'Brien (center) and mustacheless Snub.

Golf first came to America in 1657, but it wasn't until the early 20th Century that it experienced a real surge in popularity. The Professional Golfer's Association of America was founded in 1916, so the little Rolin unit was right there with one of the very first comedies set on the links. The sport quickly became fair game for other comics such as Harry Watson Jr., Paul Parrott, Larry Semon, Monty Banks, and Laurel & Hardy. They all spent time on the course, and memorable silent film examples include Charlie Chaplin's *The Idle Class* (1921) and the feature *So's Your Old Man* (1926) which captures W.C. Fields' famous Ziegfeld Follies golfing routine. Later incarnations would be Martin & Lewis in *The Caddy* (1953), *Caddyshack* (1980), and Adam Sandler's *Happy Gilmore* (1996).

One of Harold's opponents on the green is Jack O'Brien. Not to be confused with actor and director John B. O'Brien, who directed numerous shorts and features into the 1920s (often as Jack O'Brien), this Jack O'Brien was an Australian-born stuntman and bit player who worked at the Hal Roach Studio from 1915 into the sound era. He can be spotted in photos from the earliest Lonesome Lukes like this, *A Mix-Up for Maisie* (1915), *Luke Lugs Luggage* (1916), and continued on into Lloyd's glasses character shorts, in addition to the studio's Snub Pollard, Stan Laurel, Charley Chase, Our Gang, and Laurel & Hardy series.

Jack O'Brien and Harold in a frame scan from *A Mix-Up for Maisie* (1915).
Courtesy of Peter Bagrov.

Always on the edges of the shorts as grocers, street vendors, iron workers, chauffeurs, shoe shiners or prospectors, his standout role is as the devil in Our Gang's *Saturday Afternoon* (1929). As an actor whom the kids think is the actual devil, he proceeds to scare the bejesus out of them so that they obey their parents and do their chores, etc. Continuing to work for many years in the film business, the last employer listed on his 1975 death certificate is Desilu Productions.

Motion Picture News (December 25, 1915): "The Rolin Company has made a very funny number here, by employing a golf course as the setting for the picture. On the links Lonesome Luke impersonates Lord Smitem, meets Letty Lotsofcoin and is getting along fairly well when the angry lord shows up. It's a wonder that someone hasn't realized the comedy that lies in a golf club before, as Luke and his associates, continually wielding the sticks, cut a most comical appearance."

Ruses, Rhymes, and Roughnecks

Officer Earl Mohan (center) about to stop Harold's flirting in
Ruses, Rhymes and Roughnecks (1915).

Released December 15, 1915. A Phunphilm, produced by Hal Roach for the Rolin Film Company. Distributed by Pathé. Directed by Hal Roach. Working title: ***Lonesome Luke – He Has a Spell of Absentmindedness***. One reel. (Filmed from June 28-30 and August 23-4 & 28, 1915). With Harold Lloyd, Earl Mohan, Gene Marsh, Jack Spinks.

This offering tells the tale of Oscar Weeban, a fellow deeply in love with a certain Maisie. He has promised to take her to the Garbage Gentlemen's Rally, that annual society event of the small town which it is their fortune to reside, and she sends him a note to this effect. He is a rank outsider, but manages to inject himself into the spirit of

Harold shares some fruit with a child in *Ruses, Rhymes and Roughnecks* (1915).

the affair and enters into the sport of the occasion with vim. It is at this event that the ashes throwing contest is held every year, and garbage men from all sections, trained to the minute, flock to the party to compete. The contest is at its height and one of the experts is trying for a world's record when Oscar crosses the range. Of course, he and Maisie manage to get in the way of the winning throw and spoil the record which is about to be made. But what cares he? Despite the boob he made of himself at this elite affair, Maisie falls for him hard, after he has written some poetry for her, and the picture winds up with Oscar in the charming role of bridegroom. (*Moving Picture World*, December 18, 1915).

Being a "garbage gentleman" is a good indication of how low Luke was at this point on society's totem pole. He was a total outcast, although over the next couple of years Harold would work hard to update his status and appearance. Tramps were a popular comic stereotype in films, on stage, and in comic strips, with two of the best known on screen being Charlie Chaplin and Musty Suffer.

The most low-down and despicable were the team of Ham & Bud. Lloyd Hamilton and Bud Duncan appeared in more than one hundred one-reelers from late 1914 into 1917 for the Kalem Company. Their only distinguishing characteristics was that one was a big scuzzy bum and the other a little scuzzy bum, but while the films were rough and primitive an occasional sense of wild surrealism bubbled to the surface in outings like *Ham and the Sausage Factory* (1915) and *A Sauerkraut Symphony* (1916). The pair also make their own appearance as trashmen in 1915's *Ham at the Garbage Gentlemen's Ball.*

Very little is known about the missing *Ruses, Rhymes, and Roughnecks*, but historian John Bengston has identified a few of the street locations in surviving photographs. The photos were taken in Edendale, California on the northwest corner of Aaron Street and North Alvarado Street. Mack Sennett's Keystone, Selig, and the Norbig Studios were all located in Edendale, and the fledgling Rolin Company rented the Norbig Studio and laboratory. Many of the Edendale buildings and streets are still iconic today from their constant use in comedy shorts.

Since his debut in July, Luke had progressed to an up-and-coming comedy favorite. In only six months he had become the solid breadwinner for the Rolin unit, and to stress his importance the studio planted what looks like a humorously fictitious item in the trade magazines:

> The Rolin Company has been trying for two months to secure
> an insurance policy on Harold Lloyd, leading comedian appearing

in the part of Luke in the "Lonesome Luke" comedies, but owing to the many hazards this comedian takes, no company will issue a policy. A number of agents have been taken to the studio, but none have been successful in inducing their company to take a chance on Lloyd.

Motion Picture News, December 11, 1915

Motography (January 1, 1916): "Lonesome Luke attends the annual Garbage Gentlemen's Rally with Maisie. While the ashes throwing contest is in progress Luke and Maisie cross the range. Luke gets in the way of what is sure to break the record for speed and distance ashes throwing. But he makes a hit with Maisie, so he cares little for the mussing up he is subject to."

Peculiar Patient Pranks*

Released December 22, 1915. A Phunphilm, produced by Hal Roach for the Rolin Film Company. Distributed by Pathé. Directed by Hal Roach. Working title: *Lonesome Luke – He's Almost an Ostrich*. Extant: LOC. One Reel. (Filmed September 3-4, 6-7, 11 and October 9-10, 1915). With Harold Lloyd, Bebe Daniels, Snub Pollard, Phyllis Daniels, Gene Marsh, Billy Fay, Earl Mohan, Jack O'Brien, Arthur Harrison.

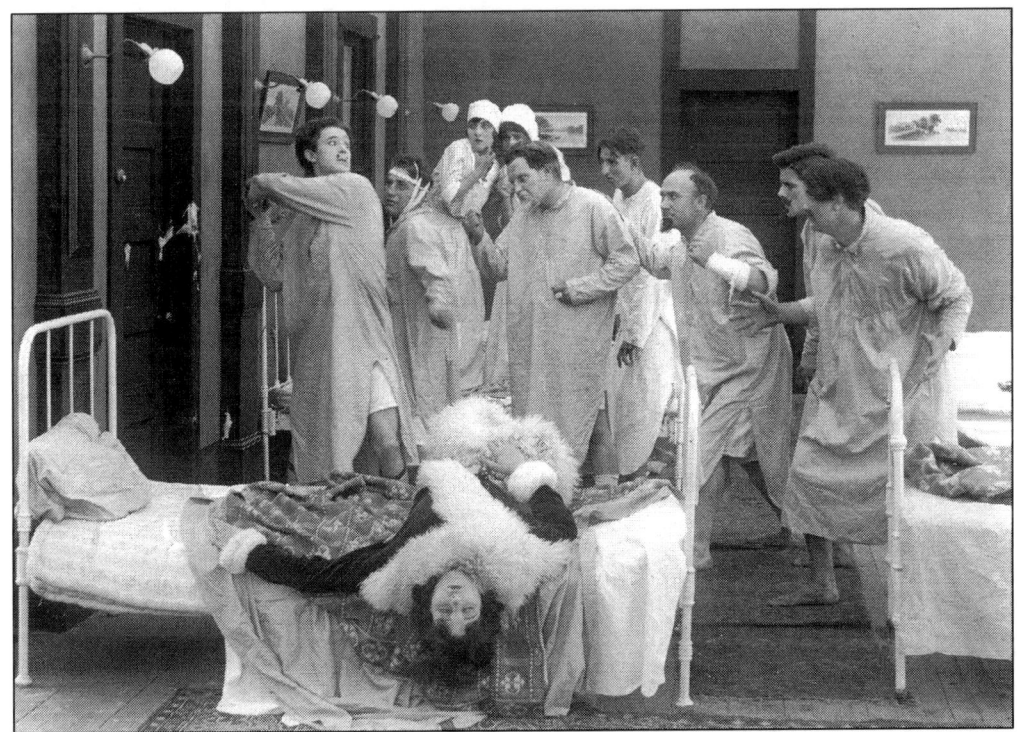

Bebe's passed out, as Harold keeps Arthur Harrison and his other ward mates at bay in *Peculiar Patient Pranks* (1915).

Luke and his partner have a head-swatting contest, in which Luke comes out second best. Chasing across a busy highway, the pal gets in the way of a sweet young lady's car and gets hit. He is taken in the car to the nearest hospital, all the way to which institution his head rests on the young lady's lap. Luke, noting the fortunate accident, endeavors to do likewise – one car misses him – the next one hits him and he is also rushed to the hospital – in an ambulance. He is allotted a bed in the ward outside his pal's private room. Peeved, he makes things miserable for the "dead ones." The revengeful doctors operate on him for something that doesn't ail him. After that he becomes demon trickster and equips himself with a quart of chloroform, and when the young lady calls to see his pal he opens the portals to dreamland via the chloroform route. The other patients attack him in close formation and receive a life free ticket to fairyland. His weapon exhausted, he is overcome by the nurses and sent to the land which Alice so well describes, when his head connects with a hammer. (*Moving Picture World*, December 25, 1915)

> "Luke, Love and Chloroform," is the title of number eleven of the "Lonesome Luke" series made by the Rolin Film Company under the Phunphilm brand on the Pathé program. In this Harold Lloyd as Luke, and Harry Pollard as Snub have an awful time with their new machine, which lands them in the hospital. Bebe Daniels is the heroine, and Gene Marsh is the head nurse. The direction is in charge of Hal Roach.
>
> *Motion Picture News*, October 9, 1915

As they had done in *Just Nuts*, the Rolin Company again moves into L-Ko Comedies territory with this "hijinks in a hospital" story. The very first L-Ko was *Love and Surgery* in 1914, a smash hit that established the series, and was quickly followed up by *Cupid in a Hospital* (1915). The pictures featured the studio's resident psychopath, Billie Ritchie, as he made life unbearable for all the other hospital patients and staff. Although Lonesome Luke is often cited as an imitation of Charlie Chaplin, there was a lot of Ritchie in his persona. Harold's character in *Just Nuts* (1915) had even been a dead ringer for Ritchie.

Luke's mean streak and penchant for hitting and kicking followed Ritchie's lead, just at the time that Chaplin was toning down his violence to explore and expand other facets of the Little Tramp's screen personality. The combative tramp figure was a holdover from the English music hall as other transplanted Brits such as Jimmy Aubrey, Sydney Chaplin, and Billie Reeves used it as well. This was precisely the tradition and style of comedy that Harold wanted to get away from when he created his young man with glasses character.

Billy Fay officiates for Bebe and Harold in 1918's *Bride and Gloom*.

Peculiar Patient Pranks is number four of the early Luke survivors, which is in the collection of the Library of Congress, and playing the head doctor is Billy Fay, a fixture of the Rolin Company from the beginning. Little and very bald – in fact Harold would often use his shiny dome as a mirror to check his teeth or fix his tie – Fay specialized in authority figures such as doctors, bosses, fathers, and especially ministers. Born William McDonald, he was a stage veteran who was billed in vaudeville as "Billy Fay – King of Clowndom." After touring in musical comedies like *The Girl from Rector's*, he joined Rolin in late 1915 and remained in support through 1919. Besides Harold's *Lonesome Luke* and glasses character shorts, Fay also worked in Dee Lampton's *Skinny* series, and became assistant director on Harold's films.

On moving out from Rolin he turned up in shorts for Earl Montgomery & Joe Rock, Jimmy Aubrey, and Mack Sennett, in addition to bits in features like *The Dangerous Moment* (1921) and *Scandal Proof* (1925). He returned to the stage in the 1920s when he toured in productions of *Abie's Irish Rose*, and came back to films briefly in the 1930s for a few Educational Comedies with Pat Rooney Jr. and Tim & Irene Ryan. Originally from Boston, he passed away in New York in 1941.

Moving Picture World (January 1, 1916): "This is one of the best of the 'Lonesome Luke' comedies, and shows Luke getting himself into a hospital for the purpose of meeting a girl whom he admires. He makes things rather more lively than usual about the hospital, and uses chloroform to stupefy doctors, nurses, etc., when he attempts to kidnap the girl. A good farce number."

Lonesome Luke, Social Gangster

Released December 29, 1915. A Phunphilm, produced by Hal Roach for the Rolin Film Company. Distributed by Pathé. Directed by Hal Roach (some sources credit J. Farrell MacDonald). Working title: ***Café Picture***. ½ reel. (Filmed September 7, 10-11, 13-14, 18 and November 10, 1915). With Harold Lloyd, Bebe Daniels, Snub Pollard, Gene Marsh, Arthur Harrison, Charles Stevenson, Earle Rodney, Billy Fay, Earl Mohan, Jack O'Brien.

Luke and his companion Tin-Horn Tommy are shooting craps on a public thoroughfare when an ugly looking pedestrian comes tramping along. Like a fox can scent the approach of the hounds – so did they feel the presence of the badge-carrier. Luke retreats to the roadway and a few seconds later finds himself astride the radiator of a swiftly moving motor-chariot. Little Miss Somebody goes motoring and sees a sign offering a hundred dollars to the best dancing partner for Mrs. Vermin Rastle.

The car on which Luke is riding bumps into the rear end of that belonging to the little millionairess and he lands in the seat beside her. She takes him in for feed and to try his feet at stepping. Tommy also meets a meal-ticket in the shape of someone not very good to look upon. In the establishment they try their feet at stepping and Luke, being able to floor the internationally famous stepper more times than anyone present, is given the razoo. But you can't keep a good man out, so he comes back with a pistol which he has taken from a policeman. When the commotion subsided there was still a few bits of furnishings that remained intact. (*Moving Picture World*, January 1, 1916).

Lonesome Luke, Social Gangster (1915) creates much mayhem in a posh eatery.

The missing *Lonesome Luke, Social Gangster* was what was called a "split-reeler" – half the length of the regular one-reel *Luke* (which was ten minutes). The split-reelers were usually combined in the theatres with a five-minute actuality or animated short. Pathé had plenty of these little "novelties" on hand, and in this case filling out the reel was *When Trees Are Stone*, a scenic look at Arizona's Petrified Forest.

Split-reel comedies were very common in the early teens; in fact the very first Keystone release in 1912 was two half-reel comedies together – *The Water Nymph* and *Cohen Collects a Debt*. Sennett would do this routinely at the beginning, but he began to produce his own actualities such as *The Kelp Industry* and *The Largest Boat Ever Launched Sideways* (both 1913) that would be paired with the short dose of slapstick. By the latter teens, two-reel comedies became the norm, and the split-reelers were phased out. One-reel cartoons and instructive films became a standard part of a cinema show.

In their favor, split-reel comedies were short and sweet – usually just one basic situation, often shot off-the-cuff. Made briskly and economically in a park or some other public location, they helped fill up the release schedule. Bebe Daniels later told authors Jill Allgood and Leslie Wood:

> We all went out in cars, with Hal Roach in the leading car not knowing what we were going to shoot, and we worked out ideas on the way. When Hal found a location he liked, we stopped, the camera was set up, and we would decide on the scene and action.
>
> *Bebe and Ben*

> We never had a script. We would start with an idea and work up the film as we went along. Lloyd and I often went out together for picnics and to fun fairs. We used to go to dance competitions, too, where we won several cups and prizes.
>
> *The Miracle of the Movies*

It seems likely that someone at the studio, thinking of Harold and Bebe winning their dancing contests, hit upon this as a good rough idea, and so the cast and crew set out and saw what developed for five minutes of screen time. This type of extemporaneous shooting helped give silent comedies the spontaneity for which they're prized today.

Motion Picture News (January 8, 1916): "Luke is especially funny, when his efforts to escape the police, who want him for shooting craps, land him in an automobile beside a young thing who is in search of a dancing partner. His pal also finds a dancing partner, and in trying out their steps in public, jealousy gives rise to a fight, the police are called and Luke is recognized as the man they have been seeking. His dancing days are ended, but not until the establishment is wrecked. On the same reel is 'Where Trees Are Stone,' which furnishes some striking views of the petrified forest of Arizona."

Moving Picture World (January 8, 1916): "The experiences of Lonesome Luke in this split-reel comedy are thrilling enough and entertaining in an elementary way. The picture will go well with audiences partial to slapstick. Completing the reel is an instructive subject entitled 'When Trees Are Stone'".

Hal Roach and Dwight Whiting (center) joins the actors on the set of
Lonesome Luke, Social Gangster (1915) for a Rolin company photo.

Lonesome Luke Leans to the Literary

Released January 5, 1916. A Phunphilm, produced by Hal Roach for the Rolin Film Company. Distributed by Pathé. Working title: *Luke Leans to the Literary*. One reel. (Filmed October 26 – 30, November 1 – 4, 6, 13, 17, 23 & 29, 1915). With Harold Lloyd, Bebe Daniels, Snub Pollard, Gene Marsh, Otto Fries.

Lonesome Luke delegates to sell some literature and receives a large folder containing general info about his wares. To become adept in that one particular line, one must be a born poet and our hero has no great difficulty to make himself that. A busy man at his office is just the proper one to trap into a deal because even his employees, in their haste, fail to have time to eject droppers in at the orders of the boss. Luke selects just such an establishment and "goes to it" with the usual selections of chin-music. He fails thrice to sell his wares, but succeeds admirably in causing havoc in the home of the pen-pushers. Later in the day unkind fate takes him to this man's home where his arguments with his wife prove futile. While in between gaps he consumes the contents of a refreshment decanter. Inclined to be spoony, Luke goes to the park to hunt himself a partner and meets with this same man's daughter. Spooning under difficulties in the park, she takes him home, telling him that her father will buy his volumes. Now as we know, Ma and Pa have seen the stranger before and very handily beat him up within a half inch of the law. (*Moving Picture World*, January 8, 1916).

Luke takes his turn as a pesky, high-powered salesman. Comics such as Monty Banks, Stan Laurel, Paul Parrott, Monty Collins, and A Ton of Fun all spent screen time peddling books, washing machines, or miracle cleaners. Some of their canvassing misadventures include *The Pest* (1922), *Paging Love*, *The Smile Wins* (both 1923), *Standing Pat*, and *The Lost Laugh* (both 1928).

Cameraman James A. Crosby plies the cinematographer's art as Hal Roach directs Harold, Ralph McComas, and Snub in 1917's *Lonesome Luke's Lively Life.*

A most important part of any comedy unit was their cameraman. Essential was the knowledge of the proper cranking speeds to get full comic effects, as well as the ability to capture all the roughhouse tumble and physical action in a concise way. Mack Sennett had some of the best comedy cameramen in the business at his Keystone Studio, but the fledgling Rolin outfit went through a good deal of trial and error. In his autobiography Harold remembered issues at the beginning:

> A counterbalance device called the Court Flight hauls passengers up and down the short steep grade of Court Street Hill at a penny fare, one car descending on a cable as the other ascends. One of Roach's early inspirations was to have Willie Work roll down this flight between the two tracks. The cameraman stationed himself at the bottom and pointed his lens up the flight. When I had rolled down, with many bruises, and the film was developed Willie Work was found, inexplicably to be rolling on a level roadway. We were so green at the business that we did not know that if you want angle in a picture you first must get angle in your lens, By inclining his camera at the same gradient as that of my descent, the cameraman had flattened it out to a spirit-level smoothness.
>
> Roach put arnica on my bruises and sirup on my vanity and we tried it a second time. Now the cameraman stationed himself in a second-story window across Spring Street at the foot of the flight. His angle was true, but there is more than one dimension to a picture; the scene had been taken at such a distance that Willie Work was a mere blob on the developed negative. We might as well have rolled a dummy down the incline. There was no third time.

As mentioned in Chapter One the first cameraman for Rolin was Fred W. Jackman. He appears to have left before the *Lonesome Luke* shorts started, so it's uncertain who started the series behind the camera. The photographer who later became synonymous with the Lloyd films was Walter Lundin, who shot the comedian's pictures for almost thirty years. Lundin was instrumental in helping to create the look of the films, in addition to pioneering the illusions for the "high and dizzy" pictures like *Look Out Below* (1919), *Never Weaken* (1921), and *Safety Last* (1923). Some sources say that Lundin shot the *Luke* films, but he didn't:

> Walter Lundin has been engaged as cameraman for Harold Lloyd-Lonesome Luke organization.
>
> *Motion Picture News*, July 21, 1917

By the time Lundin was hired by Rolin in July of 1917 all of the *Lonesome Luke* shorts had been shot and were in the can, with the final two-reelers being released amongst Harold's new glasses character one-reelers. Lundin arrived around the time of the making of *Bliss* (1917) the fourth of the new one-reel series.

So, the very first *Luke* cameramen aren't known, but as the studio became better known the trade magazines started taking notice of their comings and goings. The October 30, 1915 *Moving Picture World* shared:

> One of the cameramen, Clyde R. Cook, has left to join the Universal, and his position is taken by R.S. Rosher, formerly with Lasky, Universal and other prominent producing companies.

The Clyde Cook mentioned isn't the comedian, but a cinematographer who had worked at Selig, and moved on to Universal and Triangle features. R.S. Rosher is actually Charles Rosher who became well-known as Mary Pickford's cameraman. Being interviewed years later for *The Parade's Gone By*, Rosher told Kevin Brownlow that he had been loaned by Lasky to Rolin and shot some *Lonesome Luke*'s with a youthful Harold Lloyd. Later shooting some of the most beautiful silent films made such as *Sparrows* (1926) and *Sunrise* (1927), Rosher's time at Rolin was very brief, and probably resulted in only one or two films like *Lonesome Luke Leans to the Literary*, *Luke Lugs Luggage*, or *Lonesome Luke Lolls in Luxury*
.

Moving Picture World (January 15, 1916): "This is an extremely amusing farce comedy in which Luke does his best in the interests of a book agency. His efforts are not always appreciated by his victims, hence a great deal of the comedy of the film."

Motography (January 22, 1916): "In this comedy Luke sets out to be a book agent. He starts out with the right idea, he is persistent, but he loses this when the return for it is some pretty rough treatment. It is a laughable slapstick comedy."

Luke Lugs Luggage

Released January 10, 1916. A Phunphilm, produced by Hal Roach for the
Bebe flirts with book salesman Harold in *Lonesome Luke Leans to the Literary* (1916).

Rolin Film Company. Distributed by Pathé. Directed by Hal Roach. One reel. (Filmed October 26-30, & November 2, 6, & 23, 1915). With Harold

Lloyd, Bebe Daniels, Snub Pollard, Gene Marsh, Earl Mohan, Jack O'Brien, Arthur Harrison, Dwight Whiting.

Jack O'Brien, Snub, Gene Marsh, Bebe, Earl Mohan, Arthur Harrison, and a crowd are all unhappy with Harold's work in *Luke Lugs Luggage* (1916). General-manager Dwight Whiting helps fill out the crowd all the way in the back.

Luke takes the role of a baggage smasher at the terminal of a railroad. He got the job by answering a newspaper ad which announced the work to be "light and the pay good." But many and arduous are the duties which he is required to perform. Large and small trunks, livestock, bindles, boxes and all sorts of stuff comes under his care and he gets away with it fairly well. Yes, until a large billy goat of the long horn species comes his way. This fellow, with his well- developed tendency to buck anything and anybody in his path, leads Luke a merry chase. He is thrown hither and yon, but finally conquers him. Next, however, comes a large box of dynamite which Luke is supposed to ship. The things blows up and our hero is wafted several miles by the force of the explosion. The last we see of him is when he lands on the top rung of a friendly telegraph pole. (Pathé Bulletin, January 7, 1916).

In the early part of the 20th Century trains were the norm for most local and long-distance travel, and Luke was part of the long line of inept comedy baggage handlers that included Billy West, Hank Mann, Milburn Moranti, and even Lou Costello.

Although this film isn't known to survive, studio general manager, secretary, and treasurer Dwight Whiting can be seen in photos, helping to fill out the crowd scenes. Born in Los Angeles in 1891, Whiting came from a wealthy family and intended to go into law. After attending the Groton School in Boston and Stanford University he decided to go into business. He managed a large automobile agency in San Francisco, but at the death of his father returned to L.A. to take charge of his family's properties. Whiting's lawyer happened to be Hal Roach's lawyer, and when Rolin was looking for more funds Roach and Whiting were introduced. Whiting joined the Rolin unit at age twenty-three in 1915:

> Pathé asked for more pictures, and to continue further operation, Roach enlisted the interest of Dwight Whiting, well-known resident of Los Angeles, who acquired a one-third of the company. Mr. Whiting organized the business on a sound basis and made W.H. Doane his assistant. Messrs. Whiting and Roach became sole owners of the concern when Dan Lintheum, the third partner, jointly sold them his interests.
>
> *Motion Picture News*, January 25, 1919

That's the official version of Whiting's beginning with Rolin, but an additional reason may have been that his brother George, who had been in vaudeville with his wife Sadie Burt, acted in some of the 1915 Rolin shorts. George also wrote for the company and was still there in September of 1916. It's possible that Dwight Whiting's interest in the organization was first piqued by his brother's participation.

After setting up and running Rolin's business for four years, Whiting left the position in 1918. In 1986 Roach told film historian Glenn Mitchell that Pathé didn't like Whiting and gave Hal the money to buy him out:

> A deal was consummated on Wednesday, April 3, by which Dwight Whiting, secretary and treasurer of the Rolin Film Company, relinquishes his interests in this organization to Hal E. Roach, president of the company.
>
> *Moving Picture World*, May 4, 1918

Hal Roach's father, C.H. Roach, took over the positions of secretary and treasurer, and Harry Burns studio manager. Dwight Whiting remained in the business end of show business for many years, later as an executive at KTTV Television, Consolidated Television Sales, and Official Films.

In addition to the likes of Earl Mohan, Gene Marsh, and Jack O'Brien, another of Harold's supporting players in this film was a hungry goat, whose appetite didn't exactly endear him to director Hal Roach:

> It was necessary to employ a billy goat in a current Rolin picture. Among other amusing stunts that the "billy" did was the confiscation and swallowing of three scenarios from Director Roach's hip pocket. When Mr. Roach discovered the loss the only part of the scenarios in sight was a portion of one of the final pages which was written "finis."
>
> *Moving Picture World*, January 18, 1916

Pathé Bulletin (January 7, 1916): "For lots of action and good, wholesome fun, we heartily recommend this film – it's a laugh from start to finish."

The Leavenworth Times (October 1, 1916): "Luke, the India rubber comedian, is a scream as a baggage handler in 'Luke Lugs Luggage'.

Dwight Whiting and Hal Roach as seen in the
December 10, 1915 Pathé Bulletin. *Author's collection.*

Luke Lugs Luggage (1916) and gets some "butting in" from a bit player.

Lonesome Luke Lolls in Luxury

Released January 19, 1916. A Phunphilm, produced by Hal Roach for the Rolin Film Co. Distibuted by Pathé. Working titles: *Luke Falls in Luxury* and *Shipwrecked*. One reel. (Filmed November 6, 9-13, 20 and December 10, 1915). With Harold Lloyd, Bebe Daniels, Snub Pollard, Gilbert Pratt, Blanche White, Otto Fries, Earl Mohan, Arthur Harrison.

Gilbert Pratt (center) and Arthur Harrison (left) shoot daggers at Snub, Harold, and Blanche White in Lonesome *Luke Lolls in Luxury* (1916).

*Luke and Snub are sailors cast away on a desert island. They are captured by savages and taken to the chief. He puts them to work waving a large palm leaf over the heads of his six wives. The sailors and the wives flirt with each other. The chief is angry, and assigns the sailors to amuse his ugly wife, who has been ostracized by the others. Luke manages to temporarily force the chief to abdicate and takes his place. He rescues a white girl from slavery in the harem, but when he flirts with her, her sweetheart turns up to raise objections. The chief regains his mastery. Luke and Snub leave, swimming for home. (*Moving Picture World*, Jan. 15, 1916 and Feb. 5, 1916).*

The Rolin Company was getting established and starting to make a name for itself. As this happened the unit was able to draw on solid talent, many of whom would become regular film comedy participants for many years:

Doings of the Rolin Film Company

Gilbert Pratt, Otto Friese and Blanche White have recently joined the Rolin Film Company, all having taken part in the seventeenth of the "Lonesome Luke Phunfilms" series, which is now completed. Saturday last week, was a strenuous day at the Rolin studios, and two of the players had to be sent to the hospital as a result of the rough and tumble comedy stunts.

The Rolin Film Company is planning to build an additional stage, about 60 by 75 feet, to take care of the large sets being used by the Phunphilm pictures.

Moving Picture World, December 11, 1915.

Gilbert Pratt is a neglected figure in silent comedy. A busy writer and director of shorts, he was a solid utility man who never settled in one place but instead worked practically everywhere. In addition to Harold Lloyd, some of the other stars whose comic misadventures he piloted include Lloyd Hamilton, Al St John, Montgomery & Rock, Monty Banks, and A Ton of Fun. Originally a bank teller and an auto salesman, amateur theatricals led Pratt to the movies where he started at Kalem as an actor. He was soon playing heavies at Rolin on the *Lonesome Luke* shorts (and when not doing this he was Hal Roach's driver).

By early 1916 most of the directorial work on the *Lonesome Lukes* was taken over by Harold and Pratt, leaving Hal Roach to take care of administrative duties. Although not officially credited on the films, the trade magazines, like the following item, document Pratt's duties behind the camera:

Harold Lloyd, who has appeared in the part of Lonesome Luke in all comedies, with Gilbert Pratt will direct the second company, Lloyd appearing in the principal part.

Motion Picture News, July 1, 1916

When Harold switched to his new "glasses character" Pratt became one of the regular directors. After helming numerous Lloyd entries like *Pinched* (1917), *It's a Wild Life*, and *Hear 'Em Rave* (both 1918), he moved on and began turning up all over – Vitagraph, Federated, Fox, Jack White, Christie – and would continue for the rest of the decade. He also worked on the scripts of features such as *Clancy's Kosher Wedding* and *Two Flaming Youths* (both 1927), and in sound films it was as a writer that he did most of his work. His later credits include being a gagman on Laurel & Hardy's *Saps at Sea* (1940), and contributing to some mid-1940s Columbia shorts. He died in Los Angeles in 1954.

Luke Pipes the Pippins (1916) and is about to put the kibosh on Gilbert Pratt's muscle flexing.

The plot of Luke and Snub being shipwrecked on a desert isle would be dusted off and used again in the September 2, 1917 release *Lonesome Luke's Wild Women*. Speaking of wild women, the company got a surprise when it came time to shoot scenes with the chief's harem:

> Director Hal E. Roach of the Rolin company, failed to give specific instructions to a bevy of ten Oriental vaudeville dancers engaged for a scene to be made for a Phunphilm comedy in front of one of the fashionable mansions of the Wilshire district, Los Angeles, this week, and the owner of the property, director, and all others were horrified, when the girls appeared with scarcely more than smiles. The director was quick to correct the misunderstanding, and the scene was shortly made after the girls had donned bloomers and waists.
>
> *Motion Picture News,* December 11, 1915

Moving Picture World (February 5, 1916): "An elaborately staged farce comedy in which Luke gets into a harem and rescues a young girl from enforced slavery. The picture will be found very amusing in spite of the fact that a good deal of slapstick business is resorted to."

Luke, the Candy Cut-Up*

Released January 31, 1916. A Phunphilm, produced by Hal Roach for the Rolin Film Co. Distributed by Pathé. Working title: *Candy Cut Up*. Extant: GEM, FRANC, BOLOG. One reel. With Harold Lloyd, Bebe Daniels, Snub Pollard, Gene Marsh, Earl Mohan, Charles Stevenson, Otto Fries, Gilbert Pratt.

Luke is cook in a sweetshop. He spends his lunch hour in the park, gets into a fight with a man and steals his watch fob. Luke is making a cherry-flip for a pretty girl, when his victim comes in the shop. The man, seeing Luke wear his fob, calls a cop. But he and the cop get mixed up in the door, and the cop hits him. Luke and his co-worker get rid of the enemy by throwing food at them (*Moving Picture World*, February 12, 1916).

Charlie Chaplin's *Dough and Dynamite* (1914), where he and Chester Conklin pelted each other with flour and dough, was one of the biggest hits of his Keystone films. It launched a flurry of pastry battle comedies, and the print of *Luke, the Candy Cut-Up* at the George Eastman Museum shows it closely followed the original's recipe. Other candy shop melee clones that followed include Billy West's *Dough-Nuts* (1917) and Hank Mann's *The Gum Riot* (1920).

Keystone-style kitchen mayhem with Snub, Harold, and Earl Mohan (on floor) in
Luke, the Candy Cut-Up (1916).

Burly comic heavy Otto Fries made his debut at the Roach unit at this
time, turning up in entries like this and the previous *Lonesome Luke Lolls in
Luxury*, and would soon go on to appear all over the silent comedy map. After
a background in medicine shows and vaudeville he started in films in 1914 at
Keystone, and went on to Fox and Roach comedies. In 1920 he became the
main heavy for Jack White Comedies, and for the next six years made screen
life difficult for the likes of Lloyd Hamilton, Lige Conley, Al St John, and
Lupino Lane.

Although working steadily for White, Fries also found time to appear in
some of Stan Laurel's Metro Comedies, and Universal's *Hysterical History*
series. His silent feature appearances include *Hotel Imperial* (1927) and *Riley
the Cop* (1928), and he spent the later 1920s in shorts for Roach and Sennett.
The early days of sound saw him in memorable roles in Our Gang comedies
like *Readin' and Writin'* and *Free Eats* (both 1932). He worked non-stop in
features, including German language versions of Hollywood productions,
right up to his death in 1938.

Otto Fries (center) about to get crowned by Harold, with Bebe and Gene Marsh as bystanders in *Luke, the Candy Cut-Up* (1916).

Moving Picture World (February 19, 1916): "An exceedingly amusing slapstick farce comedy, in which Luke makes havoc in the candy kitchen. A considerable amount of taffy, caramels, flour, pulverized sugar, etc., is utilized in the making of the comedy."

Luke Foils the Villain

Released February 16, 1916. A Phunphilm, produced by Hal Roach for the Rolin Film Company. Distributed by Pathé. Directed by Hal Roach. Working title: ***Curses! Saved by Bullets!***. One reel. With Harold Lloyd, Bebe Daniels, Snub Pollard, Gene Marsh, Gilbert Pratt.

Luke is really funny as a happy miller, singing at his work from morning till night. He is loved by Maizie Nut, and they are happy in each other.

Then Luke discovers that a villain is attempting to "steal the papers." This means that Maizie's father will be in trouble, the mortgage will be foreclosed on the old home, and an innocent man will be made to pay the penalty for a crime he did not commit.

Luke rouses himself, and by stealing the papers himself, foils the villain, who is very, very angry. He makes up for it by breaking up a tete a tete between Luke and Maizie. (Motion Picture News, February 26, 1916)

The stage at the Rolin studio now contains a complete and practical saw mill, erected and equipped for a coming "Lonesome Luke" comedy of the Pathé-Phunphilm brand.

Motion Picture News, December 25, 1915

Bebe about to be sliced and diced as Harold reacts in *Luke Foils the Villain* (1916).

The cliché of the hero or heroine tied to a log or board that's approaching a giant buzz saw originated in the famous 1890 melodrama *Blue Jeans*. The immense success of the play, and its many revivals around the world, made the "buzz saw scene" one of the most imitated ever. It was so well known by the time that movies rolled around that it was a constant subject for comedy spoofs. Bebe is almost diced in this short, and there were also saw mills in *Curses* (1925) and *Sawdust Baby* (1926). Variations also proliferated such as Ford Sterling looking to make mincemeat out of Minta Durfee via a laundry press in 1915's *Dirty Work in a Laundry*.

During the early teens Ford Sterling had the market cornered on stage villainy spoofing. His big takes and florid gestures, augmented by a top hat and a variety of big mustaches, fueled popular Keystone hits like *Barney*

Oldfield's Race for a Life, *The Fatal Taxicab* (both 1913), *Double Crossed* (1914), and *A Maiden's Trust* (1917). Soon others like Chester Conklin and Mack Swain were up to no good in spoofs of their own such as *Curses! They Remarked* (1914) and *Ye Olden Grafter* (1915). Keystone's success with these parodies no doubt led to the Phunphilm crew adding their own contribution to the genre.

*Luke Foils the Villain (*1916), and after an explosion a fainted Bebe is comforted by a mustache-less Snub, as villain Gilbert Pratt cowers behind the desk.

An explosion was part of their melodramatic parody. The December 18, 1915 *Moving Picture World* reported a more powerful effect than intended - something that was almost a harbinger of the experience that Harold would have with a "prop" bomb in 1919:

> The residents of Edendale who are used to most any kind of excitement, being surrounded by half a dozen motion picture studios, were slightly startled this week when a keg of blasting powder was set off in a Phunphilm comedy scene at the Rolin studio. The explosion rocked the ground like a miniature earthquake and shattered many of the windows in the neighboring houses. Such a realistic effect had not been intended by Director

Hal Roach, who had issued orders to the property man for a small keg of gunpowder to blow the top off a barrel. The property man evidently got the wrong kind of keg and when the explosion came off the whole company was covered by dirt and debris. The assistant director had to be sent to the hospital with a piece of the barrel embedded in his leg and the Rolin Company is now busy paying for all those broken windows. Fortunately Director Roach was safely hidden behind the camera man.

Motography (February 19, 1916): "The villain tries to get some papers, but Luke foils his plans. Luke is very happy in the thought that he is loved by Maizie Nut, but when the villain comes and disturbs them many amusing incidents come to pass."

Motion Picture News (March 4, 1916): "This is a farce comedy that is fairly entertaining. As in too many instances where farce comedy is concerned there are vulgar touches that might be well eliminated, such as an accidental lifting of a woman's skirt. We do not doubt that this elimination would be made before it reached the public eye. The film is otherwise unobjectionable and amusing."

Luke and the Rural Roughnecks*

Released March 1, 1916. A Phunphilm, produced by Hal Roach for the Rolin Film Co. Distributed by Pathé. Working title: *Rural Roughhouse*. Extant: ARG. One reel. With Harold Lloyd, Bebe Daniels, Snub Pollard, Dee Lampton, Earl Mohan, Charles Stevenson, Gilbert Pratt.

The village blacksmith has a hard time holding on to his assistants. This is due, primarily, to the presence of the village belle. Finally the brawny smithy is compelled to hire as his helper a man who is without any female affiliations. He hits upon Lonesome Luke as the ideal man for the job and that well-known worthy accepts the position with alacrity. But unfortunately the queen of queens crosses Luke's path and disconcerts him. Several clashes he has with his employer in his efforts to win the affections of the girl and his position is in jeopardy. Finally Fatty, his chief rival, steals a horse whose hoofs are being manicured and runs away with the girl in true Lochinvar style. But Luke rushes to the father-in-law-he-would-like-to-have and gathers a posse to pursue the elopers. They come together far down on the road to the city and all hands get into a mixup in a delightfully muddy pool and have it out then and there in a no-decision bout. (Moving Picture World, March 11, 1916)

Harold taking orders from Gilbert Pratt in *Luke and the Rural Roughnecks* (1916).

The climax of this rare comedy was an all-out war in a giant mud puddle.

Dee Lampton, "Rolin's Fattest Boy," is not a believer of mud baths. Last week in a strenuous scene taking place in a mud puddle Harold Lloyd, Rolin's leading comedian, accidentally pushed Lampton's face deep in the mud with his foot. According to Lloyd this was accidental. Dee thinks otherwise. He gained several pounds, which he attributed to the mud he swallowed, and states that he prefers taking any such baths in the spring and externally.

Moving Picture World, January 1, 1916

This sequence may have been the start of the Hal Roach studio's fascination with mud holes. Famous examples include the large bog in *All Wet* (1924) that Charley Chase's car gets stranded in, forcing Charley to do some snorkeling to try and get it out, and there's the golf course muck trap that enables Laurel & Hardy to perform one of their tit-for-tat battles in *Should Married Men Go Home?* (1928). Most memorable are the mysterious curbside bottomless puddles that are always lying in wait for Oliver Hardy to drop into in shorts such as *Why Girls Say No* and *Putting Pants on Philip* (both 1927).

Getting the worst of this Luke mud fight was Dee Lampton, a recent addition to the Rolin stock company. At two hundred and eighty-five pounds, the seventeen-year-old Lampton was nearly a look-a-like for Roscoe Arbuckle. Coming to Hollywood from Texas, most of his four-year film career was spent working for Hal Roach. First appearing at Essanay, he got a lot of attention as the mischievous fat boy that helps Charlie Chaplin harass the onstage performers in *A Night in the Show* (1915). Lampton also worked in Essanay one-reelers like *Fun at a Ball Game* (1915) which were directed by Hal Roach. Specializing as annoying kids in shorts such as *Luke Does the Midway*, *Luke and the Bang-Tails*, and *Luke Joins the Navy* (all 1916), 1917 saw Roach star him in his own mostly split-reel series.

Dee Lampton (right) shaming Harold and his lady friend in
Luke and the Rural Roughnecks (1916).

Known as the *Skinny* series, in shorts like *Schemer Skinny's Schemes* and *Skinny Gets a Goat* (both 1917), he was a teenage version of Roscoe Arbuckle's "Fatty" character. According to Lampton's surviving contract for the *Skinnys* he was started at $100 a week, and would rise to $125 and then $150 within an eighteen-month period. This was double the salary that Roach was paying to Harold! The series didn't catch on and was discontinued after eight entries, so when Dee spent some time working for Mack Sennett in shorts like *Hula Hula Land* (1917) he was back to $20 a week. He returned to Rolin in 1918 as support to Harold's new glasses character. Playing all types of roles, like Arbuckle, Lampton was good at drag and often turned up as a woman, even in blackface as in *The Marathon* (1919). Also supporting Toto and Stan Laurel, he continued turning up in Harold's films until 1920:

Rolin Comedian Dead

Dee Lampton, 21 years of age, heavy weight comedian of the Rolin Film Company, died at the Clara Barton Hospital on September 1, of appendicitis. Lampton was born in Fort Worth, Texas, and moved four years ago with his family to Los Angeles. He soon obtained work at the Rolin studios and has since appeared as a leading player in many of the comedies produced at that plant. Dee Lampton weighed 285 pounds although he was only five feet tall. He is survived by his father and mother, and a sister and brother.

Moving Picture World, September 20, 1919

Moving Picture World (March 11, 1916): "This is a truly amusing farce comedy in which the village belle causes considerable damage to the hearts in the vicinity of the village blacksmith shop. Lonesome Luke is selected to fill the position of assistant blacksmith in the place of others who have proven unworthy. One of the most amusing incidents is a fight in a mud puddle."

Luke Pipes the Pippins

Released March 15, 1916. A Phunphilm, produced by Hal Roach for the Rolin Film Company. Distributed by Pathé. Directed by Hal Roach. Working title: ***Bums Booking Agent***. One reel. With Harold Lloyd, Bebe Daniels, Snub Pollard, Gene Marsh, Earl Mohan, Charles Stevenson, Billy Fay, Dee Lampton, Gilbert Pratt.

Lonesome Luke is a theatrical booking agency manager. Many and various are the performers who come to him for employment and many and various are the stunts that they are required to do to show their ability. Twist and Twirl, the dance sisters, are still on the hunt for an engagement and come to the Bunko Agency for a try-out. Luke puts them through their paces, and then tries out the other aspirants for places. Among them are I.B. Strong, champion strong man of the universe; and Charlie the China Chucker. Mr. Strong is a formidable individual and makes life miserable for the manager of the shop. Finally, he "cleans out" the shop in a burst of anger, and Luke is compelled to call in the help to pick up the pieces. Thus passes Luke as a theatrical booking agent. (Moving Picture World, March 25, 1916).

Luke Pipes the Pippins (1916) which includes Gene Marsh and Bebe on the far end.

Show business was a ripe source for silent comedy antics, especially since almost all of its participants had long backgrounds on the stage and knew too well the ups and downs of touring and playing in little tank town theatres. These behind-the-theatrical-scenes shorts gave ample opportunity to make fun of various acts and all kinds of theatre types. The most common scenario followed the misadventures of comics like Ford Sterling, Charlie Chaplin, Roscoe Arbuckle, and Buster Keaton with their difficulties as prop boys in entries such as *A Small Town Act* (1913), *The Property Man* (1914), *Back Stage* (1919), and *The Play House* (1921).

Like Harold in this short, Ham & Bud took over a booking office in *The Bogus Booking Agents* (1916), but the best silent show business comedy is the 1926 feature *Exit Smiling*. The British clown Beatrice Lillie stars as a girl of all trades (seamstress, prompter, cook, etc.) for a low-rent theatrical company touring the Midwest with a fragrant production titled *Flaming Women*. While the day-to-day life of a small potatoes touring outfit is parodied, there's still accurate observation to the portrayal, and with solid support from pros such as Franklin Pangborn, William Gillespie, and Dorothea Wolbert, star Lillie gives an extremely memorable comic performance.

A publicity still for *Hot Water* (1924) has Charles Stevenson (right) about to cut Jobyna Ralston's hair. *Courtesy of The Museum of Modern Art.*

Charles Stevenson joined the Rolin Company in the fall of 1915, and became the standby of the studio into the mid-1920s – possibly appearing in more Hal Roach comedies than anyone else. Born in Sacramento in 1887, this native Californian made his Luke debut around the time of *Lonesome Luke, Social Gangster* (1915), and over the years not only supported Luke, but was also in the mature Harold Lloyd shorts and features, as well as shorts with Dee Lampton, Stan Laurel, Beatrice La Plante, Snub Pollard, Eddie Boland, Gaylord Lloyd, Paul Parrott, and Our Gang. Although his film work was mostly confined to the Roach product his 1918 Motion Picture News Studio Directory entry credits him with the Vitagraph feature *The More Excellent Way* (1917).

Frequently turning up as stereotypical Jewish pawnbrokers, tailors, or studio heads, Stevenson's best roles saw him as an opponent for Harold – as the bully and rival in *Grandma's Boy* (1922) and the annoying brother-in-law of *Hot Water* (1924). He disappeared from the Roach films around 1925, with his last appearances in shorts like *Are Parents Pickles?* (1925) which were shot a few years earlier but released later. Little is known about his post-film career, but a spate of bad health led to his passing in 1943.

As previously discussed, Charles Rosher spent a very brief time doing camera work for Rolin, and when he left:

> Leon Loeb, formerly cameraman at the Lew Fields Company of the Keystone, has been engaged by the Rolin Film Company to take charge of their photographic division.
>
> *Moving Picture World*, December 18, 1915

Loeb had photographed the Weber & Fields *Best of Enemies* (1915) at the Sennett Studio, and after his own quick interlude at Rolin returned to Sennett to photograph 1916 Louise Fazenda comedies like *The Feathered Nest* and *Maid Mad*. Besides being a member of the Static Club, Loeb shot *Six Cylinder Love* (1917) and a couple of other early Tom Mix comedies for Fox. He remained in the film business, and was involved in making 16mm news releases, documentary, educational, and public relations films in Washington, D.C. into the 1950s.

Moving Picture World (April 1, 1916): "With the exception of a much-abbreviated costume worn by one of the young ladies in the play there will be found much that is pleasing in this comedy. There seems no excuse, however, for the young lady's failing to cover her lower extremities from the middle of her thighs down to her ankles. The story of the film treats of a bunko agency kept by Luke. The types that frequent the place are interesting, and much of the comedy is exceedingly good."

Motion Picture News (April 1, 1916): "Harold Lloyd, alias Lonesome Luke, here sets up as an entire vaudeville agency and his day's work is portrayed. This consists of giving a varied collection of four-a-day artists try-outs and the entire thing ends in an uproar. Lloyd gets in some uproarious business while the entire company works together in most humorous style."

Lonesome Luke, Circus King

Released March 29, 1916. A Phunphilm, produced by Hal Roach for the Rolin Film Company. Distributed by Pathé. Working title: *Luke Launches into the Legit*. One reel. With Harold Lloyd, Bebe Daniels, Snub Pollard, Gene Marsh, Charles Stevenson, Gilbert Pratt, Billy Fay, Dee Lampton, Earl Mohan, Fred Newmeyer.

Luke figures a circus is a good money-maker and goes into the business with that idea in mind. But things don't pan out exactly as he had figured and the net result is nil. He gathers around him all the necessary freaks that go with a modern up-to-date-honest-to-goodness circus – the bearded lady, the fat girl, the royal something-or-other band, the smallest man in captivity and so on. But when the beard falls off the bearded lady and reveals a young man, the fat girl proves also to be a boy, the royal band simmers down to a two piece affair, and the dwarf's fake legs are discovered the City Fathers determine on drastic action. The would-be Barnum realizes what drastic action is generally decided on by the City Fathers, and determines to save them the trouble. He then "lights out" as fast as his legs will carry him, and the last we see of him is when he leaves the confines of the village far in the rear and vows never to return. (Moving Picture World, April 8, 1916).

> The change in atmosphere has caused a hardship for the Rolin Film Company, makers of the Phunphilm brand for Pathé, in that practically all of their past week's work has been destroyed by static.
> The subject is being remade, and by special effort on the part of Director Hal Roach and members of the producing company, this can be accomplished without delay in the releasing.
>
> *Motion Picture News*, January 8, 1916

Things were getting easier for the little Rolin organization, but there were still many challenges for a unit without a permanent home base. As mentioned in the first chapter the earliest productions used the Bradbury Mansion as their headquarters/studio, but after regular production of the Luke shorts got rolling other facilities were used. Harold remembered:

> In 1915 we had to move from Court Street for some forgotten reason and Roach rented the old Norbig Studio.

From mid-1915 to early 1916 a swatch of the comedies were made at the Norbig Studios and Laboratories. This was located in Edendale, as was many other studios. In fact, Norbig was on the block between the Selig lot and Mack Sennett's Keystone Studio.

Harold and crew outside of the redecorated gate of the Norbig Studio for
Lonesome Luke, Circus King (1916)

Erected in 1913, Norbig was a rental facility and during the silent era
housed units such as Albuquerque Film Company, California Feature Film
Co., Regeaur Productions, Consolidated Film Co., Doubleday Productions,
Monarch Pictures, and the companies of Princess Mona Darkfeather and
Carlyle Blackwell. It's definite that *Lonesome Luke, Circus King* was done on
Norbig's premises as surviving stills show that the circus midway attractions
were set up and shot in front of the main studio entrance.

Charles Stevenson, Snub, Bebe, Harold and Gene Marsh are ready to fleece the suckers in *Lonesome Luke, Circus King* (1916).

Not long after the previously mentioned Leon Loeb, there was a new person in charge of Rolin's camerawork:

> Jim A. Crosby, late of the Universal photographic department, has been engaged by the Rolin Film Company to act in the same capacity.
>
> *Motion Picture News*, February 5, 1916

The Canadian-born James A. Crosby was a film industry pioneer, beginning in Chicago with Selig in the late 1880s. Coming to California with Selig, he moved on to Reliance, Bison, Universal, Ince, and the Oz Film Company where he happened to work with extras Hal Roach and Harold Lloyd on *The Patchwork Girl of Oz* (1914).

A technical innovator, Crosby patented the sprocket wheel in 1909, invented the projecting machine the Viascope, and had the commercial laboratory J.A.C. Film Co. in Los Angeles. His ingenuity and dedication as a cameraman is illustrated by this incident from August of 1916:

> Last Monday Director Roach's car was hit and demolished on its way to location, loaded with players. Bebe Daniels and Harold Lloyd were both sent to the hospital while Fred Jefferson and James Crosby suffered minor injuries. The car was completely wrecked, but the cameraman was on the job. Leaping from the

wreckage, he saw that the camera was uninjured, and at once set it up, calling meanwhile to the players the familiar phrase "Hold It!" He got a picture of the wreck, and it's going to be used in a comedy. Well, some cameramen do have a sense of humor.

1916 trade magazine ad for James A. Crosby.

Crosby remained with Rolin through most of 1916, and later founded the cameramen's organization The Static Club.

According to the Pathé Bulletin *Lonesome Luke, Circus King* was the last of the *Lonesome Luke* shorts to be advertised as a *Phun Philm*. That moniker covered *Spit-Ball Sadie* (1915) and the ensuing early *Lukes*.

Moving Picture World (April 15, 1916): "A Lonesome Luke in which Luke runs 'the best ten-cent show that was ever seen for a quarter.' Some very funny incidents occur about the circus tent where we are taken into the confidence of the manager and are allowed to view various characters making up. An entertaining number for those who like slapstick comedy."

Luke's Double*

Released April 12, 1916. Produced by Hal Roach for the Rolin Film Co. Distributed by Pathé. Directed by Hal Roach. Extant: UCLA. One reel. With Harold Lloyd, Bebe Daniels, Snub Pollard, Gaylord Lloyd.

Harold cracks himself up in *Luke's Double* (1916).

Luke falls asleep and dreams that he has a double of himself. He has an awful time about it and can't quite figure it out. They go along and Luke No. 1 gets into a "jam" with an officer of the law. The result is that No. 2 gets the blame for all the trouble. Then Luke No. 2 arouses the anger of a young lady in the park and makes his escape. The result of this is that the policeman called into the case runs across Luke No.1 and arrests him.

Finally he is thrown into jail and is languishing there when his other self appears on the outside of the cell door. His only remark to this new phenomenon is "Whether I'm me or you, or who's what, you're wrong." But while rolling around in his bed he comes to his senses and realizes that it was all a horrible dream (Moving Picture World, April 22, 1916).

Luke's doppelganger in this opus appears to have been a combination of trick photography and Harold's brother Gaylord.

> The twenty-third of the Pathé "Lonesome Luke" Phunphilms series being made by the Rolin Company will contain a very difficult piece of double exposure photography, which is something entirely new in comedy.
>
> *Motion Picture News*, January 22, 1916

A made-up Gaylord Lloyd (left) poses with brother Harold, and future movie director Robert Florey in the early 1920s. *Courtesy of The Museum of Modern Art.*

Evil doubles were a popular theme in German films, particularly two versions of *The Student of Prague* – 1913 and 1926. More of a direct ancestor for *Luke's Double* is the 1912 French comedy short *Onesime vs. Onesime*. Ernest Bourbon was a popular clown with his everyman character of Onesime. In this short Onesime randomly splits in half – one good, one bad – with the bad egg making trouble for the other – even skulking around and spying on him. In this version it's unclear if the original Onesime is the good one or bad one.

Playing Harold's double in this short was something of a dry run for his brother Gaylord, as they would also play look-alikes in *His Royal Slyness* (1920) and Gaylord would assume the mantle of Lonesome Luke in the early 1920s. Born in 1888, Gaylord was five years older than Harold, and they both got the theatre bug early. It was Gaylord who actually got Harold his first part onstage. While working as a prop master and handyman at their local Beatrice, Nebraska opera house, a boy was needed for a production of *Macbeth*, and Gaylord recommended his little brother.

The brothers were always close, and Gaylord was in some of the earliest Rolin comedies such as *Just Nuts* (1915), but went to Wyoming and spent some time working on ranches. He soon returned to California and films for Rolin, and is literally in tons of shorts with Harold, Snub Pollard and Eddie Boland. Sometimes stunting for Harold, after his own short run as Lonesome Luke Gaylord spent years working for the Harold Lloyd Corporation, often as assistant director on Harold's features. He appeared behind the scenes on other pictures until his death in 1943.

According to the May 6, 1916 *Motion Picture News* the Ohio Censor Board ordered:

> "Luke's Double." Cut out all scenes where policeman brutally strikes man with club.

It's not unusual to come across a censored print today. Slapstick comedies were frequently trimmed for violence, so you'll see someone about to be kicked in the seat, or conked on the head, and suddenly there's a jump in the action and no payoff. You may see the person reacting in pain or acting dazed, but not the moment of contact. Projectionists would often keep the snipped footage, and the Library of Congress has inherited a few reels of censored cuts. In some cases these little clips are all that exists of certain films today.

Thought lost for many years, it turns out that Harold had been given a 28mm copy of this short by the George Eastman Museum in the 1960s, but it had gone missing. While this book was being prepared, the print was located and deposited with UCLA.

Gaylord Lloyd (left) as *Luke's Double* (1916) stuns Harold and Snub
as he makes a play for Bebe.

Motion Picture News (April 29, 1916): "A bit of clever make-up, which almost looks like double exposure, is a diverting feature of this comedy."

Motography (April 22, 1916): "In this Lonesome Luke comedy the hero dreams that he has a double and to make things more uncomfortable he is both himself and his double. The escapades of one make trouble for the other, with the result that Luke is put in jail and his double goes free. Many comical situations arise from the unique state of affairs."

Them Was the Happy Days

Released April 26, 1916. Produced by Hal Roach for the Rolin Film Company. Distributed by Pathé. Directed by Hal Roach. One reel. With Harold Lloyd, Bebe Daniels, Snub Pollard, Martha Mattox, Earl Mohan, A. H. Frahlich, Gilbert Pratt, Dee Lampton, Fred Newmeyer, Charles Stevenson, Billy Fay.

Martha Mattox (as teacher) tries to control the unruly class of Rolin players in *Them Was the Happy Days* (1916).

A motion picture company is ready to start out to find a location when it is discovered that the hero, Lonesome Luke, is missing. A search is instituted. Meanwhile, Luke, who has slid to the floor of the company's auto, has fallen asleep. The picture that follows is his dream which in comedy effects far surpasses the ingenuity of the foregoing "set."

Luke dreams that he is again a schoolboy and that he and his fellow-actors are all young again. The girls are in short skirts and the boys in knee-breeches. They attend the little schoolhouse on the hill, presided over by a sour dame, the archtype of the country schoolmarm. Once in the schoolroom the real fun begins. Fatty, one of the scholars, has a "penny-dreadful" concealed in a geography book. Fatty comes to a particularly bloody part, when lo! His hair is seen to actually rise from his head and stand out like the well-known quills of the equally well-known porcupine. (*Moving Picture World*, May 6, 1916).

This *Luke* outing was most likely inspired by the success that Mack Sennett had the previous year with *The Little Teacher* (1915), where Roscoe Arbuckle, Bobby Dunn, and Sennett himself played unruly rural school students who made class life difficult for new teacher Mabel Normand. Other shorts with comics as school kids include Sennett's *The Village Chestnut*, Billy West's *The Scholar* (both 1918), and Larry Semon blackens people with ink, dumps them in mud puddles, and has them bitten by a baby alligator in the school house opening of *School Days* (1920). Of course, there were plenty of classroom antics with kids themselves from Our Gang, Mickey McGuire, Buster Brown, and even the Fox Monkeys.

The poor schoolmarm who has to contend with Luke and his pals was played by Martha Mattox, a hatchet-faced character actress who had made some of her first films for the newly-organized Rolin Company. She turns up in photos from *The Fall of Lady Sampson* and other 1915 shorts. Having come from years on stage in repertoire and stock companies, she quickly moved on to stints at Kalem and Universal where she specialized as a foil in comedy shorts as spinsters, farm wives, and general battle axes.

Playing Selina Tubbs, she was a regular in Selig's 1915's *The Chronicles of Bloom Center* comedy series, and by 1917 had become a much in-demand character performer in features such as *The Delicious Little Devil* (1919), *Beauty's Worth* (1922), *The Family Secret* (1924), and *Oh, Doctor!* (1925). Two of her best roles were as Miss Watson in 1920's *Huckleberry Finn*, and as the sinister (and ironically named) Mammy Pleasant in *The Cat and the Canary* (1927). She remained very busy in early sound films, but passed away at only fifty-three in 1933.

To date Luke had been appearing on screens a total of ten months – since July of 1915. In this short time he and his portrayer were making inroads in audience's consciousness:

> "Lonesome Luke" is proving to be a very popular fellow. Last week at the Optic Theatre in Los Angeles one of the series of the "Luke" comedies was being shown and the owner recognized Harold Lloyd, the original of Luke, in the audience. He dragged the bashful comedian to the stage and forced him to make a speech. Luke said he then really was "lonesome" for some nerve, but his talk made a great hit with the fans.
>
> *Motography*, April 22, 1916

Martha Mattox (left) about to strike as Harold and Bebe sneak pie in
Them Was the Happy Days (1916).

Likewise:

> Lonesome Luke, the comedian, has been honored by a group
> of young men back in Missouri, who have named a club for him.
> It is called "The Lonesome Luke Club."
>
> *Variety*, April 28, 1916

Motography (May 13, 1916): "Lonesome Luke and all his friends, and near friends, are in this exceptionally good comedy seen as students in the little old school. All the conventional school room happenings are burlesqued and made the basis for continued comical actions."

Luke and the Bomb Throwers

Released May 8, 1916. Produced by Hal Roach for the Rolin Film Company. Distributed by Pathé. Working title: ***Luke, Bombs and Blackhands***. One reel. With Harold Lloyd, Bebe Daniels, Snub Pollard, Blanche White, A. H. Frahlich, Gilbert Pratt, Dee Lampton, Ben Corday, Charles Stevenson, Billy Fay.

Luke starts out by stumbling into a nest of very Reds – folks whose lives are dedicated to spilling other folk's gore. Luke has a choice between instant death and becoming a malcontent and chooses the latter as being less painful – for him. The society has some important business at hand, that is, the throwing of a bomb for the privilege of which the members pick numbers. Thirteen does it, and Luke is the lucky man. He tries to substitute his thumb for the figure on his card, because he hates to deprive any of his fellow-members of their little joke, but they're all self-saving spirits, and Luke is sent on his merry way. His bomb throwing is a scream. When he comes back he is made much of by the admiring company and told that, for such distinguished service, he may now have the honor of killing a girl captive. Luke isn't keen for a degree as past master in the gentle art of murder, and in the events that follow manages to fliv the job and foil the conspirators. (Pathé Bulletin, April 28, 1916).

Anarchists and secret societies were active subjects in American tabloids of the teens and 1920s, so they were perfect fodder for the movies. Dramatic films milked them for all their melodramatic worth, so comedies ended up mocking the real stories as well as the movies that were made about them. Harold would have a rematch with a cabal in 1919's *Swat the Crook*, and they were a standard ingredient in Larry Semon's films. Larry was up against some kind of "Black Hand" organizations in *Risks and Roughnecks*, *Bombs and Blunders* (both 1917), *Rummies and Razors*, and *Pluck and Plotters* (both 1918) to name just a few.

Dee Lampton, Ben Corday (left) and Bebe Daniels show Harold that they mean business in *Luke and the Bomb Throwers* (1916).

Victor Moore got entangled with a sinister gang in *He Meant Well* (1917), and even had a hit man trailing him to make sure he took care of his own hitman duties. Billy Franey stumbles into an anarchist's cell in *The New Member* (1921), and Snub Pollard has to contend with a classroom full of assassins in *Blow 'Em Up* (1922). *The High Sign* (1921) sees Buster Keaton having a run-in with The Blinking Buzzards, and an anarchist's bomb sets the entire police force after him in *Cops* (1922).

The girl captive was Blanche White, a pretty blonde English-born actress, who was an on-and-off regular in the Rolin stock company. Her real name was Caroline McCann, and she was the real-life wife of character comedian Leo White (that is until their 1931 divorce). White can be seen in photos from *Spit-Ball Sadie* (1915), and appeared in other shorts like *Luke Lolls in Luxury* and *Luke Laughs Last* (both 1916). She also had roles in dramatic features like *Honor Thy Name*, William S. Hart's *The Dawn Maker*, and *The Chalice of Sorrow* (all 1916), plus she appeared in numerous shorts with her husband such as Billy West's *The Chief Cook* (1917), and Bulls Eye Comedies like *Help!* (1919) with Gale Henry.

Blanche White appeals for Harold's help in *Luke and the Bomb Throwers* (1916).

Making an impression in *The Chief Cook*, the September 29, 1917 *Motion Picture News* said:

> Blanche White as the slavey revealed herself as a comedienne who will bear watching as a future star. Her interpretations are strongly remindful of the work of Polly Moran.

Her last known films were the series of Pinnacle Comedies in which she and Leo co-starred, such as *Damfool Twins*, *Save a Sucker*, and *Don't Ever Marry* (all 1920). Produced by the Independent Films Association the series lasted less than a year before expiring. Ms. White passed away in 1963.

Moving Picture World (May 27, 1916): "The scenes of this farce comedy take place for the most part in the rooms of a secret order of bomb throwers. Luke, by accident, gets into the place and is held bound, released by a brave comedy citizen who holds at bay the members of the order, who are forced to give up their firearms and proceed to the street, where they are handled by the authorities."

Luke's Late Lunchers

Released May 22, 1916. Produced by Hal Roach for the Rolin Film Company. Distributed by Pathé. Directed by Hal Roach. One reel. With Harold Lloyd, Bebe Daniels, Snub Pollard, Ben Corday, Blanche White, A.H. Frahlich.

Harold attends to Blanche White as A. H. Frahlich is about to put him on the menu in
Luke's Late Lunchers (1916).

Luke starts off as the proprietor of a bean foundry, where the gentle little flies mingle with the peaceful butter cakes, so Luke feels no qualms for the flies' digestions. It does weary him though, when the beard of one of his customers gets into the soup. Luke ties the beard about its owner's neck, and the old man Niagara's on. It worries Luke again when of his customers insults his china by calling it cracked – when there's only a hair on it! The old dish rag, soaked and wrung out as occasion requires, is the source of all soup, through which, ever and anon, a resigned bean is passed, to give the dish atmosphere. Of course, Luke can't get away with this stuff, and the picture ends in a scrap that is "enjoyed by all." (*Moving Picture World*, June 3, 1916).

Lunch counters and wagons are extremely prolific in silent comedy. Everything on the menu is a recipe for a gag, and the various food items, tables, spoons, forks, pots, pans, and other restaurant equipment are just ready and waiting to be used as projectiles, or for some other kind of physical combat. Some of the more memorable hash house encounters include Vitagraph's *Hash and Havoc* (1916), Charlie Chaplin playing catch-me-if-you-can with his brother Syd in *A Dog's Life* (1918), Stan Laurel serving a motley crew in *Short Orders* (1923), and Lloyd Hamilton and Colleen Moore's difficulties with lunch wagons in *Nobody's Business* (1926) and *Her Wild Oat* (1927).

The king of culinary comedy was Roscoe "Fatty" Arbuckle. In shorts such as *Fatty's Tintype Tangle* (1915), *The Waiter's Ball* (1916), and *The Cook* (1918) he flipped flapjacks behind his back, battled ripe Limburger Cheese, and without looking tossed knives and other sharp objects with deadly accuracy. Although he always made the final result look effortless, Arbuckle related just how much work was involved in those sequences to the April 1916 *Picture-Play Magazine*:

> I spent just one week getting the kitchen scenes I was in alone. I used over ten thousand feet of film just for that. In one part of the play I had to toss a pancake up and catch it behind my back. I started at nine o'clock in the morning, did it on the first rehearsal, then started the camera and didn't get it until four-thirty. I'd hate to tell you how long it took me to catch the plate behind my back in "The Village Scandal!" I seldom rehearse since then.

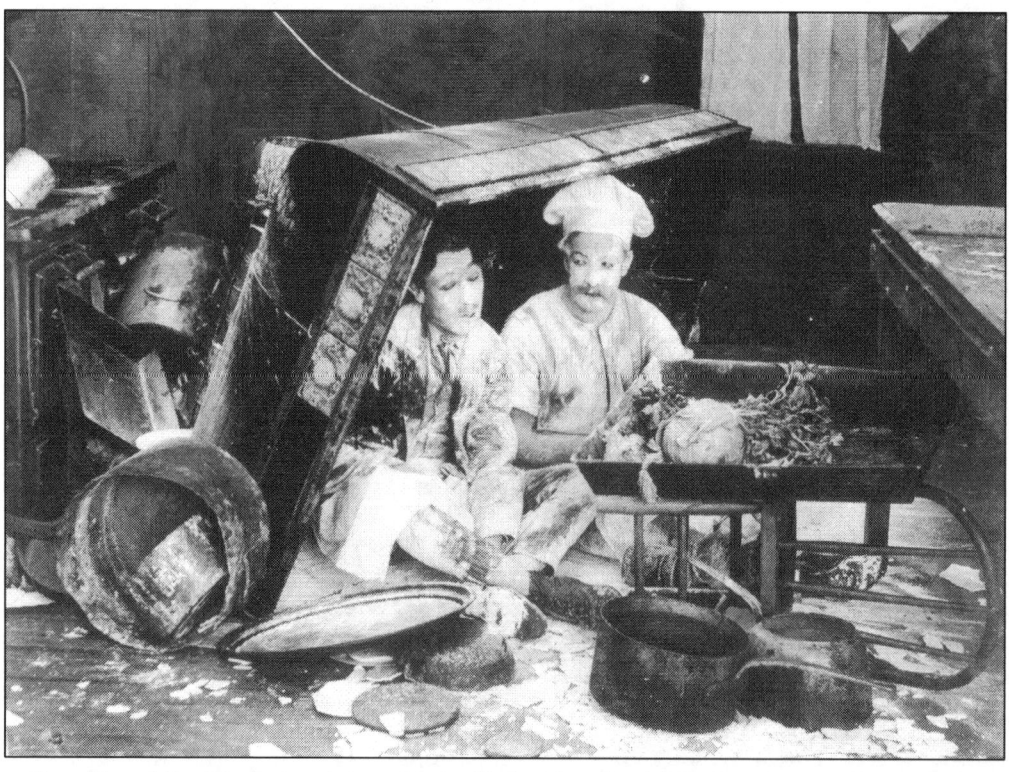

Harold and Snub have barely survived a kitchen battle with *Luke's Late Lunchers* (1916).

Later in his career Arbuckle would reprise some of these routines in *Special Delivery* (1927) and *Hey, Pop!* (1932).

The Lonesome Luke company shouldered on with a hectic pace, and continued to add new individuals to the stock company:

> Ben Corday, tallest man in this vicinity, has been added to the Rolin family of "queer ones," and is bound to make a pleasing member of the Phunphilm family. It is said that he can without assistance look over Harold Lloyd's head with Lloyd standing on Harry Pollard's shoulders. At any rate Big Ben is some tall and coupled to his length is his marked ability for good falls. He makes a good addition to the Rolin forces.
>
> *Moving Picture World*, February 12, 1916

Ben Corday was one of the most intriguing and colorful individuals making up "the Rolin family of 'queer ones.'" Born in England, he ran away at a young age to go to sea. After military duty fighting in the Second Boer War in Africa, he settled in the United States where he had a long list of occupations – wrestler, doorman, stevedore, and a stage actor. Corday is listed in the cast of 1910's *Three Million Dollars* at the Chicago Opera House, doubling in the roles of a hotel porter and a chauffeur, and he spent some time as a giant or strongman attraction with circuses. Although reports on Corday's exact height vary, he was in the seven-foot range, and thanks to this became Rolin's resident giant. For a few months he loomed over the rest of the company in shorts such as *Luke and the Bomb Throwers* and *Luke, Crystal Gazer* (both 1916).

Today Corday is best known for his contribution to the art of tattooing. Spending his last twenty years as a tattoo designer and artist he's considered a father of modern tattooing, but was as nomadic doing this as he was in the earlier part of his life. Although his work was influential, he was reportedly a notorious alcoholic, opening shops in different parts of the country in between drinking binges. Corday died in his sleep at sixty-two in 1938.

Motography (June 3, 1916): "Harold Lloyd here takes up the duties of a beanery proprietor and after extracting all the fun from one of these much laughed at and much patronized places, finds himself, as usual, in the midst of a lively scrap."

Ben Corday (center) towers over two companions in a personalized postcard.

Luke Laughs Last

Released June 5, 1916. Produced by Hal Roach for the Rolin Film Co. Distributed by Pathé. One reel. With Harold Lloyd, Bebe Daniels, Snub Pollard, Mae White, Blanche White, Dee Lampton, Ben Corday.

Luke is a butler who enjoys wearing his dress suit, but doesn't like to work. Snub, in love with the maid and in trouble with the cops, takes refuge in the house. A cop who is interested in the cook and her cooking, comes in, and Luke and Snub have trouble with him. A burglar breaks in, not because he thinks there is anything worth stealing, but because he wants to be arrested in order to get a place to sleep. He and another burglar enter madame's room, she wakens, and has a fit. The people below try to capture the gunmen, without much enthusiasm. Luke finds himself with revolver in hand and the burglars walk into them. He laughs last. (Moving Picture World, June 17, 1916).

A new supporting player had been recently added to the ensemble:

> Officials of the Rolin Film Company are congratulating themselves on securing the services of Mae White, late of the Essanay-Chaplin Company, for appearances in Pathé Phunphilms.
>
> Miss White will be remembered as taking the part of the stout woman in Chaplin's "A Night at the Show."
>
> *Motion Picture News*, March 4, 1916

Ms. White was a heavy-set vaudeville regular, and her previous work with Charlie Chaplin gave the fledgling Rolin Co. the opportunity to bask in a little reflected glory. It seems likely that Hal Roach knew White from his time at Essanay, and could have directed her there. Roach had been given Chaplin company regulars who weren't busy at the moment with Charlie to use as players in his shorts. Snub Pollard was one, and Mae White might have been another.

In an unidentified item from June 1916, Hal Roach had this to say about his company's working methods:

> We make our comedies from the barest of skeletons of stories, for I have found that it is the incidental, spontaneous, surprising little touches that bring the big laughs and that it is utterly impossible to conjure up in the making of a script. If that sounds like heresy see "Luke Laughs Last" our latest production released on the Pathé program in the week of June 5th, and which was made from a script of six lines!

ABOVE: Dee Lampton and Harold bring Ben Corday, Blanche White, Bebe, Snub, and Mae White on as reinforcements in *Luke Laughs Last* (1916). BELOW: Harold ejecting cop Ben Corday as Mae White prepares to chuck a dough bomb in *Luke Laughs Last* (1916).

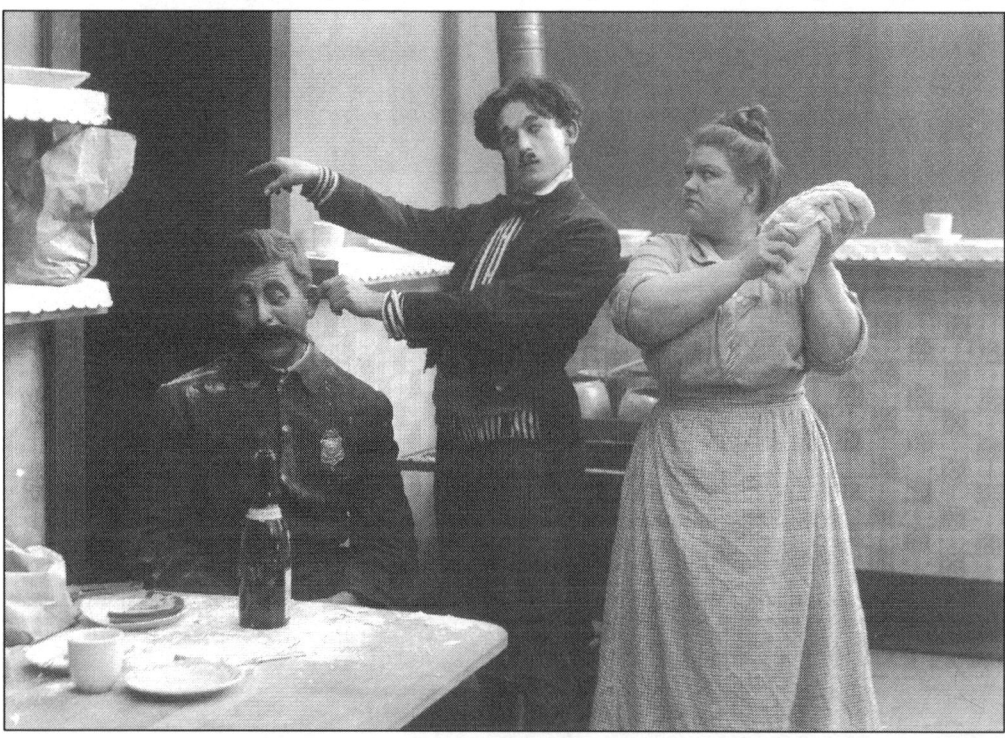

Moving Picture World (June 5, 1916): "An amusing farce comedy in which Lonesome Luke in the role of a butler is the center of a pretty mix-up, accidently capturing two burglars at the same time. Some of the comedy types in this film are unusually comical – the fat policeman, for instance, and his partner 'tall and lanky.' This is an unusually stirring comedy."

Luke's Fatal Flivver

Released June 19, 1916. Produced by Hal Roach for the Rolin Film Co. Distributed by Pathé. Working title: ***Luke's Picnic Hunches***. One reel. With Harold Lloyd, Bebe Daniels, Snub Pollard, Mae White, Blanche White, Charles Stevenson, A. H. Frahlich.

Snub tries to take out a threatening Charles Stevenson as Harold hides behind Mae White in *Luke's Fatal Flivver* (1916).

A party of fashionable people are enjoying a day in the country, when interrupted by Luke's party of fifteen people packed into a two-seater tin lizzie. The resulting confusion ends up with the food being used for combat weapons. At the end, Luke drives his car through a swamp with all fifteen of his party dragging along through the mud, to the title, "At the end of a perfect day." (Moving Picture World, June 24, 1916).

Although not known to exist today, *Luke's Fatal Flivver* was part of one of the first gifts of films given to the newly established Museum of Modern Art's Film Library. In the fall of 1935, Harold Lloyd and Warner Brothers each donated a group of eleven titles. Included in the Lloyd pictures were shorts like *Just Nuts* (1915), *Luke Joins the Navy* (1916), *Pipe the Whiskers* (1918), and *High and Dizzy* (1920), as well as his features *Grandma's Boy* (1922), *Safety Last* (1923), *The Freshman* (1925), and *Welcome Danger* (1929).

Luke's Fatal Flivver (1916) proves that four's a crowd for Harold, Snub, and Mae White.

A recent addition to the Rolin Stock Company would make a substantial, but forgotten, mark on the early film industry:

> The name of A.H. Frahlich has been added to the payroll of the Rolin studios. Mr. Frahlich has been engaged to play juveniles.
> *Motion Picture News*, January 15, 1916

Born Allen Fralick in Canada, during his brief movie acting career he was also known as Allan H. Fralick, and at Rolin was billed as A. H. Frahlich. Having started his stage career at age ten in stock companies, carnivals, and vaudeville, he entered films in 1912 with the Biograph Company. In addition to his stint at Rolin he also appeared for the Crown City Film Co., at Kalem with Ham & Bud and Ethel Teare, and in Universal's Pat Rooney one-reelers such as *Pat Turns Detective* (1918).

After five years in front of the camera, all of which is missing, he moved behind the scenes to work for the Willis & Inglis publicity agency, and then became the casting director for the Thomas Ince Studio. By 1923, he had set up his own casting agency, and as Freddie Fralick became what the *Motion Picture News* called "One of the best-known player's representatives on the coast."

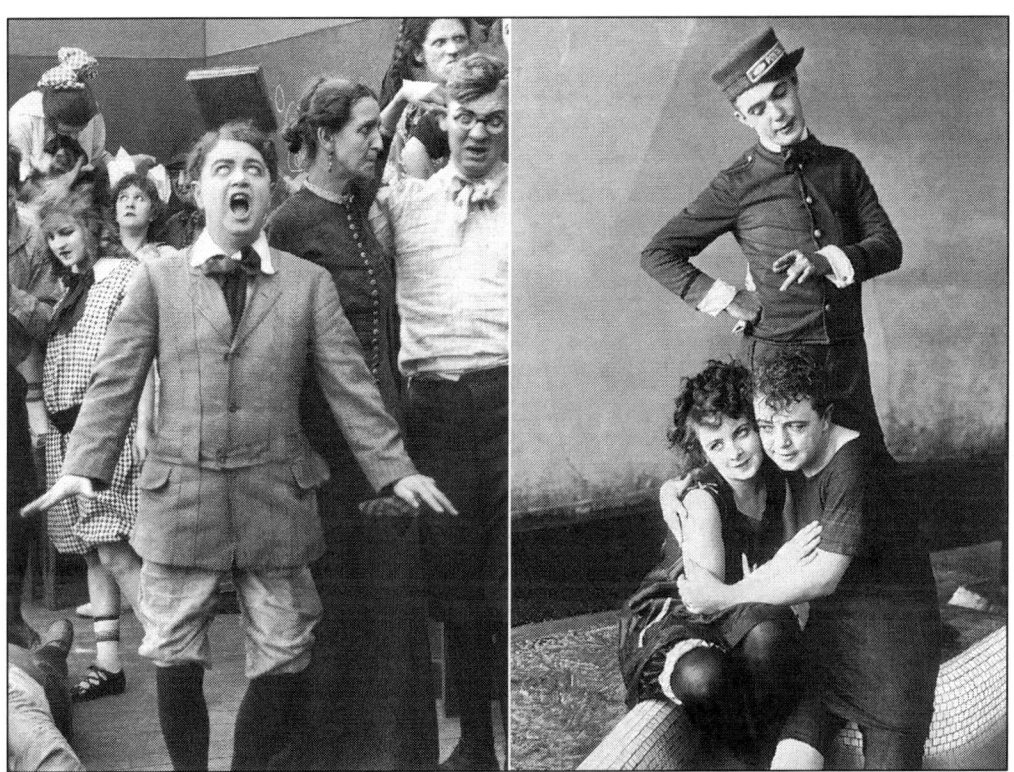

A. H. Frahlich gets chastised by Martha Mattox in *Them Was the Happy Days* (1916), and appears at Universal with Pat Rooney in *Pat Turns Detective* (1918).

From the early 1920s into the 1950s Freddie Fralick represented stars such as Leon Errol, Lewis Stone, Laura La Plante, Viola Dana, Ernest Torrence, and Edgar Kennedy. He also found the time to be editor of *The Standard Casting Guide* in the 1920s, and even had some return involvement with the former Lonesome Luke:

Sellon Goes Into "Catspaw"

Charles Sellon was engaged by Harold Lloyd yesterday for one of the featured roles in "Catspaw." Freddie Fralick handled the ticket.

The Hollywood Reporter, January 26, 1934

With his acting days long behind him, Fralick was in the company of Myron Selznick and Zeppo Marx as one of Hollywood's top agents, and remained so until his death on May 13, 1958.

The making of *Luke's Fatal Flivver* film was almost fatal for Harold according to this item from the February 5, 1916 *Motion Picture News*:

> During the making of a scene for the last current Phunphilm for the Pathé release, Harold C. Lloyd, leading man of the Rolin Company, narrowly escaped suffocation when he was placed inside the engine compartment of a large racing car with a smoke pot and the hood securely fastened. On opening the hood at the completion of the scene Mr. Lloyd was said to be found unconscious. A physician was immediately called in, and Mr. Lloyd was able to continue with his work the following day.

Motion Picture News (June 24, 1916): "This comedy is full of action of the faster sort. Luke is the pilot of an auto conveying a large party to the picnic grounds. They stop and spread their lunch, and in some way Luke's party becomes mixed with a crowd of fashionable folks out for a day in the country. When Luke's passengers see him, apparently making way with the lunch, a riot follows, in which flying articles of lunch figure importantly."

Luke's Society Mix-Up

Released June 26, 1916. Produced by Hal Roach for the Rolin Film Company. Distributed by Pathé. Working title: **Society Picture**. One reel. With Harold Lloyd, Bebe Daniels, Snub Pollard, Dee Lampton, Eva Thatcher, Mae White, Billy Fay, A. H. Frahlich, Gilbert Pratt, May Cloy, Fred Newmeyer, Charles Stevenson, Sammy Brooks.

In this comedy Harold Lloyd as Lonesome Luke is seen as a chauffeur's assistant. His wealthy employer's party promises nothing but failure because the violinist who was to appear fails to show up. Luke's style of haircut gives the hostess an idea and she presses him into service. To avoid real disaster he bandages his hand and announces his inability to perform. For the rest, his actions are a bit out of place in the drawing room and finally it is decided that he himself is entirely out of place and he is not gently helped out of the place. (Motography, July 1, 1916).

Mixing Luke with high society was always a recipe for disaster – thereby a comic success. Much like Charlie Chaplin, Luke was always ready to pretend to be something he wasn't. Sometimes in shorts like *Great While It Lasted* (1915) and *Birds of a Feather* (1917) he comes into money and ends up

Harold teases Bebe and the girls with a mouse in *Luke's Society Mix-Up* (1916).

hobnobbing with the Hoi Polloi, or just impersonates a swell in *Lonesome Luke, Social Gangster* (1915), *Luke, Rank Impersonator* (1916), and *Stop! Luke! Listen!* (1917). Even with his later glasses character Harold would be on the tramp or penniless in *Sic 'Em Towser* (1918), *Pistols for Breakfast*, and *Soft Money* (both 1919), and was more than ready to pose as a fruity classical dance teacher in *Swing Your Partners* (1918).

> The Rolin Film Company since moving into the new studio at 5813-27 Santa Monica Boulevard, has made a number of additions to its producing staff. May Cloy has been engaged to play ingénue parts assisting Miss Bebe Daniels.
>
> *Motion Picture News*, April 22, 1916

Having joined Rolin in early 1916, May Cloy was the second female lead after Bebe Daniels (together they were referred to as "the Phunphilm Girls") in a string of Luke shorts that included *Luke, Crystal Gazer, Luke Does the Midway, Luke and the Bang-Tails*, and *Luke, the Chauffeur* (all 1916). Born Mabel S. Larsen in Minneapolis, she had been a dancer in stage musical comedies. Not long after her work at Rolin she became leading lady for the comedy team of Kolb & Dill at the American Film Company.

Rolin second leading lady May Cloy.

Clarence Kolb and Max Dill were the West Coast version of Weber & Fields, and after a successful decade on stage made the jump to films in 1916. Cloy became the leading lady for their features *A Peck o' Pickles*, *Lonesome Town* (both 1916), and *Beloved Rogues* (1917). She married Clarence Kolb that year and continued to work with the team onstage in shows such as *Wet and*

Dry, Pair of Fools, and *Queen's High,* all through the 1920s. Ms. Cloy later retired, and in the sound era her husband Kolb became a character actor in tons of films like *His Girl Friday* (1940) and *Adam's Rib* (1949), even playing his old stage self in the Lon Chaney biography *Man of a Thousand Faces* (1957). Clarence Kolb passed away in 1964 and May Cloy in 1977.

Motion Picture News (June 24, 1916): "Lonesome Luke, chauffeur in the home of a wealthy family, is called in to take the place of a guest of honor at a reception and the resulting complications are side-splitting, unless we have lost our sense of comedy. There are pretty girls too, one of them who is quite bewitchingly so, has a prominent part, which she fully deserves."

Motion Picture News (July 22, 1916): "Harold Lloyd and Bebe Daniels are featured in this amusing comedy of the newly rich. The famous violinist fails to show up at the reception and the hero acts as a substitute. There is some funny small business running all through this, and some knockabout work at the close."

Luke's Washful Waiting

Released July 3, 1916. Produced by Hal Roach for the Rolin Film Company. Distributed by Pathé. Working title: *Chinese Laundry*. One reel. With Harold Lloyd, Bebe Daniels, Snub Pollard.

Luke gets an afternoon off and calls on his fair one. They have an untimely accident, however, and when they pick themselves out of the mud hike to the nearest tailor shop. The girl can't be accommodated by the tailor, because he's not that kind of tailor; so she goes next door to a Chinese laundry to be washed and ironed. The places adjoin, there is considerable mixup and the film ends in a medley of trousers and flat irons. Luke, a fire-hose, Bebe, a fire-hose, pig-tails, a fire-hose, and so on. (Motion Picture News, July 8, 1916).

July of 1916 marked a year since *Spit-Ball Sadie* and the regular release of *Lonesome Luke* films. *The Moving Picture World* acknowledged this milestone a few months later on November 11, 1916:

Pathé's "Luke" Comedies Have Successful Year

The "Lonesome Luke" comedies on the Pathé program are making an enviable reputation. It is only about a year ago that the first one made, "Just Nuts," played to remarkable business and established a record for repeat viewings. Harold Lloyd, the star, "Snub" Pollard, his able assistant, and Bebe Daniels, the charming sixteen year old ingenue were at that time unknown, but under the able direction of Hal Roach, of the Rolin Company, they have developed into what many persons consider is the ablest comedy cast of the day. As to Harold Lloyd, the exhibitors themselves call him one of the two greatest comedians in the business.

Harold and Bebe decide to take advantage of Charles Stevenson, Sammy Brooks, and Fred Newmeyer's services in *Luke's Washful Waiting* (1916).
Courtesy of the Academy of Motion Picture Arts and Sciences.

In the short span of a year Rolin and the *Luke* comedies became firmly established, and Harold was on his way to becoming a true audience favorite.

Luke's Washful Waiting takes Luke into the world of Chinese laundries, which was a standard short comedy setting. Ham & Bud are terrible workers in *The Winning Wash* (1915), and much of the action in *Fatty's Faithful Fido* (1915) takes place in Frank Hayes' laundry shop. Wearing a long pigtail as "One Lung," he's the butt of many jokes and on the receiving end of much slapstick.

Ethnic stereotypes were a staple in silent comedy, just as it had been in vaudeville. Besides comical Asian characters, there were African-Americans, Jews, Irishmen, and Germans as well. Laundries, of course, were always run by Chinese people, pawn shops operated by Jewish proprietors, and nine times out of ten black characters are scared, or always ready to roll dice or whip out giant razors. At the same time, the comedies also made fun of policemen, country rubes, ministers, criminals, scholars and even race car drivers, so in their attitude that everyone and everything was fair game for laughs they were equal opportunity abusers.

Since these stereotypes so casually permeated the genre there are plenty of examples of it in the early Lloyd and Roach films. But they are the kind that was standard for the day – they never go to the extremes of racism that were a feature of Larry Semon's comedies. Still demeaning caricatures turned up in film comedies through the 1950s, and for modern audiences there are a few cringe-worthy moments in Harold's later *Safety Last* (1923) and *Feet First* (1930), but overall his films are fairly light on extreme ethnic stereotyping.

Motion Picture News (July 22, 1916): "Slapstick action is here staged in a laundry and a tailor store adjoining one another. There have been better Lonesome Luke comedies, although this one manages to create a deal of laughter. Harold Lloyd and Bebe Daniels are the principals."

Luke Rides Rough-Shod*

Released July 10, 1916. Produced by Hal Roach for the Rolin Film Company. Distributed by Pathé. Extant: BRUS. Working title: *Luke's Western Romance*. One reel (Filmed from March 14-21, 1916). With Harold Lloyd, Bebe Daniels, Snub Pollard, Charles Stevenson, Billy Fay, Fred Newmeyer, A.H. Frahlich, Sammy Brooks, Eva Thatcher, Rose Mendel, Ben Corday, Dee Lampton, C.A. Self, L.A. Gregor, Ray Wyatt, C. Spikeman, Winna Brown, F. Ward, L McCormack, H. Minnishaw, H. Granger, Gilbert Pratt.

Luke Rides Rough-Shod (1916) and strikes fear into the hearts of hombres Sammy Brooks, Ben Corday (in doorway), Fred Newmeyer, Dee Lampton, Billy Fay and A. H. Frahlich.

Luke is discovered on a donkey. He learns by means of signs posted conspicuously that there's a certain bad man at large for whom a fat reward is offered. Luke, handling his shooting iron gingerly, meets up with the wicked one, who, thinking he is covered, points to the wide expanse of blue overhead. Luke changes clothes with him and rides into town on the blackleg's pony. He does some spectacular riding and erratic shooting until chased by the mob, he takes refuge in a barn. "Behold the Indian" comes up behind him, pushes him off the loft, and Luke, hurtling through plenty of cubic feet, lands on the back of a bull. (Moving Picture World, July 15, 1916).

Like comedies, westerns were a cinematic staple from the very beginning, and the genre certainly expanded after the American film industry settled in California and had the perfect locations for cowboy opuses right at their fingertips. As soon as the screen's wild-west conventions were set they were ready targets for parody.

The most frequent recipe was to take an established comic personality (who would generally fill the role of tenderfoot) and send them to the wide-open spaces with expected results. In shorts Roscoe Arbuckle did *Fatty and Minnie Hee-Haw* (1914)*, Out West* (1918), *The Sheriff* (1918), and *A Desert Hero* (1919). Not to be outdone Hank Mann, Lupino Lane, Larry Semon, Johnny Arthur, Jimmie Adams, the Hallroom Boys, and Edward Everett Horton rode the range in *Guns and Greasers* (1918), *Way Out West* (1920), *Two Faces West* (1921), *Some Scout, Whoa Emma! Honest Injun* (all 1926), and *Find the King* (1927). Features like *Wild and Wooly* (1917), *The Round-Up* (1920) and *Go West* (1925) saw the likes of Douglas Fairbanks and Buster Keaton fending for themselves.

A few companies specialized in western comedies with one of the longest running being Essanay's 1910 to 1916 series of *Snakeville* Comedies. Soon-to-be Rolin regulars Harry Todd and Margaret Joslin made their names in these one-reelers where they shared the screen with Augustus Carney and Victor Potel. A rip-off of the *Snakevilles* came from the St. Louis Motion Picture Co. who put out some 1913 – 1914 *Frontier Films* that starred a young Lloyd Hamilton as a character named "Pretzel." In the late Teens Mack Sennett developed a *Sheriff Nell* series for broad and boisterous Polly Moran, with support from Ben Turpin and Slim Summerville. Over at the Al Christie Studio Fay Tincher put on cowboy hat and boots for two-reelers like *Wild and Western, Go West, Young Woman*, and *Rowdy Ann* (all 1919).

The mid-1920s saw Universal produce two comedy western series. The first was *W.C. Tuttle Western Comedies* with Pee Wee Holmes and Ben Corbett playing two always-feuding ranch hands in the mythical western 'burb of Piperock. The two years of their shorts included titles like *A Man-Sized Pet* (1926) and *Cow is Cows* (1927). Universal's other claim to comedy western fame was some 1928/1929 *Tenderfoot Thrillers* two-reelers which featured character player George Chandler doing a Buster Keaton imitation as an Eastern dude persona usually named Bertie or Cuthbert. Sadly, none of these are available today, but contemporary critics referred to his Keaton portrayal, and Chandler continued doing it in sound shorts like *The Back Page* and *The Lure of Hollywood* (both 1931) before finally dropping it.

Harold keeps the town at bay in *Luke Rides Rough-Shod* (1916).

Luke Rides Rough-Shod was Rolin and Harold's first western parody, but it opened the flood-gates as Harold would continue with *From London to Laramie* (1917), *Two-Gun Gussie* (1918), *Billy Blazes, Esq.* (1919), and *An Eastern Westerner* (1920). From here, Roach would send practically all of his stable of comics to the lone prairie, which included Snub Pollard in *Whirl O' the West* (1921) and Eddie Boland's *Hurry West* (1921). Paul Parrott double-billed in *Blaze Away* (1922) and *The Uncovered Wagon* (1923), so did Stan Laurel in *The Soilers* (1923) and *Wide Open Spaces* (1924), and Will Rogers in *Two Wagons, Both Covered*, and *The Cowboy Sheik* (both 1924). Our Gang ventured out west in *War Feathers* (1926), as did Laurel & Hardy in their famous feature *Way Out West* (1937). Even the monkeys, dogs, and ducks of the Dippy-Doo-Dads followed Horace Greeley's advice in *Go West* (1923).

Winna Brown was one of the regular supporting players with Rolin at this time, and *Luke Rides Rough-Shod* was right up her alley as she was one of the most expert horsewomen to ever work in Hollywood. Winnifred Brown was born in 1885 in Wyoming County, Pennsylvania, and soon traveled to Texas and New Mexico, along the way becoming an expert equestrian and champion relay rider. In 1914, she entered pictures in New Mexico with the Albuquerque Film Company:

"Reuben's Busy Day," an Albuquerque comedy-drama picturing remarkable stunts with an automobile. Buck Connors and Winna Brown are the leads.

Moving Picture World, November 14, 1914

Winna came to Los Angeles with the company, co-starring with Dot Farley in films like *When Quality Meets* (1915) that was set around a recent Los Angeles rodeo. Moving on to other studios she appeared in other 1916 *Luke* shorts such as *Luke, Crystal Gazer, Luke, the Chauffeur*, and *Luke, the Gladiator* (whose chariot race may also have taken advantage of her equestrian skills). After settling in California, she acquired a large expanse of land, which also came in handy for movie cowboy Tom Mix:

> For staging Mix subjects Mr. Fox has leased a large tract of land on the Winna Brown ranch near Los Angeles, erected a complete western city, from dance hall to undertaking establishment, and arranged for the maintenance of a large stock farm to furnish horses and cattle for the films.
>
> *Motion Picture News*, January 13, 1917

Winna Brown's ranch became Mixville – Tom Mix's studio for making his western pictures. Only minutes from Los Angeles on Glendale Boulevard, a shopping center now occupies the wide open spaces where Mix once rode. *Courtesy of Robert S. Birchard.*

Becoming known as "Mixville" this location was in use for many years, as was Winna. She specialized in stunts such as racing a horse alongside a speeding railway train and swinging from it to the cab of the engine, and doubled for a wide array of stars that included Bebe Daniels, Priscilla Dean, Colleen Moore, Norma and Constance Talmadge, Betty Compson, Marie Prevost, and even Joseph Schildkraut. Known as "Fred" by her friends, she suffered many serious injuries in the line of duty over the years but continued working until 1946's *My Darling Clementine*. Cancer sent her to the Motion Picture Country Home, where she died in March of 1947.

Moving Picture World (July 15, 1916): "The ending is too funny for description, it must be seen to be appreciated."

Luke, Crystal Gazer

Released July 24, 1916. Produced by Hal Roach for the Rolin Film Company. Distributed by Pathé. Working titles: ***Luke and the Fortune Teller*** and ***Lonesome Luke Crystal Gazer***. One reel. (Filmed from March 23-31, 1916). With Harold Lloyd, Bebe Daniels, Snub Pollard, Eva Thatcher, Harry Todd, Bud Jamison, Charles Stevenson, Rose Mendel, Fred Newmeyer, Sammy Brooks, Dee Lampton, Billy Fay, A.H. Frahlich, Gilbert Pratt, Rose Mendel, Ben Corday, Ray Wyatt, C. Spikeman, Winna Brown, Lionel Comport, May Cloy, Della Mullady.

Harold improvises a snake charm tune for Bebe in *Luke, Crystal Gazer* (1916) as Eva Thatcher and Gilbert Pratt fall under its spell.

Four "chicken" fanciers, looking over the metropolitan farm, come upon a dame who would have looked better had they been cross-eyed, and they elect Snub to "feed" her while they go their merry ways. Luke stumbles into an occult shop, where he gets a job. The chief spiritualist is the mother of the nicest girl Luke has ever seen, and Luke decides to stick around.

The four "chicken" fanciers float in and the old lady "goes into the silences" while the daughter behind the screen, plays the departed spirit for any one who has the price. She gets Luke to substitute for her while she goes outside, and one of the boys, who has seen her behind the curtain, comes up and grabs a hand – Luke's hand. Of course there is a riot that ends with the crystal ball doing duty for shrapnel. (*Moving Picture World,* July 29, 1916).

A vaudeville advertisement for Eva Thatcher, where she was known as "The Irish Lady."

Playing Bebe's fortune teller mother was silent comedy veteran Eva Thatcher. Part of the ensemble in a number of the 1916 *Luke* shorts such as *Luke, Rides Rough-Shod, Luke's Lost Lamb* and *Luke's Newsie Knockout,* Thatcher specialized in older dowager characters with a rumpled face that looked like someone had slept in it. She had worked for years in vaudeville as Evelyn Thatcher. Billed as "The Irish Lady," she came to films around 1914 for Universal appearing in their *Frontier Films* and opposite Augustus Carney in his *Universal Ike* series (plus stayed after Carney left for the *Universal Ike Jr.*'s).

Her appearance with Charlie Chaplin in *The Count* (1916) gave her relatively new film career a boost and she soon became a regular at the top comedy outfit of the day – the Mack Sennett Studio. Soon she was working everywhere – Fox, Larry Semon, Al Christie, and Jack White. Her feature film appearances included Lois Weber's *A Chapter in Her Life* (1923), a number of Leo Maloney westerns, and Buster Keaton's *College* (1927). After retiring in 1936 she passed away in 1942.

During the making of *Luke, Crystal Gazer* producer Hal Roach was off on one of his periodic business trips to meet with the Pathé bigwigs. In the days before air travel was common, trains were the way to go and a trip from California to New York took four days each way. Most correspondence between the coasts was done by telegram, but to really iron out business details face-to-face meetings had to be scheduled. These trips were a good excuse for publicity photos and items:

> Phunphilm Director Hal Roach, who has been producing some screamingly funny comedies for Pathé release, has departed for the great New York.
>
> He was given a rousing farewell at the depot by members of his fun company. Mr. Roach goes to the East to confer with the heads of the firm which is marketing Phunphilms. While away the players are working under the direction of Gilbert Pratt who has been playing leads.
>
> *Moving Picture World*, March 25, 1916

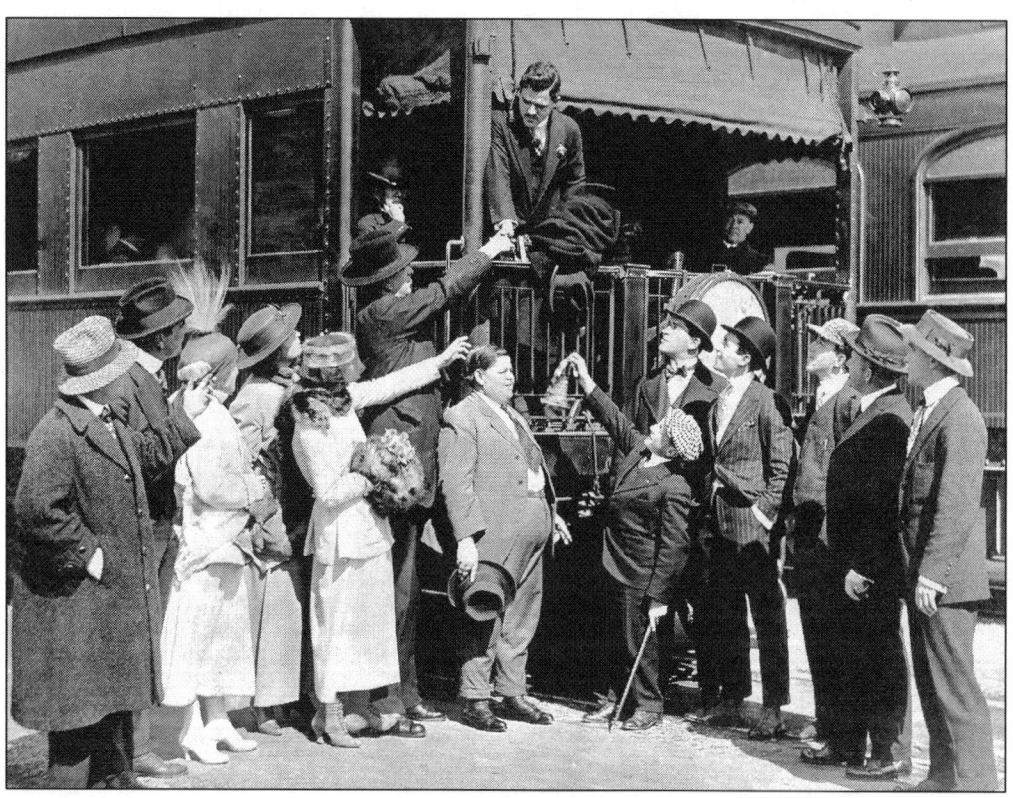

A natty Harold (right) and the rest of the Rolin ensemble see Hal Roach off on a trip to confer with Pathé in New York.

As previously mentioned, Harold was not all that happy with the Luke character, and items like this from the February 1917 issue of *Picture-Play Magazine* must have reinforced his frustrations:

> No, that was not Charles Chaplin that you saw in "Luke, Crystal Gazer." It was Harold Lloyd, of the Rolin Film Company. He makes up to look a lot like our friend Charles, but there is quite a difference in their work – and salary.

Moving Picture World (August 5, 1916): "An amusing farce comedy in which Luke happens into the house of a spiritualist and substitutes for a pretty girl, whose place is behind the curtain. Discovered by a pal Luke is hauled out and from here quick action characterizes the picture. This will be found extremely amusing."

Motography (July 29, 1916): "In this true-to-form Luke comedy Harold Lloyd and his supporting company, which includes the vivacious Bebe Daniels, indulges in some very swift action."

Luke's Lost Lamb

Released August 7, 1916. Produced by Hal Roach for the Rolin Film Company. Distributed by Pathé. One reel. (Filmed from March 31 – April 5, 1916). With Harold Lloyd, Bebe Daniels, Snub Pollard, Sammy Brooks, Bud Jamison, Charles Stevenson, Rose Mendel, Fred Newmeyer, Eva Thatcher, Dee Lampton, Billy Fay, Harry Todd, Margaret Joslin, May Cloy, Mrs. Halliburton and baby.

"Lonesome Luke" as Harold Lloyd is known, takes his wife and child to the beach, there to disport himself. His wife can't see that stuff though and sets him to mind the baby. There's another little family there, namely, Snub and his wife. Also some girls. Luke forgets about the baby in observing the girls, with the usual disastrous result to himself. (Moving Picture World, August 12, 1916).

Here Luke and & Co. finally get around to one of the major subgenres of silent slapstick – the beach comedy. Created by Mack Sennett as the logical location for his bathing beauties to romp, he started as early as *The Diving Girl* (1911) while he was still directing for Biograph, and half of the very first Keystone release was *The Water Nymph* (1912). Over the years Sennett never strayed very far from the surf with regular outings that included *Mabel's New Hero* (1913), *Miss Fatty's Seaside Lovers* (1915), *A Bedroom Blunder* (1917), *She Sighed by the Seaside* (1920), *Water Wagons* (1925), and *The Beach Club* (1928).

Harold takes care of Junior in *Luke's Lost Lamb* (1916).

Everyone from Fatty Arbuckle to Harry Langdon, even Charlie Chaplin in *By the Sea* (1915), spent time kicking up sand. Harold mentioned in his autobiography that one of the very first Rolin efforts was built around two mischievous boys with Harold as a chauffeur who had to look after them at the seaside. He would go back to the beach in his later glasses character comedies *By the Sad Sea Waves* (1917), *Why Pick on Me?* (1918), and *Number Please* (1920).

A memorable performer who had recently joined the Rolin ranks was Sammy Brooks. At about four feet high, Brooks was an adept comic foil who found a ready place in silent slapstick as his miniscule figure made him a walking sight gag. Born Samuel Rockenberg in Brooklyn in 1891, Sammy began acting onstage in productions such as *Snow White and the Seven Dwarfs*, and *Katzenjammer Kids* with the World of Mirth Company, as well as toured vaudeville as part of *Lasky's Hoboes*. His initial film work included playing with Mary Pickford in the Famous Players feature *Cinderella* (1914), in addition to Heinie & Louie and Hans & Fritz shorts for Starlight and Lubin.

> Sammy Brooks, height four feet, two inches, and weighing ninety-six pounds, is the latest freak discovered by Manager D. Whiting and Director Hal Roach, of the Rolin Film Company.

Brooks appeared on the Orpheum circuit as one of Lasky's Hoboes, and had other stage experience.

At the studio giant Ben Corday uses Brooks for his morning exercise, lifting him first with one hand and then the other.

Harold Lloyd, who appears as Lonesome Luke in the Rolin Phunphilms, has a standing wager that he and Brooks can both get into the same suit of clothes without the ruse being apparent.

Motion Picture News, March 11, 1916

Sammy Brooks gives Harold a lift on his bike during the making of *Chop Suey & Co.* (1919).
Courtesy of the Museum of Modern Art.

Becoming a *Lonesome Luke* regular in early 1916, Brooks appeared in practically every Harold Lloyd film through *Grandma's Boy* (1922). He also appeared non-stop in the Roach comedies of Snub Pollard, Paul Parrott, Our Gang, and Stan Laurel, and took a lot of punishment in the name of comedy – frequently kicked, vaulted over, knocked down, and trod upon. But as a comic reversal, he would usually end up laying waste to the comic that thought he would be a pushover. After 1926, as the Roach comedies became more situational and realistic, he appeared on screen less, but worked in other capacities at the Roach lot. His last known film was *Swiss Miss*, and he died on May 16, 1951.

Mahoney City Record (October 4, 1916): "The comedy is a 'Lonesome Luke,' 'Luke's Lost Lamb.' This is really funny and will delight the children as well as grownups. Send them here."

Luke Does the Midway*

Released August 21, 1916. Produced by Hal Roach for the Rolin Film Co. Distributed by Pathé. Working title: ***Lonesome Luke at the San Diego Exposition***. One reel. (Filmed from April 6 -12, 1916). Extant: GOS. With Harold Lloyd, Bebe Daniels, Snub Pollard, Bud Jamison, Dee Lampton, Harry Todd, Margaret Joslin, Sammy Brooks, Charles Stevenson, Billy Fay, Fred Newmeyer, May Cloy, Mrs. Haliburton.

Luke goes to see the sights at the exposition, and he wouldn't be Luke if he didn't get into trouble immediately. There isn't a side show or an amusement device in the whole park that Luke doesn't try to get ready for the scrap-heap as soon as he sees it. Moreover he accords the same treatment to the other visitors to the fair. The result may be imagined. Luke leaves the exposition via the back of a wild ostrich, and the exposition heaves a sigh of relief when he departs. (*Moving Picture World*, September 2, 1916)

Bebe and Harold checking out a sideshow in a frame scan from
Luke Does the Midway (1916). *Courtesy of Peter Bagrov.*

The Rolin Phunphilm players have had a great trip to San Diego and Mexico this week. They enjoyed the little journey immensely and well they might, for the sights that they saw were new and novel. Everyone got to see the 1916 Exposition as well as the Army and Navy headquarters, both on land and sea.

Moving Picture World, May 6, 1916

The Midway that Luke does was part of the Panama – California Exposition at San Diego's Balboa Park. This ran from 1915 to 1917 as a celebration of the opening of the Panama Canal, and was an extended plug for San Diego as the first U.S. port of call for ships sailing north from the canal. Luke gets mixed up in all the crowds, festivities, booths, and exhibits at the fair, just as Roscoe Arbuckle and Mabel Normand did a year before. *Fatty and Mabel at the San Diego Exposition* (1915) was something of a blueprint for this comedy, and when the earlier film was made Harold was working for Mack Sennett. He also shared a little screen time with Arbuckle in *Miss Fatty's Seaside Lovers* (1915), but in his 1928 autobiography he had this to say about working with the large comic:

> Once or twice I worked with Fatty Arbuckle, but with little success. Arbuckle had the star bumpers on the lot and he led them in person, taking Brodies that shook buildings. I could bump with any of them, but he surrounded himself with a group of regulars who knew his methods so well that they did not need to be told what to do, and weren't, leaving a new man to guess and flounder.

During the shoot, the Rolin actors were as much of an attraction as the midway shows:

> The exposition officials gave the players a whole basket of passes to all the concessions, and when the actors attended the many shows there were many visitors who went in just to be with the comedy gang.

Photoplayers Weekly, April 29, 1916

This surviving *Luke* short resides at Moscow's Gosfilmofond Archive. It was publicly shown there in a 2016 festival program, but hasn't circulated otherwise.

Motography (August 26, 1916): "A slapstick comedy which presents Harold Lloyd in happy surroundings. The bathing beach resort is a good setting and Lloyd as Lonesome Luke has plenty of opportunity to be funny."

Moving Picture World (August 26, 1916): "An amusing farce comedy in which Luke's adventures on the midway end in rough handling for himself as well as others. Many will find the introduction of the usual midway sights coupled with Luke's funny personality very entertaining."

Harold (center), Joe Bordeaux (right) and Edgar Kennedy (left) are penniless swains that court the titular heiress (left) in *Miss Fatty's Seaside Lovers* (1915).
Courtesy of the Library of Congress.

Luke Joins the Navy*

Released September 3, 1916. Produced by Hal Roach for the Rolin Film Company. Distributed by Pathé. One reel. (Filmed from April 17-21, 24, 26 & May 2, 1916). Extant: MoMA, EYE. With Harold Lloyd, Bebe Daniels, Snub Pollard, Bud Jamison, Harry Todd, Margaret Joslin, Dee Lampton, Charles Stevenson, Fred Newmeyer, Billy Fay, Sammy Brooks, Gilbert Pratt, May Cloy.

Lonesome Luke here joins the Navy not so much from the promptings of a patriotic spirit as from a desire to gain prestige in his hometown and particularly with the one and only girl. He and his pal are put through the regular paces on shipboard, and between the two of them diversion is afforded the spectator. (Motography, September 2, 1916).

Luke Joins the Navy (1916), but Snub can't get away from his battle axe wife Margaret Joslin. *Courtesy of the Academy of Motion Pictures Arts and Sciences.*

Luke Joins the Navy, along with *Luke's Movie Muddle* (1916) and *Lonesome Luke, Messenger* (1917), is one of the most accessible of the series today – but unfortunately in a cut-down version. New York's Museum of Modern Art has the complete short, but sadly it's rarely screened. Missing are sequences of Luke and Snub having trouble with lifeboat drills and a long routine of them trying to "drop anchor"- which involves them carrying an immense anchor up a ladder and tossing it unconnected over the side. The pair join up to get away from their hum-drum civilian lives, but have nothing but trouble aboard ship. Most of the real sailors didn't take their extra work very seriously and mostly stand around gawking at the action and the camera. Harold remembered:

> The Navy lent us the use of a battleship deck and were cordial hosts. Bebe may have had something to do with that.

Luke is one of the innumerable movie comics who ended up being nervous in the oceangoing branch of the service, and his nautical misadventures here would be revisited in Harold's first feature *A Sailor-Made Man* (1921). Many movie comedians spent time on the briny. Charlie Chaplin got *Shanghaied* (1915) as did Harry Langdon in *Shanghaied Lovers* (1924). Stan

Laurel spoofed the maritime drama *All the Brothers Were Valiant* (1923) in his *Brothers Under the Chin* (1923), suffered through *Navy Blue Days* (1925), and was a memorable sea dog with Oliver Hardy in 1928's *Two Tars* (and then was immediately imitated by Snub Pollard and Marvin Loback in the next year's *Here Comes a Sailor*).

Silent comedy's main silly sailor was former vaudevillian Billy Dooley. Starting in 1925 he was Al Christie's "goofy gob" in four years' worth of shorts like *A Salty Sap* (1926), *A Mooney Mariner* (1927), and *Water Bugs* (1928) to prove it. His sailor suit was Dooley's calling card, and in his few outings without it he seems naked and devoid of any comic personality.

The following inauspicious item noted the beginning of one of the all-time most valuable members of the Harold Lloyd team:

> Fred Newmeyer has been added to the stock company.
>   *Motion Picture News*, December 25, 1915

Starting as an actor, Newmeyer became possibly Lloyd's most important writer and director – collaborating on seminal pictures like *Grandma's Boy* (1922), *Safety Last* (1923), and *The Freshman* (1925).

Newmeyer was born in 1888 in Central City, Colorado, and knew Harold as a boy. In fact, they shared the same school house. His aim was to be a baseball pitcher, and he did well, ending up in the major leagues with the Philadelphia Athletics until an injury ended his sports career. Moving to the West Coast with the hopes of recovering his arm strength, he instead reconnected with Harold, who brought him into movies. Since he had some acting experience in stock companies, he started out in the *Luke* shorts as an all-purpose character player.

Years later Newmeyer told historian Sam Gill that after a falling out with Hal Roach he left Rolin and went over to Fox where he worked with Henry Lehrman and William S. Campbell. This seems to have developed his comedy creation skills, and on returning to Roach he began writing and directing, cutting his teeth on some 1920 Snub Pollard comedies like *Slippery Slickers*, *All Lit Up*, and *Raise the Rent*. Soon he was back working on Harold's films, where shorts like *Now or Never* and *Never Weaken* (both 1921) led to features.

Often sharing directorial credit with Sam Taylor, Newmeyer stayed with the Lloyd unit through *The Freshman* (1925), and then branched out to the wider world of silent comedy. His track record with the huge Lloyd hits put him in demand with some of the biggest comedy names of the day. Newmeyer directed Douglas MacLean, Larry Semon, Leon Errol, and

Reginald Denny in features such as *Seven Keys to Baldpate, The Perfect Clown* (both 1925), *The Lunatic at Large* (1927), *The Night Bird* (1928), and he even went to the East Coast to helm *The Quarterback* (1926) with Richard Dix and *The Potters* (1927) with W.C. Fields.

Fred Newmeyer and Harold during the making of *Among Those Present* (1921).

With the arrival of sound, he initially directed "A" features like *Fast and Loose* (1930), but was soon stuck in lower budgeted productions for independent outfits like Screencraft Productions and Commonwealth. 1936 and 1937 saw him return to the Hal Roach fold to helm Our Gang two-reelers, as well as their only feature *General Spanky* (1936). His last film was the Fred Scott PRC western *Rodeo Rhythm* (1942), and his last days were spent at the Motion Picture Country Home in Woodland Hills, California. There he was interviewed by historian Sam Gill about his early days in the movie business, and passed away in 1967.

Billboard (September 2, 1916): "Luke Joins the Navy is another screaming slapstick comedy, made by the Rolin Company. Luke as a Jackie will coax laughs from the grouchiest. The majority of scenes are taken aboard a U.S. man-of-war, and, besides being a corking comedy, the scenes on board are very interesting."

Motion Picture World (September 9, 1916): "A slapstick comedy in which Luke joins Uncle Sam's fleet and has diverse, peculiar and fairly funny experiences. There is a deal of rough and tumble work in which respect the offering is similar to others of this brand. Harold Lloyd and Bebe Daniels are the principals."

Luke and the Mermaids

Released September 17, 1916. Produced by Hal Roach for the Rolin Film Company. Distributed by Pathé. Working title: ***Luke Asleep in the Briny Deep***. One reel (Filmed from April 27 – May 3, 1916). With Harold Lloyd, Bebe Daniels, Snub Pollard, Bud Jamison, Harry Todd, Charles Stevenson, Fred Newmeyer, Sammy Brooks, Dee Lampton, Billy Fay, Margaret Joslin, May Cloy, J. Weiss, Tod Cregier, Mary Henderson, Florence Rose, Ruth Marzer, Aileen Allen, Vera Steadman, Victoria Wolf, Cora Webb, Naola Burrell, Nina Burrell, Nina Glaze, Del Manley, Ed Egel.

Luke and his pal dream of seeking the briny depths and meeting there a flock of mermaids, clad in one-piece bathing suits. Their adventures with the girls and several sons of Neptune are funny though disconnected. (Motion Picture News, September 30, 1916).

The Rolin Company was always ready to work attractive women into their proceedings. The idea of mermaids was particularly good as that meant bathing beauties. Beach girls had become a comedy staple after Mack Sennett filmed Mabel Normand in her one piece for *The Diving Girl* (1911) and *The Water Nymph* (1912). Sennett basically came up with a more refined version of the "French postcard," and moved to the logical conclusion that if one girl in swim wear on the screen caused a sensation – a bevy of them would become an industry standard.

Something looks fishy to Harold in *Luke and the Mermaids* (1916).

And they did – like his Keystone Cops, every comedy unit had to have their own versions. As with the L-Ko Girls and the Fox Sunshine Beauties, the Rolin Company had their own beauty squad, whose highlights would include *Ragtime Snap Shots* (1915), *Lonesome Luke Lolls in Luxury*, *Luke Pipes the Pippins* (both 1916), *Luke's Wild Women*, *Lonesome Luke Loses Patients*, and *Clubs are Trump* (all 1917). Besides the opportunity for bathing girls, the undersea idea brought an opportunity for novelty:

> Atmosphere has been added to the ocean bed scenes by taking them through a glass tank in which varieties of fish are always moving about.
>
> *Motion Picture News*, September 30, 1916

French filmmaker George Melies was very fond of shooting undersea fantasies such as *Divers at Work on the Wreck of the Maine* (1898), *The Kingdom of the Fairies* (1903), *The Mermaid* (1904), and *Under the Seas* (1907) through a tank that would add swimming fish and crustaceans to the foreground of a shot. This process is lovingly illustrated in the recreation of the Melies studio in Martin Scorsese's 2011 feature *Hugo*, where a prop man is dropping lobsters in the tank as the camera moves to shoot through the tank and show the effect. George and Ernest Williamson brought breathtaking actual underwater photography to films in features such as *20,000 Leagues under the Sea* (1916), making the old fish tank effect more appropriate for spoofs and comedy shorts.

Luke and the Mermaids (1916) has Harold ruling the undersea kingdom. His subjects include Charles Stevenson, Snub, Bud Jamison, Margaret Joslin, Dee Lampton, Fred Newmeyer, May Cloy, Bebe, and Harry Todd.

Since bathing beauties were all the rage, two athletic girls were making the rounds of the movie studios. Many of the beach girls were just decoration, but Aileen Allen and Vera Steadman were record-holding divers and swimmers. The Canadian-born Aileen Allen had a relatively short stay in movies in between diving competitions, but during the teens she swam and did stunts for Rolin, Mack Sennett, and Triangle Comedies:

> Thrills and deeds of daring, all performed in pursuit of comedy, fairly tumbled over one another during the past week at the Mack Sennett-Keystone Studios.

In one scene Aileen Allen, the Keystone champion diving girl, was called on to make a fall over a balcony rail onto the floor below.

After battling with the villain, Miss Allen made the fifteen-foot fall all right, but instead of going over the rail, the rail gave way, and the girl, the villain, the hero rushing to her rescue and two extra people went with it. Fortunately the net below held, and no one was seriously hurt.

Moving Picture World, February 24, 1917

Swimming champ and long-time Christie Comedies leading lady Vera Steadman.

Besides some Luke shorts, the athletic Ms. Allen also appeared in *Settled at the Seaside* and *Those Bitter Sweets* (both 1915) for Mack Sennett, Vitagraph's *He Got Himself a Wife* (1915), and the western *Mister 44* (1916). Her busy sports career saw her win many medals and championships for fancy and high diving. She also competed in the 1920 Summer Olympics, was the women's director of the Pasadena Athletic Club, became the assistant coach of the U.S. women's track team in 1928 and 1932, and from 1931 to her retirement in 1949 was swimming instructor and director of women's athletics at the Los Angeles Athletic Club. During that time, she trained Esther Williams, who became MGM's big swimming star.

Like Ms. Allen, Vera Steadman was also a record holding diver and swimmer from the Los Angeles Athletic Club, but unlike her contemporary Steadman eventually became a busy silent comedy leading lady on dry land. Born in Monterey, California in 1900, she had no previous experience on the stage or screen when she joined Keystone in 1915. Her devotion to water sports and her good looks brought her to Sennett's attention. Showing her swimming prowess in Sennett comedies like *Those College Girls* (1915), *The Surf Girl* (1916), and *Her Native Dance* (1917), she eventually became an ingénue in *Her Blighted Love* and *The Summer Girls* (both 1918). She also made the rounds of the other comedy units, hence her one-time appearance with Lonesome Luke, but she also turned up in shorts at Universal and with comic Larry Semon.

In 1919 she settled in at the Al Christie Studio and stayed there through the 1920s where she was leading lady to every comedian on the lot – Bobby Vernon, Jimmie Adams, Neal Burns, and especially "goofy gob" Billy Dooley. In addition to shorts such as *Exit Quietly* (1921), *Fool Proof* (1923), *Getting Gertie's Goat* (1924), and *A Mooney Mariner* (1927), she appeared in Christie features like *Stop Flirting* (1925) and *The Nervous Wreck* (1926). The arrival of sound saw a drop off in her career, and the rest of her work was as an uncredited extra. This came to an end in 1941 when she was struck by an automobile. Told that she would never walk again – she did two years later. Although she left the movie business, she was on hand for many of the Sennett company reunions before her death in 1966.

Moving Picture World (September 30, 1916): "While there is nothing entirely new about this farce-comedy number, it is at the same time very amusing and interesting. That portion in which Luke and his pal follow the mermaids to their submarine home is cleverly contrived and entertaining."

Luke's Speedy Club Life

Released October 1, 1916. Produced by Hal Roach for the Rolin Film Co. Distributed by Pathé. Directed by Hal Roach. Working title: ***Luke and the Club Loungers***. One reel. (Filmed May 3-6, 1916). With Harold Lloyd, Bebe Daniels, Snub Pollard, Earl Mohan, Bud Jamison, Dee Lampton, Sammy Brooks, Charles Stevenson, May Cloy, Billy Fay, Fred Newmeyer, Harry Todd, Margaret Joslin, Aileen Allen, Victoria Wolf, Cora Webb, Naola Burrell, Nina Glaze, Harvey L. Kinney, Tod Cregier, M. Harrington, Elmer Ballard, Sidney Fiske, Beth McAlister, Jay Irvine.

Luke is chief bellhop in a club, and his experiences with all the members are some of the most humorous that he has undergone in these comedies (Motion Picture News, October 7, 1916).

Harold, Bebe (left), Charles Stevenson, May Cloy (right) watch Dee Lampton, Bud Jamison and Sammy Brooks (center) turn up much worse for wear in *Luke's Speedy Club Life* (1916).

A popular, but now forgotten, comedy player and Hal Roach regular of the Teens was Harry Todd. Born in Alleghany, Pennsylvania in 1865, he started his stage career at age fourteen in a production of *Uncle Tom's Cabin*. After working in vaudeville, he entered films in the early days of Essanay, and then joined Selig in 1909 where he worked with Roscoe Arbuckle in shorts like *Ben's Kid* (1909). The next year he returned to Essanay and became one of the leads in their successful *Snakeville* comedies.

Todd played "Mustang Pete" opposite Augustus Carney as "Alkali Ike" and his real-life wife Margaret Joslin as "Sophie Clutts." Comedies such as *Alkali Ike's Auto* (1911), *Alkali Ike Plays the Devil* (1912), *Sophie's Hero* (1913), and *Sophie Picks a Dead One* (1914) had Todd and Carney battling over the favors of the zaftig Ms. Joslin. Carney left the company at the end of 1913, but Todd and Joslin continued headlining in the shorts until the unit closed down in 1916.

Harry Todd (right) Evelyn Selbie, Augustus Carney, and Victor Potel (left) all check out Fred Church's trance in *Alkali Ike and the Hypnotist* (1913).]

From there the pair had a brief stay at L-Ko before roosting at the young Rolin Studios and becoming mainstays in the *Lonesome Luke* and Lloyd's later glasses character shorts, as well as the Rolin series with Dee Lampton, Toto, and Stan Laurel. Moving on from Roach, Todd played supporting roles in features. He's very funny as comic relief in Fred Humes' 1927 western *A One Man Game*, but with the arrival of sound his roles in features like *It Happened One Night* (1934) grew progressively smaller. Todd kept working up to his death in 1935.

Luke's Speedy Club Life was Luke's second go-round as a bellboy, the first being 1915's *Bughouse Bellhops*. Harold would don the service uniform again, but this time wearing glasses, in *On the Jump* (1918). The Rolin Company and its output was quickly growing in popularity, and this manifested itself in the press – such as this item from the April 29, 1916 *Photoplayers Weekly*:

Harold Lloyd, known to screen fans as Lonesome Luke, is certainly a funny player. On the set the other day he was preparing to do a scene, and before the scene was filmed the action had been changed so much at his suggestion, that it was entirely different and much longer. He and Director Roach worked harmoniously, putting business here and there, and taking out action wherever it is not needed. They are doing some fine work.

Luke had even become enough of an established screen favorite to have an imitator! Sammy Burns was a British-born dancer and comedian with a background in the English music hall and American vaudeville. He hit films in 1915. Not having much of a comic persona of his own, his first film, *Sammy's Scandalous Scheme* (1915), had him imitating Charlie Chaplin. For the next couple of years he took advantage of the Luke make-up and costume in shorts for Vogue and L-Ko such as *An Innocent Crook, Sammy's Dough-Full Romance* (both 1916), and *Bombs and Bandits* (1917). When Lloyd dropped the Lonesome Luke character so did Burns. The rest of his career was sporadic – King Cole Comedies made on Staten Island, his own company that went bankrupt, and the grade-Z independent feature *Fun on the Farm* (1926) – but for the most part he returned to the stage – dancing, teaching, and choreographing low-budget acts and productions.

The Look of Luke: Sammy Burns in an ad for *An Innocent Crook* (1916), and with Vera Reynolds (a.k.a. Dolly Dimples) in L-Ko's *Bombs and Bandits* (1917).

Moving Picture World (October 7, 1916): "An amusing farce comedy in which Luke makes his entrance and exit as a bell boy at a certain club. The business of this picture is in many instances original. The fun is clean, and the action not overdone."

Motion Picture News (October 7, 1916): "The new stunts devised are truly uproarious, and the good part about it is that one is sprung every few feet or so."

Luke and the Bang-Tails*

Released October 15, 1916. Produced by Hal Roach for the Rolin Film Company. Distributed by Pathé. Directed by Hal Roach. Photographed by James Crosby. Extant: MoMA. Working title: *Luke and the Tia Juana Races*. One reel (Filmed April 13-17, 22, 24, & May 19, 1916). With Harold Lloyd, Bebe Daniels, Snub Pollard, Harry Todd, Bud Jamison, Charles Stevenson, Fred Newmeyer, Sammy Brooks, Dee Lampton, Billy Fay, Margaret Joslin, May Cloy, Clark Irvine.

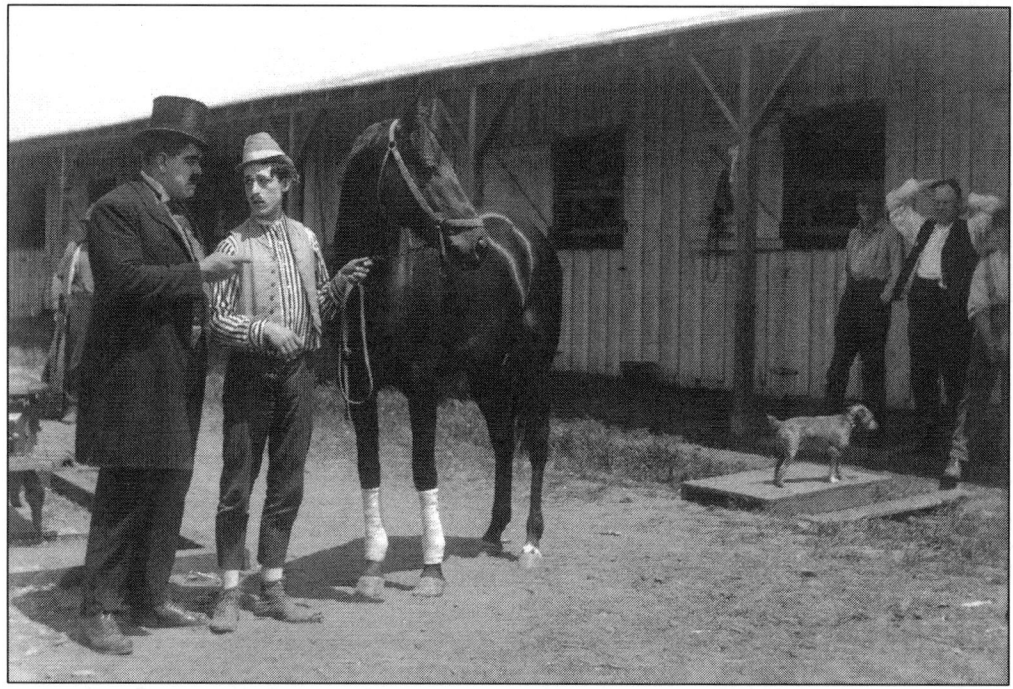

Harold and Bud Jamison play a scene for *Luke and the Bang-Tails* (1916) as real folks take a gander. *Courtesy of the Academy of Motion Picture Arts and Sciences.*

At the race track, Luke and Snub are stable boys. A scheme is hatched to fix the race by giving the favorite, "Little Eva," some dope to slow her down. When Snub can't get her to drink it, he sprays it on with a spray gun. A fat man who wants to be a jockey is put to work to lose weight. He falls with a bale of hay on his back. Some scenes of mayhem in the race track café, Luke steals beer from the waiter's tray. The race begins and the favorite wins. In the café Snub admits that he sprayed the horse, and Luke wins the blow intended for Snub. (Eileen Bowser, description based on print at The Museum of Modern Art)

This is another rare Luke survivor which is in the collection of The Museum of Modern Art. Detailing Luke and Snub's misadventures at the stables and behind the scenes of a big race track, the film was shot on location during a company trip to San Diego and south of the border:

> The "Phunphilm" crowd was down at Tia Juana, Mex., at the reopening of the big race track, and worked out some interesting films on that side of the international boundary line. Some say that certain members of the company dropped some good coin while "playing the ponies." However, they were able to make their return to San Diego, as they had their own automobiles with them
> *Motion Picture News*, May 13, 1916

A few weeks later, Harold and company returned to shoot more footage:

> Hal Lloyd, who is currently creating quite a character in Lonesome Luke in Rolin-Pathé Comedies, together with Director Hal Roach, cameraman Jim Crosby and Harry Pollard went to Tia Juana again this week to get additional scenes for the comedy which they made there last month.
> *Moving Picture World*, June 17, 1916

Most of the action in this one-reeler revolves around Luke and Snub's efforts to secure the winning of the big race for their old, swaybacked nag. In order to do this the main favorite, "Little Eva," has to be doped to slow her down. Luke disappears, and this is left for Snub to do. The almost five minutes spent on his difficulties with the horse essentially becomes a Snub Pollard comedy. Then Luke returns and it's back to the main plot. Similar sequences occur in other survivors like *Luke's Shattered Sleep* (1916) and *Luke's Wild Women* (1917) – Harold has a coffee break while Snub takes over the picture.

Motography (October 7, 1916): "This is an uproarious comedy put out in the best Rolin style. Luke's comical bits of 'business' get the laughs in every scene, and the story itself, if it may be styled a story, is up to a splendid standard in that elusive element which causes us to sometimes exclaim "what fools we mortals be."

Moving Picture World (October 21, 1916): "A farce comedy in which Luke and his pal do service at a racing stable. The manner in which the horses seemingly take part in the business of the play is very amusing. This number will be a welcome addition to the program of any picture theatre."

Luke, the Chauffeur

Released October 29, 1916. Produced by Hal Roach for the Rolin Film Company. Distributed by Pathé. Working title: *Luke's Taxi*. One reel. (Filmed from May 9-15, 1916). With Harold Lloyd, Bebe Daniels, Snub Pollard, Margaret Joslin, Gilbert Pratt. Winna Brown, Charles Stevenson, Billy Fay, Fred Newmeyer, Sammy Brooks, Harry Todd, Bud Jamison, May Cloy, Earl Mohan, Nina Glaze, Sidney Fiske, Tod Cregier, Harvey L. Kinney.

A wild sort of comedy in which a fortune hunter marries a fat widow believing her to be an heiress – but she isn't. Luke figures in an incidental role of a chauffeur. His machine is all decorated up like wash day and the tricks it is made to perform are original as well as humorous. (Motion Picture News, October 28, 1916).

Harold, Bebe, Snub and Margaret Joslin are clocked at over 15 miles an hour by constable Gilbert Pratt in *Luke, the Chauffeur* (1916).

The "fat widow" of *Luke, the Chauffeur* was played by the sturdily built Margaret Joslin, a very important member of the Rolin stock company. She had come to prominence with the Essanay Company playing Sophie Clutts, the most desirable woman (and basically the only one) in the studio's Snakeville Comedies. Ms. Joslin was born in Cleveland, Ohio in 1883, and her entry into show business seems to have been due to her marriage to actor Harry Todd. She spent a little time with him on stage and when he entered films for Essanay in 1910, she did too. Their first appearances with the studio was in Colorado and then G.M. Anderson moved the outfit to California. Their 1911 hit *Alkali Ike's Auto* established the rivalry of Augustus Carney and Harry Todd for the favors of Ms. Joslin, and the series continued until 1916 in entries such as *Alkali Ike's Pants* (1912), *Sophie Picks a Dead One* (1914), and *Snakeville's Beauty Parlor* (1915).

When Essanay closed its Niles, California plant in 1916, Joslin and Todd spent a brief time at Universal supporting Ernie Shield and Billie Ritchie. Their next stop was the young Rolin unit where they dove into the ensemble for *Lonesome Luke*. Resembling the character of Mama from *The Katzenjammer Kids* comic strip, Joslin was perfect as matrons or mothers-in-law. In *Luke Joins the Navy* (1916) she's so overbearing as Snub Pollard's wife that he's more than happy to join the Navy to get away from her.

Besides the *Lukes* she was a regular in the Dee Lampton *Skinny* series, and was also a foil for Toto and his replacement Stan Laurel. Both Joslin and Todd continued to work with Harold Lloyd until 1919, and after leaving Rolin she appeared in a few features such as *Girls Don't Gamble* (1920), *The Danger Point* (1922), and *Three Jumps Ahead* (1923). She retired from the screen soon after and passed away in Glendale in 1958.

Luke, the Chauffeur (1916) has Snub ordering him where to go.

Chauffeuring or taxi driving was a common profession for silent comedians. Both Snub Pollard and Eddie Boland took turns behind the wheel, Oliver Hardy and Bobby Ray were rivals for fares in *Hey, Taxi* (1925), and Harry Langdon even struggled with a horse and buggy in *The Hansom Cabman* (1924). In the late 1920s director Del Lord oversaw the *Dan the Taxi Man* series at the Mack Sennett Studio, which focused on the misadventures of Jack Cooper's cabbie.

A few years later in sound Lord reworked the series for Hal Roach. Starting with *What Price Taxi?* (1932), *The Taxi Boys* encompassed ten entries and included Clyde Cook, Franklin Pangborn, Billy Bevan, but mostly Billy Gilbert and Ben Blue among its drivers. Harold Lloyd himself returned behind the wheel in his 1928 feature *Speedy*, giving Babe Ruth a memorable ride to Yankee Stadium.

Moving Picture World (November 4, 1916): "Luke is the guardian of the taximeter. Seated on his benzine buggy's throne he 'rips' her into 'high' and describes some geometrical figures not recognized by Newton in his laws of gravitation."

Motography (October 21, 1916): "Harold Lloyd and his company of supporting players are not funny in this comedy because their scenario failed to provide them with the opportunity. Luke's jitney-bus is good for a smile and so are one or two other things but on the whole this is only a passable sort of Lonesome Luke comedy."

Luke's Preparedness Preparations

Released November 5, 1916. Produced by Hal Roach for the Rolin Film Company. Distributed by Pathé. One reel. (Filmed May 15-18, 1916). With Harold Lloyd, Bebe Daniels, Snub Pollard, Bud Jamison, Charles Stevenson, Harry Todd, Fred Newmeyer, Dee Lampton, Gilbert Pratt, Margaret Joslin, Sammy Brooks, Billy Fay, Earl Mohan, Ed Nettle, Mary Henderson, Zetta Robson.

The picture features Lonesome Luke, who comes on the scene where Colonel Earache is momentarily expected to drill the soldiery of the city, volunteers from all walks of life. Luke is mistaken for the major and is presented with a sword. He accepts and puts his "company" through all kinds of outlandish drills until the real major shows up and puts Luke to rout. He is literally shot off the earth. (Photoplayers Weekly, June 17, 1916).

Preparedness figures in a comedy made by the Rolin Company for release by Pathé. A camp has been built near the studio, and practically all of the scenes are laid around this. Harold Lloyd, as Lonesome Luke, is the unfortunate one on whom all accidents fall.

Moving Picture World, June 10, 1916

Harold reviews his Yap's Crossing troops (all the male members of the Rolin stock company) in *Luke's Preparedness Preparations* (1916).
Courtesy of the Academy of Motion Picture Arts and Sciences.

With World War I raging in Europe, many people in America were preparing for the country's eventual entrance into the fray. This was a "preparedness movement" where groups were formed to drill and defend in case of any invasion – even in Hollywood there was the Lasky Home Guard, where Paramount studio employees uniformed up and marched around under the command of self-appointed leader Cecil B. DeMille. Wartime themes dominated all kinds of popular culture, including movies. In fact, an exhibitor ad slogan at this time for the *Luke* series was "*If fun was shrapnel, he'd win the war!*"

Subjects such as rationing and looking for U-Boats were ripe subjects for comedies, and another that poked fun at preparedness was Victor Moore's *Home Defense* (1917). This chronicled a group of husbands who used it as a cover to meet once a week and play cards. This worked well until their wives got wise and demanded to see their drills and maneuvers. The most famous World War I comedy was Charlie Chaplin's *Shoulder Arms* (1918), whose huge success spawned the genre of the "service comedy." For years every comic from Larry Semon to Bob Hope to Martin & Lewis to Pauly Shore made at least one picture in uniform. Harold answered the call with his own *Kicking the Germ Out of Germany* (1918).

Harold and Snub play "hot potato" in *Luke's Preparedness Preparations* (1916).

An unidentified item from August 1916 describes Harold's experience with a non-film-wise bystander:

> Harold Lloyd, the "Lonesome Luke" of the Lonesome Luke Comedies produced for Pathé by the Rolin Film Company has been wearing a soldier suit lately. It was his garb for the "Preparedness" comedy just completed. Lunch time came before he knew it one morning, and Luke, who had just completed his make-up, didn't care to take it off to go to lunch. So he went out with it on. He was seated in a restaurant, busily engaged in assimilating nourishment, when he was accosted by a nearsighted old lady, who putting a kindly hand on his shoulder addressed him thus: "I am so glad to see you have heeded your country's call and mobilized. Besides, it's so much better than loafing around the street corners!"

Motography (October 28, 1916): "Lonesome Luke comedy in which Harold Lloyd surrounds himself with a number of freakish characters who place themselves under his charge to become soldiers. The picture has some amusing spots."

Motion Picture News (November 4, 1916): "Lacking the story that is usually present in the Rolin release, this Lonesome Luke comedy with its rough and tumble tricks can hardly rank with other releases in which this comedian has appeared. The gags are mostly old, and there is much kicking and falling resorted to as a means for comedy."

Moving Picture World (November 11, 1916): "A good tumble-about comedy."

Luke, the Gladiator

Released November 12, 1916. Produced by Hal Roach for the Rolin Film Co. Distributed by Pathé. Directed by Hal Roach. Working title: *Lonesome Lukius, Gladiator*. One reel. (Filmed from May 20 to June 10, 1916). With Harold Lloyd, Bebe Daniels, Snub Pollard, Gilbert Pratt, Margaret Joslin, Dee Lampton, Bud Jamison, Billy Fay, Earl Mohan, Fred Newmeyer,

In old Rome *Luke, the Gladiator* (1916) is about to lay out Gilbert Pratt as Bebe, Harry Todd, and Margaret Joslin stand by.

Sammy Brooks, Charles Stevenson, Harry Todd, Haika Carle, Capitola Holmes, Gene Hershaw, H. Saunders, J. Stevenson, J. Jenks, C.H. Butter, Thelma Daniels, Beatrice Peskett, Ester Bennett, Aileen Ware, Robert Wooley, Winna Brown.

The misadventures of Lonesome Lukius as a gladiator amidst the togas, dancing girls, chariots, and baths of ancient Rome.

Lonesome Lukius basks in the favor of the Roman girls in *Luke, the Gladiator* (1916).

The Rolin Company finally got around to spoofing stage productions like *Ben-Hur*, and popular spectacular Italian films such as *The Last Days of Pompeii* (1913) and *Cabiria* (1914). In 1918, they would mount a similar production for Toto with *Cleopatsy*. Because of the bigger budgets usually needed for more elaborate sets and costumes not many of the comedy companies tackled these types of period spoofs. Notable exceptions were Buster Keaton's first feature *Three Ages* (1923), and Lupino Lane's *Roaming Romeo* (1928). The June 24, 1916 issue of *Motion Picture News* gives a picture of some of the difficulties the Luke unit had in making their epic:

> The Rolin Company are finishing the Lonesome Luke burlesque of "Julius Caesar" for Pathé. One of the scenes to be made was that of the chariot race, and before it was completed the

sets in use were practically smashed to pieces. The cause of the breakage was the catching of Lonesome Luke's whip on a chandelier. The horses dashed madly through a fountain and thus the stage was flooded. Several days the players worked on exterior locations for this, and the costumes worn gave old Sol the opportunity of his life to perpetuate a goodly number of sun blisters.

Hopefully, some of the above destruction was able to be used as comedy material in the final cut of this missing film.

Motion Picture World (November 11, 1916): "A Lonesome Luke comedy that is really funny and full of action, as most of the Luke comedies are. As a Roman gladiator Luke certainly is a scream, and his shield and pointed helmet make a foil which baffles the bravest. As a burlesque on Roman times this is diverting. The audience will find real novelty in the comedy."

Motography (November 11, 1916): "This is a remarkably good Luke comedy. Chariots, Roman baths and Roman gladiators of more or less questionable courage make up a single reel of much merriment. The picture has some elaborate settings."

Santa Cruz Evening News (December 16, 1916): "Now everybody knows that Luke is sure to make a fine gladiator, so come out and have a hearty laugh at one of the two greatest of screen comedians."

Luke, Patient Provider

Released November 19, 1916. Produced by Hal Roach for the Rolin Film Company. Distributed by Pathé. Working title: *Lonesome Luke, Calamity Merchant*. One reel. (Filmed May 31 – June 3, 1916). With Harold Lloyd, Bebe Daniels, Snub Pollard, Bud Jamison, Harry Todd, Charles Stevenson, Fred Newmeyer, Sammy Brooks, Dee Lampton, Billy Fay, Earl Mohan, Margaret Joslin, Winna Brown, Estelle Harrison, Gilbert Pratt.

The situation which indirectly brings about the comedy is the misfortune of a certain doctor, who, because he has no patients for months, is obliged to dismiss his pretty nurse. Luke then steps into the breach and volunteers with the aid of his flivver to supply patients. (Moving Picture World, November 25, 1916).

The Rolinites are now filming a physician's story. A city ambulance and other hospital equipment was secured for use in the comedy, and some real thrills were taken when an ambulance run was made that ended in a collision with a streetcar.

Motion Picture News, July 1, 1916

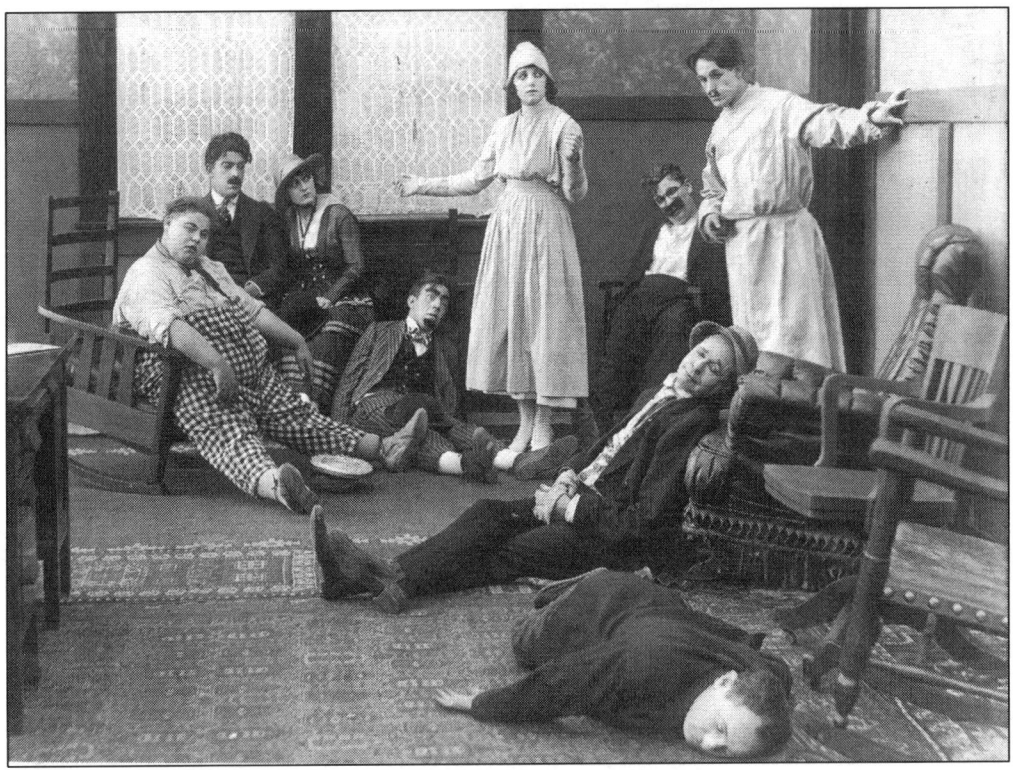

Luke, Patient Provider (1916) has Dee Lampton, Gilbert Pratt, Fred Newmeyer, Earl Mohan,
Harry Todd or Sammy Brooks to pick as next.

The main idea of this Luke one-reeler was eventually reworked twice by Harold. In 1920's *High and Dizzy* he's the doctor who can't get patients, and when he does it is poor little rich girl Mildred Davis, whom he falls for. The second, and closer, re-do came in *Never Weaken* (1921). Harold works next door to an osteopath's office. His girl Mildred is the nurse, but as there are no patients she's going to get canned. To help her out Harold gets an acrobat friend, and armed with a pile of the doctor's business cards they stage "accidents" where his pal takes bad spills. Then Harold comes along, does a few osteo maneuvers, fixes the victim, and passes out cards. He also takes advantage of a passing street washing wagon to spread soap powder in its path to create a street full of slipping and falling pedestrians who all receive cards.

This gag situation was hardly new – in 1913's *A Healthy Neighborhood* Ford Sterling played a new doctor who had no patients so he hires thug Bill Hauber to leave banana peels all over the sidewalks around his office, and soon money comes limping in. *Oh! Doctor!* (1917) has Roscoe Arbuckle as another doctor who happens to see a crowd on the street gathered around someone selling a miracle soap that ensures the user will never get sick. Fatty counteracts the situation by sending his car into the crowd and then passing out the cards to the people mowed down. Finally, in *Hey, Doctor!* (1918) Alice Howell is the nurse who's going to get the axe, so she goes out with a huge bunch of bananas, drops them all over, and helpfully distributes the obligatory cards.

Harold and Bebe in the process of making Fred Newmeyer a new patient in *Luke, Patient Provider* (1916).

Motion Picture News (November 18, 1916): "In this Lonesome Luke undertakes to furnish a hospital with patients, and goes about it by 'running wild' in his flivver. The picture winds up with a wild sort of chase which is fairly diverting, although not as funny as other of Luke's mishaps. The business in the main part of the reel is well up to standard."

Moving Picture World (November 25, 1916): "One of the most amusing of the Luke comedies. Children as well as adults will enjoy this comedy."

Motography (October 20, 1917): "Luke is great. This went over like a whirlwind. I can't say too much for Luke. Many stunts and a laugh or yell every second. He is all right. Don't be afraid to book it."

Luke's Newsie Knockout

Released November 26, 1916. Produced by Hal Roach for the Rolin Film Company. Distributed by Pathé. One reel. (Filmed from June 5-12 & 19, 1916). With Harold Lloyd, Bebe Daniels, Snub Pollard, Bud Jamison, Charles Stevenson, Sammy Brooks, Eva Thatcher, Earl Mohan, Billy Fay, Fred Newmeyer, Harry Todd, Leon Leonhardt, Harvey L. Kinney, Ray Thompson, Mrs. Hilda Limbeck, Sidney Fiske, H.L. O'Connor, Mrs. Estella Short.

There are no synopsis available.

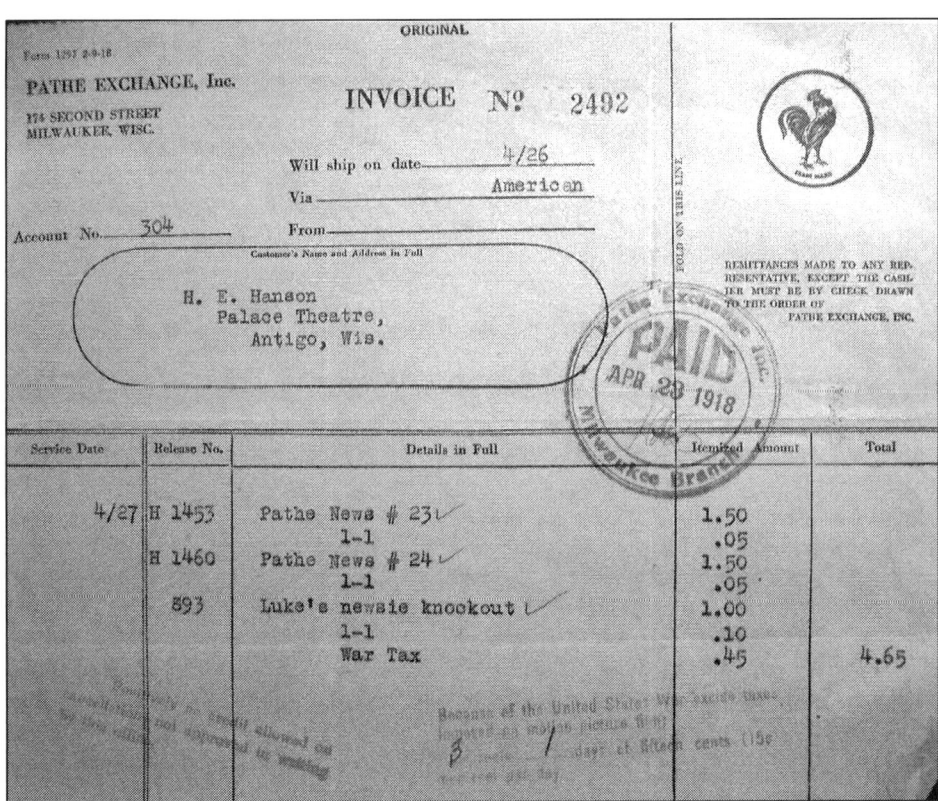

Invoice, complete with War Tax, for the elusive *Luke's Newsie Knockout* (1916).

This is the great *Lonesome Luke* mystery film. Although the title is listed in the trade magazine release schedules and the Rolin Company ledgers, there are no plot descriptions, or photos that are available. The few reviews available give very little plot information. Elmira, New York's *The Telegram*'s report of "Luke's Newsie Knockout – Biggest laugh yet" could be prejudiced as it was Hal Roach's hometown paper.

Luke Wins Ye Ladye Faire also has no info, but there are plenty of photos and descriptions that give a good idea of the subject. The title *Luke's Newsie Knockout* suggests that he could be a newsboy, a reporter, a boxer, or even a combination of all three. Hopefully more info, or even better the film itself, will someday turn up.

Hal Roach in full polo regalia.
Courtesy of The Museum of Modern Art.

By this time Hal Roach was no longer involved in the day-to-day direction of the *Luke* shorts. Like Mack Sennett before him, the running of his expanding studio took up a good deal of his time and energy, which included focusing on new features such as the Dee Lampton series. As described in the July 1, 1916 *Motion Picture News*, Harold, Gilbert Pratt, and their regular crew took over the making of the *Lukes*:

The Rolin Film Company organization has been increased to two companies. One composed of D. Lampton, the fat boy, Harry Todd, Mary Joslin, Fred Newmeyer, Billy Fay, Estelle Harrison and others, will be under the direction of Hal Roach, who is responsible for the success of the "Lonesome Luke" series by Pathé. Harold Lloyd, who has appeared in the part of Lonesome Luke in all comedies, with Gilbert Pratt, will direct the second company, Lloyd appearing in the principal part. Others in this organization will be Bebe Daniels, Harry Pollard, Bud Jamison, Earl Mohan and Charles Stevenson.

The Salt Lake Tribune (December 5, 1916): "A comedy with the ginger of a clever newspaper story."

Altoona Times (December 8, 1916): "Luke's Newsie Knockout' – one of the Luke famous comedies. Bring the kiddies and they will enjoy it."

Luke's Movie Muddle*

Released December 3, 1916. Produced by Hal Roach for the Rolin Film Company. Distributed by Pathé. Extant: GEM, EYE, BFI, ACAD, ESM, OTT. Working title: *Luke's Model Movie*. One reel. (Filmed June 13 -17, 1916). With Harold Lloyd, Bebe Daniels, Snub Pollard, Bud Jamison, Margaret Joslin, Dee Lampton, Harry Todd, Gilbert Pratt, Billy Fay, Estelle Harrison, Earl Mohan, Fred Newmeyer, Ray Robertson, Harvey L. Kinney, H. L. O'Connor, Mrs. Hilda Limbeck, Jewel Mason, Peggy Heinse, J. J. Martin.

Luke as the combination box office man, doorman and usher of a picture theater cuts an unusually ludicrous figure in this comedy. Humor is extracted from everything to do with a house, ushering, operating and piano playing come in for burlesque and the whole is done in highly amusing style. (Motion Picture News, December 12, 1916).

Today, *Luke's Movie Muddle* is the most accessible of the *Luke* films. Long-available on 16mm and 8 mm (often under the title *The Cinema Director*), over the years it has surfaced on various public domain home video collections and is all over the internet. As a surviving example of the series it's a very knockabout affair. The cinema portrayed is a two-man operation: Snub is projectionist and Luke everything else, although his main duties are flirting with every woman and fighting with all the men. Like Billie Ritchie, Luke is especially combative in this entry. Snub has a few moments on his own – unspooling film all over the booth, falling asleep while cranking the picture, and even cooking an egg on the hot projector. Thanks to a fire, the film ends with a big exodus from the theatre, which leaves Luke and Snub choking each other in the crowd's wake. The short even gets in an opening plug in for their distributor Pathé when Luke puts a company standee out in front, and even demonstrates how the rooster crows for the cop on the beat.

Harold and Snub have some difficulty with their film rewinder in *Luke's Movie Muddle* (1916).

As soon as audiences started going to cinemas there were comedies that portrayed and parodied the movie-going experience. Best known of the early examples is D.W. Griffith's 1909 *Those Awful Hats*. Poking fun of women wearing ridiculously large and adorned hats to the cinema and obstructing the view of the rest of the audience, the theatre has a giant claw that descends from the ceiling to snatch the offending headgear. The final woman to come in (Flora Finch) has the largest hat yet, and when the claw comes down it clamps on her neck to hoist her skyward.

Soon Keystone got into the act, having Mack Sennett disrupt a show when he sees his ex-girlfriend Mabel Normand being mistreated onscreen in *Mabel's Dramatic Career* (1913). This is finally too much for Mack to bear, so he pulls out a gun and shoots at the movie villain, and of course empties the house. In the 1917 Sennett comedy *A Movie Star*, Mack Swain is a cowboy matinee idol who visits a smalltown theatre that is showing his latest picture. He plays the big shot and makes time with the local girls, until his battle-axe wife shows up to cart him home.

Roscoe Arbuckle was very fond of the plot of *Fatty at San Diego* (1913) where Fatty's out on his own and gets into trouble fighting and flirting with women. When he returns to his wife with a black eye, he makes up an elaborate tale in which he's a hero. Unfortunately for Roscoe, he doesn't know that his hijinks were filmed by a cameraman, and when he and wifie go to the picture show the newsreel reveals the truth. Arbuckle starred in this plot again in *A Reckless Romeo* (1917), and later he gave it to Al St John when he directed *Never Again* (1924). Other movie theatre comedies include *Her Screen Idol* (1918), *Pop Tuttle's Movie Queen* (1922), *This Way Out* (1923), *Sherlock Jr.* (1924), and *The House of Flickers* (1925).

Estelle Harrison and Harold outside the Hal Roach Studio.

After the departure of May Cloy, Estelle Harrison took over the position of second Rolin leading lady. Born in Florence, Alabama as Ruby Estelle Harrison, she and her family moved to Los Angeles in 1906 where the pretty, blue-eyed blonde made a perfect ingénue in local L.A. stock companies before moving over to doing the same thing for Kalem and Biograph. She joined the Rolin organization around the time of *Luke, the Gladiator* (1916), and frequently as Snub's girl, she fulfilled the function of the second banana's sweetheart. She was also busy playing nurses, party guests, maids, ladies in waiting, and girls' school co-eds.

In 1920 she began branching out, and after supporting Jimmy Aubrey in his Vitagraph short *His Jonah Day*, she became the regular leading lady to comedian George Bunny. George was the son of the late John Bunny and had a brief stint as the star in Capitol Comedies two-reelers produced by the National Film Corp. and distributed by Goldwyn. Estelle was Bunny's love interest in 1921 titles that included *You'd Better Get It*, *Food for Thought*, *Homebrewed Youth*, and *Blue Friday*.

Following Capitol Comedies' quick demise, she returned to the Roach lot and Lonesome Luke, although this incarnation of Luke was played by Harold's brother Gaylord Lloyd. Estelle was Gaylord's main support in 1921's *The Lucky Number*, *A Zero Hero*, and *Dodge Your Debts* (more in Chapter 3). Finally finished at Roach, she appeared in the western features *A Knight of the West* (1921) and *Fighting Hearts* (1922), and then disappeared from the movies' radar screen. One of the last items about Ms. Harrison was in 1925 about a reunion lunch in the Hal Roach commissary:

> **Talk of Old Days at Reunion Lunch**
> For old times' sake –
> It wasn't so terribly long ago that Bebe Daniels, Estelle Harrison and Marie Mosquini started their careers together at the Hal Roach Studios.
> Miss Mosquini is still with Hal Roach, while Miss Daniels has traveled through various fields of film endeavors and Miss Harrison has dropped from public view in retiring to private life.
> *Exhibitors Trade Review*, January 17, 1925

Motography (November 25, 1916): "This is one of the most boisterous 'Lonesome Luke' comedies yet filmed. Luke, as the proprietor, cashier, ticket taker, usher, etc., of a movie theatre keeps things humming. The picture is replete with novel bits of comedy and it also makes good use of some of the older slapstick stunts. Right through from first to last 'Luke's Movie Muddle' is a procurer of prolonged laughs."

Luke, Rank Impersonator

Released December 10, 1916. Produced by Hal Roach for the Rolin Film Company. Distributed by Pathé. Working title: ***Luke's Social Splash***. One reel.

(Filmed from June 20-23, 1916). With Harold Lloyd, Bebe Daniels, Snub Pollard, Gilbert Pratt, Bud Jamison, Charles Stevenson, Estelle Harrison, Fred Newmeyer, Sammy Brooks, Billy Fay, Earl Mohan, Harry Todd, Margaret Joslin, Marjorie (Peggy) Prevost, Jewel Mason, Peggy Heinse, Mrs. Estella Short, Vesta Marlowe, Villatta Singley, Madeline Vintin.

Luke is a bum who tries to break into society. In a "borrowed" suit he poses as Lord Helpus at a posh dinner.

Gilbert Pratt and Bebe catch Harold either sneaking in or sneaking out in
Luke, Rank Impersonator (1916).

By the time of *Luke, Rank Impersonator* Harold had worked hard to try and clean Luke up. Originally, he was quite the tramp, but in Harold's quest to make his screen persona more of an everyman his clothes improved and his hair became less wild and more maintained. Or as Harold put it himself:

> Not only was the get-up imitative but it was an offense to the eye originally. I cleaned it up as time went on until it was self-respecting before it died.

> *An American Comedy*, 1928

Luke would even occasionally be gainfully employed in plots that were excuses to dress him up, and looked positively spiffy in some exhibitor ads.

This upscale movement would continue, and in his last films Luke would turn up as a gentleman's valet, a fancy barber, and a legitimate detective.

Silent comedy was rife with comics posing as some kind of royalty. Charlie Chaplin was fond of it for *Caught in a Cabaret* (1914), *A Jitney Elopement* (1915), and *The Count* (1916). Often used was the old *Prince and the Pauper* plot of the lead being a dead ringer for a certain noble person, who then swap places and cause confusion. Harold takes advantage of that theme for *His Royal Slyness* (1920) when he switches places with the look-a-like Prince of Razzamatazz. Eddie Lyons in *Meet the Doctor* (1924) and Lupino Lane in *Howdy Duke* (1927) also helped themselves to that story.

Harold and Bebe spark, as Bud Jamison and Gilbert Pratt conspire in
Luke, Rank Impersonator (1916).

In 1921 Harold and company remade *Luke, Rank Impersonator* with his glasses character as *Among Those Present*. This time our hero is a hotel bellboy who poses as the horseman and hunter Lord Algernon Abbott Aberdeen Abernathy in order to attend the fox hunt of the newly rich Mr. and Mrs. O'Brien. The three-reel length gives room for many misadventures, but after falling for the rich couple's pretty daughter Harold finally admits his masquerade and wins over the O'Briens.

Making a few appearances in the Rolin shorts at this time was Marjorie Prevost, the younger sister of Mack Sennett star Marie Prevost. Having also begun her career with Sennett, after her Rolin stint she branched out to

Foxfilm Comedies. As Peggy Prevost she was the leading lady there for Hank Mann, Charles "Heinie" Conklin and Sidney DeGray in shorts such as *The Film Spoilers* and *His Merry Mix-Up* (both 1917). Moving on from Fox she appeared in Universal brands like L-Ko and Century Comedies for *Hello Trouble* (1918), *Hearts in Hock* (1919), and *Uncle Tom's Caboose* (1920), and then made the jump to features. Before her career ended in 1925 she supported Charles Ray in *The Old Swimmin' Hole* (1921) and Mildred Harris in *The Fog* (1923). She later worked on stage in Ziegfeld's *Palm Beach Follies*.

Motion Picture News (December 9, 1916): "Fast comedy stuff on the order of early Keystone Chaplins. Dining room scene with soup slinging and table tossing by company in evening dress. Stupid cop and semi-conscious vagrants get laughs in the exteriors. Luke plays Lord Helpus with a decidedly alcoholic slant which is not without its funny moments."

Moving Picture World (December 16, 1916): "Luke's attempts to break into society start the comedy rolling in this one-reel picture. The fun is speedy all through."

Moving Picture World (December 16, 1916): "Luke is a busy Beau Brummel. He is the paprika in the social baked potato and when they dress him up in an open-faced suit, he puts pep in a pitiful party."

Luke's Fireworks Fizzle

Released December 17, 1916. Produced by Hal Roach for the Rolin Film Company. Distributed by Pathé. One reel. (Filmed from June 26 – July 1 & September 16, 1916). With Harold Lloyd, Bebe Daniels, Snub Pollard, Bud Jamison, Sidney DeGray, Dee Lampton, Charles Stevenson, Earl Mohan, Fred Newmeyer, Billy Fay, Sammy Brooks, Vesta Marlow, Marjorie (Peggy) Prevost, Villatta Snigley, Madeline Vintin, William N. Brown, Frank Lake.

Luke lands a job in a fireworks factory and fearlessly flirts with fate in the shape of enough gunpowder to send him so far away that it would take four dollars to send him in a postal card. He finally ascends to the clouds astride a giant skyrocket. (*Moving Picture World*, December 23, 1916).

It seems that Director Hal Roach of Rolin-Pathé funny pictures is always taking big timely topics and converting them into comedies, for this week the company started working on a roaring (honest roars) picture in an ammunition factory. Fourteen stacks of dynamite, twenty-seven large cans of black powder, eighty-three fuse caps, and 300 feet of fuse was delivered to the studio and put in the ice box for safe keeping. Hal Roach is preparing burn-ointment by the barrel for the Rolin players.

Photoplayers Weekly, July, 15, 1916

In *Luke's Fireworks Fizzle* (1916) Sidney De Grey, Dee Lampton, Charles Stevenson, Bud Jamison, Earl Mohan, Fred Newmeyer, Billy Fay and Snub all wait for Harold and Bebe to blow sky-high.

The perfect job for a silent comedian is working in a gunpowder factory – what could possibly go wrong?? Luke's occupation in this outing paved the way for the employment of Lloyd Hamilton in *Dynamite* (1920) and Bobby Dunn in *No Danger* (1923). There were also plenty of individual fireworks in films such as *The Rivals* (1923), where Slim Summerville attaches Bobby Dunn to a skyrocket that shoots him across the Culver City sky. The king of explosions and explosive comedy was Larry Semon, as big bangs were a stock ingredient in his pictures alongside chases, crashes, and spectacular falls from high places. Houses, train cars, and Frank "Fatty" Alexander were regularly blown up in Semon's slapstick ballets.

One of Luke's co-workers at the fireworks plant is Sidney DeGray, a silent film veteran who's totally forgotten today. Born in England in 1866, he was appearing on stage in the United States by 1909. Some of his shows include the 1911 Chicago production of *The Girl from London*, and Kolb & Dill's 1913 musical comedy *Lonesome Town*. He made his movie debut that same year for the Majestic Motion Picture Company, where he appeared with Fred Mace, Carrie Clark Ward, and Billie West in shorts such as *One Round O'Brien's Flirtation*, *Mrs. Brown's Burglar* (both 1913), and *A Riot in Rubeville* (1914).

Soon he followed Fred Mace over to the Apollo Company for items like *Apollo Fred Becomes a Homeseeker* and *The Cheese of Police* (both 1914), before headlining in some of the Alhambra and Santa Barbara brand comedies that were distributed by the Kriterion Sales Corporation:

> Sidney DeGray, who is directing the Alhambra brand of comedies released on the Kriterion program has completed several of his series, "The Painted Anarchist," "Syd's Love Affair," "Syd as a Detective," and "Syd the Masher." Mr. DeGray also plays the leads in these comedies, Miss Marty Martin playing opposite.
>
> *Moving Picture World*, February 6, 1915

Sidney De Grey (right) getting the worst of it from Heinie Conklin in the Charles Parrott-directed *The Film Spoilers* (1917). *Courtesy of Cole Johnson.*

His starring series, which also included *Light Fingered Syd* and *Syd, the Athlete*, lasted through 1915. This was the beginning and end of his directorial career, and he settled into supporting the stage stars Blanche Ring and Charlotte Greenwood in their features *The Yankee Girl* and *Jane* (both 1915). At this point he joined the Rolin stock company, but six months later he did a stint at Foxfilm Comedies to work with Hank Mann, Charles Parrott, and Heinie Conklin in two-reelers like *A Bon-Bon Riot* and *The Film Spoilers*.

From here most of his screen time was spent in feature films, most notably *Jes' Call Me Jim*, *The Mark of Zorro* (both 1920), and *The Nut* (1921). He even later returned to the Roach organization for *The King of the Wild Horses* (1924), and the Thelma Todd/Patsy Kelly short *Slightly Static* (1935). His work in sound films was as an uncredited player, but he remained busy up to his death in 1941.

Motion Picture News (December 16, 1916): "A characteristic slapping and kicking picture in which Lonesome Luke and his associates cavort about in a fireworks factory. There is a good bit of conventional horseplay such as smoking around explosives, and there is some original humor when Luke gets into a rocket fight with another. All in all a highly diverting release in which the Rolin supporting company scores as good effect as its star."

Moving Picture World (December 16, 1916): "A bull in a china shop is a mild engine of destruction compared to Luke among the fireworks. Everything goes with a bang and the last seen of the cause of the trouble shows him seated astride a huge skyrocket and headed for the moon. This one-reel farce is among the best of the brand."

Luke Locates the Loot

Released December 24, 1916. Produced by Hal Roach for the Rolin Film Company. Distributed by Pathé. One reel. (Filmed July 6-10, 1916). With Harold Lloyd, Bebe Daniels, Snub Pollard, Bud Jamison, Estelle Harrison, Sammy Brooks, Dee Lampton, Earl Mohan, Billy Fay, Charles Stevenson, Gilbert Pratt, Enid Markey, Sidney De Gray, Jack O'Brien, Otto Fries.

Luke is a detective's assistant, but when a hurry call comes in for the boss to attend a masque ball and locate two crooks who are stealing everyone's jewels, he goes himself. He gets into various mixups there and the arrival of his boss makes things worse for him. (*Motion Picture News*, December 23, 1916).

Rolin to Burlesque Sherlock Holmes

Sherlock Holmes tales are to be burlesqued by the Rolin Lonesome Luke Company, under the direction of Hal Roach; Harold Lloyd appearing as the supreme criminologist, and Bebe Daniels as Lady Raffles. The picture is nearing completion, and has a big cast of Rolin Players.

Motion Picture News, August 26, 1916

In *Luke Locates the Loot* (1916) sleuth Harold fingers Estelle Harrison as the culprit, with stunned responses from Bebe, Bud Jamison, and the rest of the party guests.

Arthur Conan Doyle's Sherlock Holmes stories were such a world-wide phenomenon that it led to adaptations on stage and in films. The most famous early portrayer of Holmes was William Gillette (who in England had a young Charlie Chaplin as Billy the newsboy). Gillette put his version on film in the 1916 feature *Sherlock Holmes* for the Essanay Company. Other Holmes in silent films included 1915, 1920 and 1929 versions of *The Hound of the Baskervilles*, and a British series of shorts.

Holmes was also ripe for parody, and almost every movie comic did a turn as a "defective detective." In addition to Harold there was Douglas Fairbanks as "Coke Ennyday" in *The Mystery of the Leaping Fish* (1916), Max Asher as master of disguise "Detective Duck" in the comedy serial *The Adventures of Lady Baffles and Detective Duck* (1915) and Joe Rock as master investigator "K.N. Pepper" in *Footprints* (1920).

Luke Locates the Loot (1916) and sees that Snub and Bebe get run in by Otto Fries (left).

Others included Stan Laurel as *The Sleuth* (1925), the Ebony Company's *A Black Sherlock Holmes* (1918), *Sherlock Jr.* (1924) with Buster Keaton, and Solax's *The Detective's Dog* (1912) where a sleuth's pooch solves the crime and saves the day. Later on the Hal Roach lot, Snub Pollard would get his turn to detect in *The Mystery Man* (1923), Our Gang was on the trail of *The Mysterious Mystery* (1924), and in 1927 Laurel & Hardy asked the question *Do Detectives Think?*

Moving Picture World (December 23, 1916): "Although lacking in the novelty the speedy work of the cast and the business put into this one-reel farce will ensure the laughs. Luke turns detective and has an amusing encounter with a gang of crooks that get into a social gathering and relieve the guests of their valuables."

Luke's Shattered Sleep*

Released December 31, 1916. Produced by Hal Roach for the Rolin Film Co. Distributed by Pathé. Extant: MoMA. Working title: ***Luke, Asleep at Last***. One reel. (Filmed July 11 – 15, 1916). With Harold Lloyd, Bebe Daniels, Snub Pollard, Bud Jamison, Charles Stevenson, Fred Newmeyer, Sammy

Brooks, Billy Fay, Earl Mohan, Noah Young, Gus Leonard, Margaret Joslin, Harry Todd, Gilbert Pratt, Vesta Marlowe, Sidney DeGray, Ray Thompson, Norman DePure, Minnie Eckert, Lillian Avery, Maybelle Beringer, Gusta Berg, Beth Darwin, Villatta Singley, Lola Walker, Helda Lunbeck, Annette Hatten, Frances Scott.

Lonesome Luke and his weird associates here disport themselves in a cheap rooming house that furnishes beds for ten cents and beds with springs for fifteen. The humor is rather low on the whole concerning itself with the discovery of an odor surrounding a gentleman's feet, rats and fleas in the bed, and the breaking of various obstacles over heads. (*Motion Picture News*, December 30, 1916).

Flophouses in silent comedy are predominantly associated with Charlie Chaplin. *Luke's Shattered Sleep* survives in the collection of The Museum of Modern Art and was definitely patterned after Chaplin's flophouse sequence in *Police* (1916) – with the addition of Bebe as the poor slavey who has to take care of the mopping and spittoons. The Little Tramp also got a bed for a dime in *Triple Trouble* (1918) and *The Kid* (1921), but Charlie's most memorable doss house stay was in the unreleased *The Professor* (circa 1921) which was unearthed by Kevin Brownlow and David Gill in the 1980s. Other silent comedy flophouses include the 1916 *Mishaps of Musty Suffer* "whirl" *Look Out Below*, and the Fred Ardath two-reeler *Wild Women and Tame Men* (1920).

Recently added to the Rolin performer's roster was Gus Leonard. Born in France in 1859, as Amedee Theodore Gaston Lerond, Leonard emigrated to America as a boy and began his stage career in San Francisco around 1880. For the next thirty-plus years he toured the West Coast with the companies of Tony Pastor and Ed Armstrong, as well as soloing in vaudeville doing German dialect comedy and a popular drunken waiter act. Sometimes billed as "The Odd Musical Musician," he first hit movies in 1914 for Balboa and Powers.

> Gus Leonard, veteran of the vaudeville stage, is now a member of the Kalem comedy company in Los Angeles, and will play with Ethel Teare and Jack MacDermott.
>
> *Picture-Play*, July 1916

In addition to appearing with Ethel Teare in titles like *A Molar Mix-Up* and *Romeo of the Coal Wagon* (both 1916), he also supported the studio's knockabout team of Ham & Bud. By the end of 1916 he found his way to the Hal Roach lot, where he would work regularly for the next twenty years.

Seemingly born old, as part of the regular Rolin stock company Gus often turned up in walk-ons such as a guest in a hotel lobby, but other times he would have nice bits like his elderly spinster who's looking for a man (any man) in *Bumping into Broadway* (1919). Besides working for Harold Lloyd for many years, Leonard appeared frequently in Al Christie shorts and racked up an impressive number of feature film credits that included *Homer Comes Home* (1920), *The Battling Orioles* (1924), Buster Keaton's *Go West* (1925), and *The First Auto* (1927).

Gus Leonard in vaudeville, and on the right supervising Harold's delivery service. in *On the Jump* (1918).

He remained just as busy in talking films, and thanks to constant television showings of "The Little Rascals" Leonard is remembered as Old Capp in *Mush and Milk* (1933) and Scotty Beckett's Grandpa in *The Lucky Corner* (1936). Sound revealed his natural warmth, which made him ideal to be paired with the Our Gang kids. Gus ended his long career in 1937 and passed away two years later at eighty, even though he had already seemed that age for the bulk of his screen appearances.

Motion Picture News (December 30, 1916): "On the whole a funny picture."

Moving Picture World (January 6, 1917): "Audiences may think Luke with his St. Vitus movement never sleeps, but they are dead wrong. Like Bill Shakespeare Luke 'blesses the man who first invented sleep.' After a screamingly comical search for slumber he finally hits the hay and sleeps without moving to Brooklyn."

Bebe, Snub, and Harold share a quiet moment before *Luke's Shattered Sleep* (1916).

Luke's Lost Liberty

Released January 7, 1917. Produced by Hal Roach for the Rolin Film Company. Distributed by Pathé. (Filmed from June 26 – July 1, and September 15, 1916). One reel. With Harold Lloyd, Bebe Daniels, Snub Pollard, Gilbert Pratt, Estelle Harrison, Charles Stevenson, Earl Mohan, A. H. Frahlich, Max D. Hamburger.

A burlesque on prison reformers. The convicts sit around, smoke good cigars and imbibe rare wines, while others less fortunate serve them dutifully. (*Motion Picture News*, January 1, 1917)

Another Rolin comedy soon to be finished is that laid around a prison. The Los Angeles East Side jail is serving for scenes, special arrangements having been made with the warden. Scores of the comedians of the Rolin aggregation are appearing in stripes for Lonesome Luke comedies, the titles have not been definitely decided upon.

Motion Picture News, August 26, 1916

Bebe and Estelle Harrison visit Harold and Snub as Earl Mohan, Charles Stevenson, Max D. Hamburger, A. H. Frahlich, and Gilbert Pratt look on in envy in *Luke's Lost Liberty* (1917).

Whether innocent or guilty, most silent comics spent time in jail. Although Harold wasn't behind bars much, his colleagues did plenty of time. Buster Keaton was *Convict 13* (1920) and Larry Semon *The Star Boarder* (1919), plus Billy West made *A Rolling Stone* (1919) and Marcel Perez *You're Next* (1919). Usually the situation in lock-up was better than they were used to outside, so if they got out they would spend the rest of the short trying to get re-arrested.

Chaplin is the most extreme example of this – always in and out of stir. In *Police* (1916) he's just been released, and in *The Adventurer* (1917) and *The Pilgrim* (1923) he's busted out and is on the lam. He goes to prison for helping the blind girl in *City Lights* (1931), and in *Modern Times* (1936), his last film as the Little Tramp, the 1930s are so threatening that jail's a safe haven. On the Hal Roach lot Stan Laurel was in the pokey in the missing *No Place Like Jail* (1918), Snub Pollard was *Doing Time* (1920) and *The Jail Bird* (1921), and Laurel & Hardy were "guests of the state" in *The Second Hundred Years* (1927) and their feature *Pardon Us* (1931).

Max D. Hamburger (front right), as well as Dorothea Wolbert, Evelyn Paige, Harry Todd, Gilbert Pratt, Lottie Case, Harold, Nina Speight, and Billy Fay, are all suffering from Sammy Brooks' tonsil athletics in *Birds of a Feather* (1917).

One of the men in stripes in *Luke's Lost Liberty* is Max D. Hamburger. Although he had a great name for a comedian, Hamburger never rose above playing bit parts. He appeared in the *Lonesome Lukes*, Harold Lloyds and other Roach shorts from 1917 to 1920, but was always on the periphery as an elevator operator, sailor, telegram messenger, diner, train passenger, or bar patron (or any other kind of patron). By the time of his death in 1939 he had been out of films for many years, and his coroner's report listed he was working as a stage property man.

Moving Picture World (January 6, 1917): "High life behind bars is the subject of this one-reel farce. Luke and his pal find existence in prison so amusing that they depart with regret. The reel is well played and filled with slap-dash comedy."

Luke's Busy Day

Released January 21, 1917. Produced by Hal Roach for the Rolin Film Company. Distributed by Pathé. (Filmed from July 24-29, and August 5, 1916). One reel. With Harold Lloyd, Bebe Daniels, Snub Pollard, Bud Jamison, Marie Mosquini, Sammy Brooks, Earl Mohan, Sidney De Gray, Gus Leonard, Max D. Hamburger, C. G. King, W. L. "Bumps" Adams, Fred Jefferson, Norman Napier, William N. Brown, H. Granger, J. Irvine, Frank Lake, Beth McAlister, Virgil Owens, Harry Russell.

The story concerns the rivalry of Luke and Snub for the police chief's daughter. Snub stoops to all kinds of treachery to win out but Luke manages to sail through with flying colors. (*Motion Pictures News*, January 30, 1917).

Snub Pollard was extremely important in the development and success of the *Luke* series. Having started his stage career at age fourteen with companies such as Pollard's Lilliputians, Snub was a seasoned comedy pro, and at this point much more experienced than Harold. Of course, Lloyd was learning quickly, and must have absorbed a good deal of comedic technique and knowhow from Mr. Pollard. Onscreen the pair were sometimes rivals – other times pals – and often a combination of both. Even after Harold transitioned to his glasses character their movie relationship remained more or less the same, but with less hitting and kicking.

Since we're discussing Snub's role in the comedies, it's a good place to talk about the Rolin player who would become the leading lady of his starring series. Marie Mosquini started as the "gal Friday" of the Rolin Studio at age fourteen – acting as secretary, answering phones, ordering props, checking out costumes, even patching films – and soon began playing various bit roles in the *Luke* comedies.

Harold keeping busy making a cop think that he's Dee Lampton.

"I didn't care for it particularly at first," she confessed. "I went right back to my shorthand and stenography and probably would have been there today but for Mr. Roach. I owe everything to him."

Motion Picture Classic, November 1920

Marie Mosquini and Harold in the early 1920s.
Courtesy of The Museum of Modern Art.

Eventually she became a full-time actress, and was teamed with Snub in 1920. Besides appearing in umpteen shorts with him, she also found time to support Stan Laurel, Paul Parrott, and Will Rogers. After leaving the Roach lot in 1924 she worked in Universal shorts with Charles Puffy and a few features, the most famous being *Seventh Heaven* (1927). She retired from movies in 1930 when she married Dr. Lee DeForest of Audion tube and Phono-Films fame.

Another busy comedy player in this film is Harry Russell, a tall, thin, and bald actor. Playing character roles in Universal brands such as Frontier and L-Ko, Russell also spent time at Keystone. Around the time that *Luke's Busy Day* was shot it was announced:

Rolin Company Expands

The success of Pathé's "Luke" comedies has caused the Rolin company, which produces them, to expand. A new company has just been formed under the direction of Harry Russell, formerly of Keystone. "Fatty" Lampton and little Gertrude Short will play the leads.

Motography, August 19, 1916

It doesn't appear that Russell remained with Rolin for very long – the Lampton series was extremely short-lived – and after this he continued appearing in shorts until 1923.

Motion Picture News (January 30, 1917): "Some original gags such as the manner in which Luke's machine calls for him in the morning, unassisted, makes this number highly diverting."

Luke's Trolley Troubles

Released February 4, 1917. Produced by Hal Roach for the Rolin Film Company. Distributed by Pathé. One reel. (Filmed from July 31 and August 5 & 16, 1916). With Harold Lloyd, Bebe Daniels, Snub Pollard, Bud Jamison, Gus Leonard, Sammy Brooks, Sidney De Gray, Harvey L. Kinney, Vera Reynolds, Max D. Hamburger, W.L. "Bumps" Adams, Billy Fay, Joe Turner.

Luke and his side partner steal a trolley car and proceed to make trouble for everyone who boards the car. (*Moving Picture World*, February 3, 1917).

Studio on Trolley Car

One of the most unusual studios on record was that used by the Rolin Company while making a "Luke" comedy for Pathé. The entire picture was staged on a trolley car which for most of the time was in motion. The cameras were set up between the seats and in spite of the handicaps the photography is excellent. "Snub" Pollard and Harold Lloyd, the well-known comedians, acted as motorman and conductor respectively.

Motography, September 16, 1916

Harold and Snub's streetcar antics seem to have gone so well that they revisited them a year later in *Off the Trolley* (1917). Gaylord Lloyd would rework this picture as *Trolley Troubles* (1921) when he took over as Lonesome Luke, and Harold would do another spin on trolley problems, this time with the addition of a live turkey, in the opening of his 1924 feature *Hot Water*.

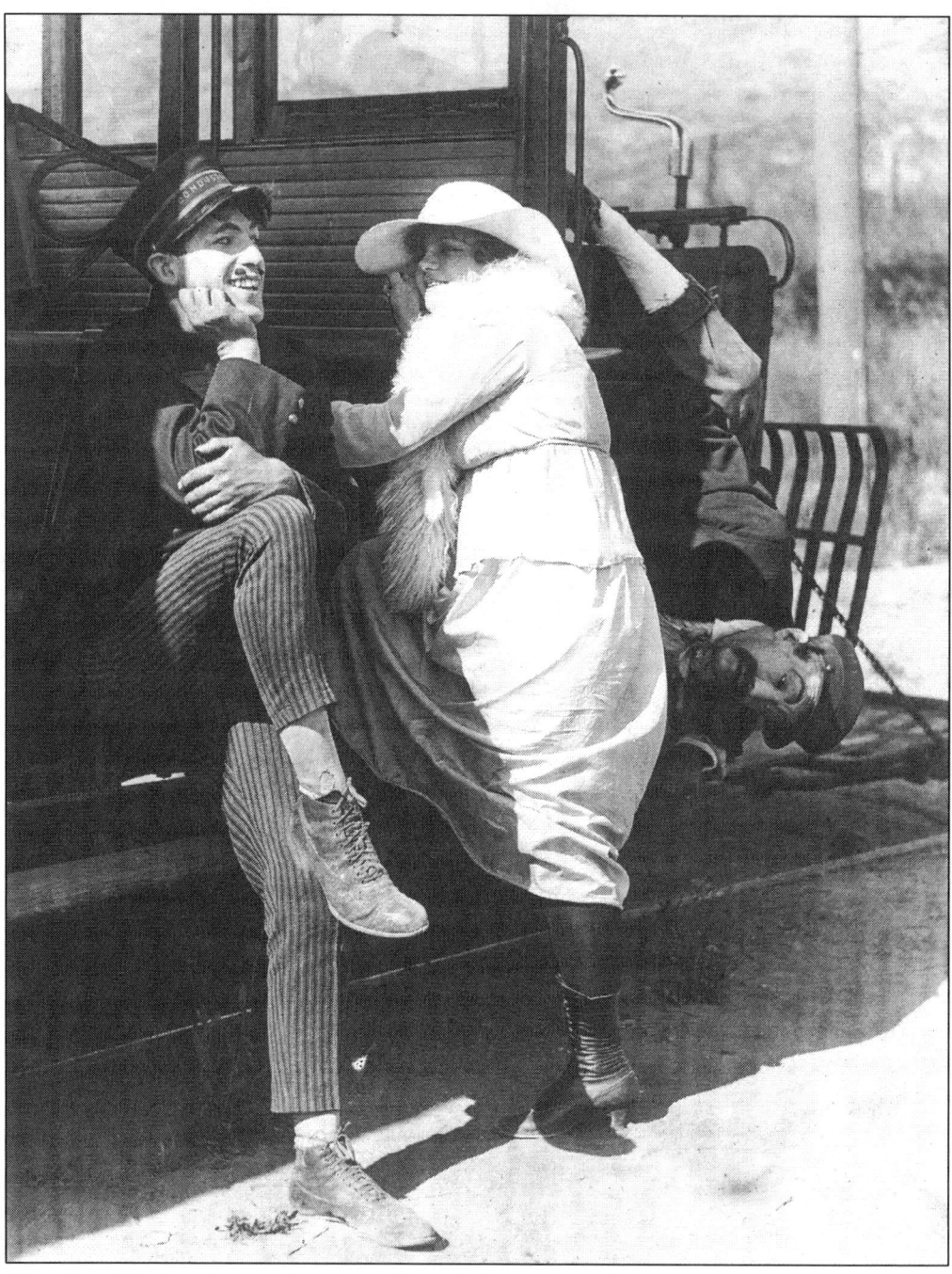

Harold and Snub welcome Vera Reynolds on their trolley car in *Luke's Trolley Troubles* (1917).
Courtesy of the Academy of Motion Picture Arts and Sciences.

A pretty ingénue on the trolley was a recent graduate of L.A.'s Polytechnic High School. Vera Reynolds was turning up in shorts for Rolin, L-Ko, and Sennett, and soon had leading roles in one-reel Triangle Comedies like *A Self-Made Failure* and *Caught in the End* (both 1917). She moved on to more shorts – Gayety Comedies such as *Dry and Thirsty* and *Parked in the Park* (both 1920) with Billy Bletcher, a number of Al Haynes Atma Comedies, a slew of Morris Schlank-produced Broadway Comedies teamed with Eddie Barry, and even a gig supporting Stan Laurel in *The Pest* (1922). She was also married to Earl Montgomery, half of Vitagraph's star comedy team of Montgomery & Rock, from 1919 to 1926.

Vera Reynolds and Al St John (center) are surprised by Charles Force (left) in the Triangle Comedy *A Self-Made Hero* (1917). *Courtesy of Sam Gill.*

By 1923 she'd moved to features in dramas like *Icebound* (1924), as well as comedies such as *The Night Club* (1925) and *Wedding Bill$* (1927) with Raymond Griffith. In the late 1920s she hooked up with Cecil B. DeMille and appeared in comedy-dramas like *Sunny Side Up, Corporal Kate* (both 1926), and *The Main Event* (1927) for his P.D.C. production company. After the switch to sound she appeared mostly in low-budget features such as *The Monster Walks* and *The Gorilla Ship* (both 1932) before leaving films that year.

Motion Picture Magazine (April 1917): "A street car full of silliness, but you will laugh just the same."

Moving Picture World (February 3, 1917): "A good rough-and-tumble 'comic.'"

Lonesome Luke, Lawyer

Released February 18, 1917. Produced by Hal Roach for the Rolin Film Company. Distributed by Pathé. Directed by Hal Roach. One reel. (Filmed from August 5 to August 28, 1916). With Harold Lloyd, Bebe Daniels, Snub Pollard, Bud Jamison, Charles Stevenson, W.L. "Bumps" Adams, Estelle Harrison, Sidney De Gray, Gus Leonard, Earl Mohan, Lottie Case, Sammy Brooks, Merta Sterling, Dorothea Wolbert, Harry Rattenbury, Charles King, Norman Napier, Max D. Hamburger, Billy Evans.

Harold and Snub stand on more than ceremony in *Lonesome Luke, Lawyer* (1917).

The greater part of this comedy is laid in a courtroom, where opportunities innumerable are offered the Rolin comedy organization for staging a burlesque trial scene. The judge, the jury, the court attendants, and last but not least the attorneys present such comical appearances that the spectator will indeed be laughing every minute of the time. Harold Lloyd is seen as the attorney whose client is old and ugly and he gets all the worst of it because the opposing party is prettiness personified by the charming Bebe Daniels. (Motion Picture News, February 24, 1917).

> In Hal Lloyd's newest picture a street car accident is used as a base for the story which shows how each person who saw the wreck explained it in court. Dissolves are done and the different versions shown on the screen in the courtroom. A great mob is used here and some very funny situations arise during the arguments. The different versions of the wreck causes many laughs.
>
> *Motography*, September 2, 1916

It's unusual for Luke to be on this side of the law. Here he's a lawyer, and while not a good one, he'd usually be on the receiving end of a court case. Like Chaplin, Keaton, Laurel & Hardy, and his other silent comedy contemporaries, Luke was an underdog, and generally on the wrong side of the law. This short was remade five years later in 1922 as a vehicle for the Roach Studio's current star Eddie Boland. In *Good Morning, Judge* Boland is the titular lawmaker who favors the pretty defendant over the old woman who was the victim of her poor driving. Again, the varying versions of the accident are reported to the judge.

A sure sign that the Rolin Company was coming up in the film industry food chain is shown by their opportunity to cast two silent comedy mainstays like Merta Sterling and Harry Rattenberry in this comedy. Only a couple of years before the studio would have been too fly by night to secure the services of players of their caliber. Today, round and fully packed Merta Sterling is unjustly overlooked, but in 1917, she was busy making audiences laugh. Born in a log cabin in Wisconsin, she was often referred to in the trade magazines as Myrta or Myrtle Sterling, and according to the March 10, 1917 *Motion Picture Weekly* this is how her career got started:

> Eight years ago, she was a stenographer in the office of Klaw and Erlanger. They decided to revive "The Prince of Pilsen," and she had a hunch that she was just cut out to play the character woman. She succeeded in convincing her employers that she was right, and they told her she might learn the part and attend rehearsals. When they

saw her work, they gave her the chance, inexperienced as she was, and she made good. She had a lot of vaudeville experience after that, and two years ago deserted to the movies.

The overlooked, and not to mention demure, Merta Sterling. *Author's collection.*

She made her film debut in 1914 for Universal, appearing in some of their Joker Comedies, but soon became a regular in Kalem Comedies. Spending a couple of years in shorts such as *The Actress and the Cheese Hound* and *The Bandits of Macaroni Mountain* (both 1915) as support of the studio's headliners like Ham & Bud and Ethel Teare, she was small, and as big around as she was tall. Built like a cannonball, she was bug-eyed and boisterous, and specialized in female authority figures like fussy mothers, suspicious wives, excitable spiritualists, or, as in *Raskey's Roadshow* (1915), even lion tamers. In 1917 she relocated to Universal's L-Ko and Century brands, doing featured roles and occasional leads in titles such as *The Little Fat Rascal*, *A Prairie Chicken* (both 1917), and *Rough on Husbands* (1918). Known as "the rotund and reckless comedienne," practically all of her starring films have vanished.

She can still be seen in *King of the Kitchen* (1918), *The Freckled Fish* (1919), or playing second fiddle to the Century Lions in *A Lion's Alliance* and *Lion Jaws and Kitten Paws* (both 1920). This stint at Universal was the peak of her career. It culminated with her making *The Sage-Brush League* (1919), a five-reel feature for the short-lived Romayne Super Film Co. From this point she free-lanced all over, appearing with Hank Mann, Bobby Dunn, Lloyd Hamilton, Monty Banks and at the Hal Roach Studio in *The Janitor, The Messenger* (both 1919), *Years to Come* (1922), *Scorching Sands*, and *All is Lost* (both 1923). By the mid-1920s her appearances became sporadic. She lost a lot of weight, but was still very effective as the wife that drives Charles Puffy to murder in *Not Guilty* (1926), in addition to supporting the Fox Monkeys in their starring feature *Darwin Was Right* (1924), and working in other pictures such as *Star Dust Trail* (1924) and *Paid to Love* (1927) into the late 1920s.

Harry Rattenberry takes a look at some lower limb evidence in *Lonesome Luke, Lawyer* (1917).

Harry Rattenberry was a busy comedy regular in the Teens, who spent much of his film career in the films of Al Christie. Born in Sacramento, California in 1858, Rattenberry began his stage career twenty years later as an actor and opera singer, as well as in musical comedies like *The Chorus Lady*. He began working in pictures in 1913 for Bison and Universal, and it was in their Nestor brand that Mr. Rattenberry specialized in playing farmers, police commissioners, sea captains, but more often than not the leading lady's crusty father. At 5'11' and two hundred pounds, he cut a formidable figure, and had just the right amount of authority to create the needed comic tension.

One of his funniest surviving Nestor comedies is 1915's *Pruning the Movies*. A parody of Chicago's well-known head of movie censorship Major Metillius Lucullus Cicero Funkhouser, Rattenberry plays "Major Bunk," who with his band of bluenosers descends on a studio projection room and cuts out all the "objectionable" items in an underworld drama. Flowers are substituted for knives and prunes for cocaine – until the film makes absolutely no sense.

In 1917, the actor moved out from Christie shorts and had nice supporting roles in features, working with stars like Mary Pickford and George Beban in titles that included *M'Liss* (1918), *The Delicious Little Devil* (1919), *Huckleberry Finn* (1920), and *Soul of the Beast* (1923). After this lone appearance with Harold in *Lonesome Luke, Lawyer* he returned to the Hal Roach lot right before his death in 1925 for shorts such as *Hard Knocks*, *Zeb Vs. Paprika*, and *Tire Trouble* (all 1924).

Moving Picture World (February 17, 1917): "This one-reel farce is one of the best of the series. The courtroom scene contains an unexpected amount of new business, and speedy action keeps everyone on the run."

Motion Picture News (February 24, 1917): "This is decidedly the best of the recent Luke comedies."

Luke Wins Ye Ladye Faire

Released February 25, 1917. Produced by Hal Roach for the Rolin Film Company. Distributed by Pathé. Working title: **Land Ye Ladye Faire**. One reel. (Filmed August 16 -22, 1916). With Harold Lloyd, Bebe Daniels, Snub Pollard, Bud Jamison, Charles Stevenson, W.L. "Bumps" Adams, Estelle Harrison, Sammy Brooks, Sidney De Gray, Gus Leonard, Lottie Case, Dorothea Wolbert, Alice Davenport, Maybelle Beringer, Brownie Brownell, Rose Eghers, Clara Lucas, George Marion, Enid Markey, H. Smith.

Luke is a Robin Hood type, with Snub as his merry man, in "olde" England, doing his best to battle the villain and his armored henchmen to win the hand of the faire damsel.

This was another period piece for the company – this time set in "Merrie Olde England." Although missing, photos show that "period" exteriors were found and used at the baronial entrance and elaborate grounds of Los Angeles' Castle Sans Souci. Built in 1912 by Dr. A.G.R. Schloesser, this castle-like mansion was a memorable location in silent comedies such as *Father was a*

ABOVE: Luke Wins Ye Lady Faire (1917), but he and Snub are hard-pressed by Bud Jamison and his knights at the main gate of L.A.'s Castle Sans Souci. BELOW: Harold and Snub beg Bud Jamison for mercy in *Luke Wins Ye Ladye Faire* (1917).

Loafer (1915) with Billie Ritchie, and most famously Mack Sennett's *Tillie's Punctured Romance* (1914). The September 9, 1916 *Motion Picture News* described some of the drawbacks in making this kind of period film:

> He is engaged in making a comedy with early English settings and costumes, and an important part of the wardrobe necessary for this are a number of suits of armor. The comedians are finding the designers did not take into consideration any falls when the armor was made, and practically every one of the players has a number of cuts on various parts of the anatomy as the result of the metal pinching when they alighted.

Luke Wins Ye Ladye Faire was the final Lonesome Luke one-reeler released, and as it doesn't appear to have been screened for the press there are no trade magazine reviews available – only scattered newspaper items.

The Daily Advance (March 26, 1917): "Don't fail to see Luke in this great comedy."

Lonesome Luke's Lively Life*

Released March 18, 1917. Produced by Hal Roach for the Rolin Film Company. Distributed by Pathé. Working title: **Luke's Lively Life**. Two reels. (Filmed August 28 to Sept. 11, 1916). Extant: GEM. Copyrighted March 16, 1917 (LU10389) by Pathé Exchange, Inc. With Harold Lloyd, Bebe Daniels, Snub Pollard, Bud Jamison, Dorothea Wolbert, Sammy Brooks, Sidney DeGray, Charles Stevenson, Gus Leonard, Ralph McComas, Ray Thompson, Jack Perrin, Elmer Ballard, Larry Adams, Virgil Owens, Harvey L. Kinney, Max D. Hamburger, Thomas Cassidy, Frank Darcy, Golda Marden, Lottie Case, May Ballard, Maybelle Beringer, Gladys Kinney, Beth Darwin, Beaulah Peyton, Ana McDermott, Clara Morris, Florence Burns, Lucille Smith, H.Y. Goldberg, Ben Goldberg, J.P. Pearce, A. Perluss, Rose Eghers, Pearl Sharkey, Iraee Claire, Billy Clarke, Maxine Whitford, Albert Stein, Wilma Morris, Myrtle Webb.

Lonesome Luke as hat-check boy in the Broadway Café. A gentleman arrives with a hat, coat, cane, muffler, and gloves and Luke makes him check each article separately. Luke has a different thing for each customer as they pour into the place. Snub arrives much worse for wear and proceeds to cause varieties of pandemonium in the café. Later after things are going smoothly, trouble starts in the kitchen and Luke is pressed into service there, where he works in well with that crew as they toss the food to the waiters to show their efficiency in speed and accuracy. However, Luke soon gets in wrong with the French chef while juggling some soup and is chased out. He finds a horse on the street and rides back into the café but the horse does not like this and starts for home. On arriving there the horse proceeds to throw off Luke into the watering trough and there he is left. (Copyright description)

Lonesome Luke's Lively Life (1917) finds Snub jealous as Harold attends to Bebe's shoe.

Luke had become so popular that an expansion was in order:

> Owing to the repeated requests from exhibitors for these "Luke" comedies, in two reel lengths, Mr. Berst (vice-president and general manager of Pathé) decided some months ago to discontinue the release of the one reelers and put the comedies in two reels only. Arrangements were made with the Rolin Company to this end and Pathé has now on hand seven two-reel "Lonesome Luke" comedies, that everyone who has seen declares to be "great." The first to be released will be "Luke's Lively Life," which has been put on the program for March 18.
>
> *Motography* March 3, 1917.

Lonesome Luke's main critic was Harold. Although busy working and turning out films that were making him a household name, he wasn't happy. He described the situation in a mid-1920s career piece in *Photoplay Magazine*:

I was trying to find a new character. Even after Pathé started us making two-reelers, I was all wrong on him. I just couldn't stand him any longer. I had an idea for a more natural character – the sort of kid that everyone knows. I wanted to make comedies where people would see themselves and their neighbors. It was then that I hit on the straight make-up with the glasses.

Lonesome Luke's Lively Life (1917) includes Harold painting on an unusual canvas.

Always determined, it would just be a few months before Harold would get his wish. *Lonesome Luke's Lively Life* does survive today, in a Pathéscope cut-down that runs ten minutes – basically half of the original length. Harold has much funny business as the hat check boy – when a woman isn't allowed in because her gown exposes her bare back, Harold paints on her back to create a clothing pattern. The funniest business occurs when Harold is pressed into service in the kitchen with Luke, the chef, and various waiters juggling and tossing food back and forth with the greatest of ease.

The large and temperamental chef is played by Ralph McComas, a five-foot eleven, two hundred and ninety pound local Los Angeles boy who made good in the film industry of the teens. Starting in vaudeville as a comic, he was snagged for movies by Universal's *Joker Comedies* in 1913 where he supported Gale Henry and Max Asher. After a brief turn with Fred Mace at Majestic, he settled in at the Selig Company to become a key member of their *Chronicles of Bloom Center* comedies. Following the misadventures of the denizens of a small rural town, McComas played Chubby Green, the village prankster and bad boy.

Ralph McComas suffers from Napoleon and Sally's musical disabilities in
Twin Cupids (1916). *Courtesy of Robert James Kiss.*

This was in 1916, and afterwards McComas was bouncing all over – besides Rolin, he became regular support for the chimps Napoleon and Sally at E & R Jungle Films, and returned to Universal to work with Eileen Sedgwick and little Milton Sims in shorts such as *The Shifty Shoplifter* and *The Butler's Blunder* (both 1918). At this point his career suddenly dropped off and he only made sporadic appearances. The short *Three Pairs of Stockings*, and the Maurice Tourneur feature *The Great Redeemer* (both 1921) are the last known films before his death at thirty-five in 1924.

A sequence with a horse in the nightclub makes the climax for the film. Although lasting just a few seconds, it took a lot longer to shoot:

> The larger sets used for this were of the interior of a New York café, and a big scene was that in which a wild-eyed individual rode a fiery horse into the place, while it was at the height of its cabaret merriment. Everything went lovely until the horse reached the foot of the stairs leading to a mezzanine floor, where it stopped, and all the persuading of the scores of ingenues, male and female, could not induce it to climb the steps. The director tried out a number of different horses, and finally found a docile one which would march up, but arriving at the top it would not have enough "pep" to buck as the scenario provided. It then became necessary to get a horse and lift it to the floor where it would do the bucking as a double of the one with the sweet disposition that climbs the stairs.
>
> *Motion Picture News*, October 14, 1916

Motion Picture News (March 17, 1917): "Lonesome Luke is the hat check boy in a Broadway café. He burlesques the grasping race of the hat check boys to an uproarious degree.

Later in the picture Luke is pressed into service in the kitchen, and here the whole company proceeds to show itself off as an expert juggling aggregation. One speaks of 'riots' guardedly, but this picture can be frankly so termed."

Motion Picture Magazine (June 1917): "Recommended as a sure cure for the blues. You just can't help laughing at Luke's restaurant escapades."

Lonesome Luke on Tin Can Alley*

Released April 15, 1917. Produced by Hal Roach for the Rolin Film Company. Distributed by Pathé. Directed by Hal Roach. Extant: MoMA,

BRUS, NAZ. Two reels. (Filmed from December 8, 1916 to January 19, 1917). Copyrighted March 16, 1917 (LU10390) by Pathé Exchange, Inc. With Harold Lloyd, Bebe Daniels, Snub Pollard, Marie Mosquini, Margaret Joslin, Bud Jamison, Harry Todd, Sammy Brooks, Billy Fay, Fred Newmeyer, Charles Stevenson, Gus Leonard, Dorothea Wolbert, Earl Mohan, Gilbert Pratt, David "Slim" Voorhees, W.L. "Bumps" Adams, Della Mullady, S.B. Smith, Joe Turner, Elmer Ballard, Sandy Roth, Joseph Kelly, Max D. Hamburger, Irene Tyner, Leila Jocelin, May Ballard, Emma Carrington, P.L. Howard, James Williams, Dink Johnson, Earl Dower, Chink Snowden, Nita Davis, Wilma Morris, Nina Trask, Lois La Pearl, Walter Howell, Vivian DeLadd, Dave Higgins, F. Bartell, Earl Dancer, Harry Rindfleish, Billy Gilbert, Frank Terry.

The policemen on the beat have a hard time with the obstreperous characters who inhabit the slum alley. Luke is a pickpocket, living on his wits, who uses a fake arm to distract victims while his real arm slips into their pockets. To escape from the police, he frequently has to take refuge in the basement café, where Snub Pollard is a waiter and Bud Jamison the big boss. The café has a dance hall, a back room where illegal card playing goes on, a kitchen, and a room for prizefights. Bebe Daniels, in cap and sweater, is a tough dame who can take care of mashers by herself. Luke creates mayhem in all these areas while escaping the police. He hides under the gaming table, smoking the player's butts and drinking their drinks. He dances with his own coat on the dance floor.

In the street, he gets in a fight with a man over a cigarette butt, then saves the man's life from a passing car and is rewarded with a thousand dollars. However, the police chase him, and riding a bicycle to escape, he ends up in the boxing ring. He plays poker with the boss, who cheats openly. Luke bets on the boxing match, and influences the outcome by making one fighter think he has torn his pants. The entire place is in confusion, the police arrive, and Luke flees, chased by Bebe, who is after his money. She steals it, and he chases her through a tunnel. (1974 description by Eileen Bowser based on the print at The Museum of Modern Art)

On the surface this is the *Luke* comedy that seems the most like an answer to a recent Charlie Chaplin film: February 5, 1917's release of *Easy Street*. But Chaplin had started production only about two weeks ahead of *Lonesome Luke on Tin Can Alley*, so Harold and company couldn't have seen any footage. Most likely they were going on whatever the trades were reporting on the film, and they could have hired extras that had just worked on the Chaplin picture. It appears Rolin just decided to put Luke into a similar slum neighborhood, as there's no specific liftings from *Easy Street*.

Exhibitor ad for the new two-reel *Luke* series.

Chaplin had started exploring his "lower depths" vision of life with its flophouses, seedy dance halls, and underworld riff-raff with *Police* (1915), and would continue with *A Dog's Life* (1918), *The Professor* (circa 1919), and *The Kid* (1921). Other comics followed suit such as Monty Banks in *Peaceful Alley* (1921) and Lloyd Hamilton's *Careful Please* (1926), as would Harold in *From Hand to Mouth* (1919), and the feature *For Heaven's Sake* (1926).

Slim Voorhees towers over Bebe, Charles Stevenson, Harold, and Sammy Brooks in
Lonesome Luke's Honeymoon (1917).
Courtesy of the Academy of Motion Picture Arts and Sciences.

David Voorhees has been added to the large force of people making Rolin comedies. Dave is six feet nine inches tall and is correspondingly thin.

Motography, December 9, 1916

The incredibly tall and super thin Voorhees was nicknamed "Slim" for obvious reasons, and without any kind of known performing background seems to have been tapped for films for his unique physical characteristics, such as in this surviving short where he makes a ridiculously undernourished-looking boxer. Voorhees appeared in the *Lukes* and early glasses character shorts from the beginning of 1916 into 1917 when he was called up for army duty:

David "Slim" Voorhees, one of the tallest, if not the tallest of actors on the screen, has been called to the colors and on July 15th reported for duty at a certain post in California. "Slim" is now drum major in one of the army bands. He was born in Kansas in 1890 and stands 6 feet, 7 ¾ inches tall. He is a nephew of the late U.S. Senator Voorhees of Indiana, and has been playing in Pathé's "Lonesome Luke" comedies. He is said to be the tallest man now enlisted in Uncle Sam's army.

Photo-Play Journal, October 1917

The silent Billy Gilbert.

After being discharged, he returned to the Roach lot for a couple of shorts like *An Eastern Westerner* and *High and Dizzy* (both 1920), but left the film industry. Later he worked as a chauffeur for Southern California Edison and as a truck driver for the Consolidated Rock Company before his death in 1939.

In addition to Voorhees, the silent comedy regulars Billy Gilbert and Frank Terry are seen in the cast. Gilbert, known in silent comedy circles as "Little Billy Gilbert" (to differentiate him from the familiar roly-poly Billy Gilbert of sound films), was small with a standing-up batch of thick brown hair who started his show business career at five years old. An all-around daredevil and roustabout, he spent time as an aeronaut, jockey, acrobat, and show manager. Before joining Keystone as one of the original Keystone Cops in 1913, he worked at Coney Island as a clown at the Steeplechase and a diver at Dreamland Pier. All this experience came in handy doing stunts for Mack Sennett, and he spent the bulk of 1913 to 1933 working there.

One of his forays from Sennett was a brief stint as a director for Harold on some of the early glasses character one-reelers like *Rainbow Island*, *The Flirt*, *Pinched*, *Move On* (all 1917), and *The Tip* (1918). Lloyd wasn't happy with his work, and refers to him (although unnamed) in *An American Comedy*:

> I had to think up story and gags, direct and play the lead at the rate of a picture a week – a judgement, some might have thought, upon my willful head. I was desperate enough to take on a former Keystone cop actor as director. Then Pollard suggested Alf Goulding, another former member of Pollard's Lilliputians. Goulding was hired on the theory that if he was any good at all I would alternate him with the former Keystone actor, giving each a week to work out his story. Goulding proved to be innocent of any camera knowledge; but an old vaudevillian, he could pull gags out of the air, and thin air at that, and was a tremendous help. With his alternative, I had to supply the gags as well as virtually direct for the week he presided.

Not long after, Gilbert returned to Sennett, and sensibly old standby Gilbert Pratt took his place. Billy Gilbert later spent some time working for Schiller Productions in Yonkers, NY, where he supported Marcel Perez and Bud Duncan. Besides doing bits at Sennett and working behind the scenes, he freelanced in shorts for Fox, Joe Rock and Weiss Brothers, and turned up in features such as *The Missing Link* (1927) and *Welcome Danger* (1929). Having spent much time doing props, in 1930 he became chief property master at the Sennett Studio, and continued when Mascot and Republic took over the lot. His last known screen appearance was in 1935's *Keystone Hotel*, and he died in 1961.

Frank Terry was perhaps the oddest and most colorful man of mystery to end up in Hollywood. This music hall veteran was born in Worcestershire, England as Ernest Dovay, but was soon touring as an acrobat and singer-songwriter under the names Ernest Edwards, Nat Clifford, and others. As he toured the world he's said to have married multiple woman and was involved in numerous scandals. In the teens he ended up as Frank Terry in American vaudeville with a popular drunk character known as "Mr. Booze," and also offered his services as a sketch writer and script doctor. His earliest known film work is in 1917 for Mack Sennett, but his on-and-off again home for almost twenty years was the Hal Roach Studio.

Frank Terry (left) and Stan Laurel will soon find out that *There's No Place Like Jail* (1918).
Courtesy of the Library of Congress.

After doing bits like this, he became the main collaborator for Stan Laurel in his first stay at the studio – directing, writing, and co-starring in *No Place Like Jail* (1918) and *Hustling for Health* (1919). When Laurel left, Terry moved over to Harold's unit, and stayed for around two years:

> "I have seen Lloyd improvise a piece of business on the spur of the moment that would prove the biggest laugh in an entire production," said Terry, in a reminiscent mood. "A sudden twist

of his shoulders, maybe a fall, any one of fifty different things that would come to him suddenly, and he would "break us up" as they say in show parlance. Usually the effect is the same on the audience."

Detroit Free Press, March 6, 1921

Unfortunately, Terry was the person that handed Harold the prop bomb that was actually a live bomb and exploded during a photo shoot at the Witzel Studio. Remaining with the comedian after his recovery, Terry can be glimpsed on screen in the shorts *High and Dizzy* and *Get Out and Get Under* (both 1920). Through the 1920s he moved around – sometimes at Roach, but also racking up credits for Special Pictures, Universal, Bray, and Sennett. In sound he also worked for Paramount, Larry Darmour Productions, and Harold Lloyd features like *Movie Crazy* (1932). His last verified screen appearances are in 1935's *The Bride of Frankenstein* and *The Great Impersonation*. Finding religion, he became the missionary Reverend Frank Edwards and spread the word in Hawaii and California up to his death in 1948.

Moving Picture World (April 14, 1917): "The comedy shows Luke as a pickpocket with a fake arm, the boss of Tin Can Alley and the backer of the most screamingly ridiculous prize fight ever filmed. How Luke wrests victory from seeming defeat is told in a hilarious manner."

Arkansas Democrat (May 24, 1917): "'Lonesome Luke,' that ever-popular Pathé player, will be seen in his second two-reel feature comedy. This one is entitled 'Lonesome Luke on Tin Can Alley,' and is one of the most excruciatingly funny comedies ever shown in this city. Many people think that 'Lonesome Luke' is as funny as Charlie Chaplin, the greatest praise that be awarded any comedian."

Lonesome Luke's Honeymoon

Released May 20, 1917. Produced by Hal Roach for the Rolin Film Company. Distributed by Pathé. Working title: *Luke's Honeymoon*. Two reels. (Filmed October 3 – 18, 1916). Copyrighted March 16, 1917 (LU10391) by Pathé Exchange, Inc. With Harold Lloyd, Bebe Daniels, Snub Pollard, Bud Jamison, Sammy Brooks, Dorothea Wolbert, Charles Stevenson, Slim Voorhees, Marie Mosquini, Sammy Burns, Estelle Harrison, Arthur Mumas, W.L. "Bumps" Adams, Gilbert Pratt, Max D. Hamburger, Florence Burns, Margaret Strong, Beth Darwin, Sis Mathews, Wilma Morris, Harvey L. Kinney, W.B. Turner, Harry Swisher, George Murphy, May Ballard, Babe Lloyd (Harold's father James Darsie Lloyd, a.k.a. "Foxy").

Bud Jamison looks doubtful about Harold and Bebe's marital status in
Lonesome Luke's Honeymoon (1917). *Courtesy of the Academy of Motion Picture Arts and Sciences.*

Lonesome Luke, an iceman, is pressed into service to marry the daughter of a rich man because she wants to get rid of a titled suitor. At the church they strike another wedding party and get soaked by mistake and a sign pinned on them. They arrive at a hotel and cause much merriment by the sign. They finally get a room but are continuously annoyed by bellboys. Luke has a fight with the count, and thinks he has killed him and goes for a doctor. He does not get one but returns just in time to knock the count out again as he is coming to. Finally disgusted with the annoyances, he grabs his girl and rushes out of the hotel through the mass of bellboys and guests only to meet the girl's father on the sidewalk. After a few minutes he becomes reconciled and accepts Luke instead of the count. (Copyright description)

The premise for this film was re-used a couple of years later in *Haunted Spooks* (1920), where Harold marries Mildred Davis so that she can inherit an estate. Honeymoons, real or pretend, are usually recipes for disaster in screen comedies. Harold and Bebe are bumpily just married in *That's Him* and *Bride and Gloom* (both 1918), and when they set off on a shipborne wedding trip in *A Jazzed Honeymoon* (1919) they are forcibly separated with the poor groom thrown into the engine room and made to work as a stoker.

Other difficult post-nuptials include Buster Keaton in *One Week* (1920), *My Wife's Relations* (1923) and *Spite Marriage* (1929). In *His First Honeymoon* (1921) Monty Banks has troubles with his bride's cooking, a hulking iceman, and a pesky book salesman. Definitely the worst after-wedding events play out in the Roscoe Arbuckle-directed *Honeymoon Trio* (1931). Poor Al St John and his bride head off on their honeymoon trip with Al's former rival in tow. This megaphone-voiced blowhard takes great relish in emasculating the hapless new husband, and Al, powerless to thwart or even shut him up, is symbolically cuckolded in a never-ending honeymoon from hell.

A recent recruit to the Rolin stock company was the small and bird-like Dorothea Wolbert, who immediately cornered the market on snoops, mean mothers-in-law, and henpecking wives. Having started her career on stage as an ingenue in the hit *Charley's Aunt*, she spent many years on the boards working for producers such as Charles Frohman, and appearing with names like A.S. Willard in popular shows such as *The Masquerader*, *The Little Minister*, and *The Butterflies*. She made her film debut in 1916, and the next year took her place in the Lonesome Luke comedies.

Dorothea Wolbert and her children are chauffeured by Hilliard Karr and Little Napoleon in *A Small Town Hero* (1922). *Courtesy of Robert S. Birchard.*

Wolbert stayed with the Lloyd unit during Harold's transition to his glasses character, and played regularly in other Hal Roach shorts through 1919. After branching out into features such as *Cupid Forecloses* (1919) and *La La Lucille* (1920), in 1920 Universal gave her a series of starring Star Comedy one-reel shorts that included *Shapes and Scrapes* (1920), *Fresh from the Country*, and *A Model Made* (both 1921). From here she became a ubiquitous face in silent comedies all through the silent era, working everywhere supporting the likes of Beatrice Lillie, Pola Negri, Louise Fazenda, Laurel & Hardy, and A Ton of Fun in shorts and features like A *Woman of the World* (1925), *The Heavy Parade, Exit Smiling* (both 1926), *Anybody Seen Kelly?* and *Their Purple Moment* (both 1928). She kept busy after the move to sound, and worked steadily in bit parts until 1957.

Motion Picture News (March 17, 1917): "Luke is an iceman who is pressed into service to marry Bebe Daniels, who wants to get rid of a tilted suitor. Their experiences with the bell hops in the hotel and the manner in which the whole tangle is finally straightened out and the irate father appeased form two reels of superlative comedy."

Motography (May 19, 1917): "The attempts of an heiress to marry Luke in order to destroy the chances of a wily villain are excruciatingly funny."

Patterson Morning Call (August 3, 1917): "Lonesome Luke's Honeymoon" is the comedy attraction, and it is such a one to make you forget your troubles."

Lonesome Luke, Plumber

Released June 17, 1917. Produced by Hal Roach for the Rolin Film Company. Distributed by Pathé. Directed by Hal Roach. Working titles: *Luke's Plumbing Blunders* and *Lonesome Luke's Plumbing Mishap*. Two reels (Filmed from October 20 – November 8, 1916). Copyrighted June 7, 1917 (LU10905) by Pathé Exchange, Inc. With Harold Lloyd, Bebe Daniels, Snub Pollard, Bud Jamison, Margaret Joslin, Marie Mosquini, Charles Stevenson, Gus Leonard, Marguerite Nichols, Sammy Brooks, Gilbert Pratt, Arthur Harrison, W.L. "Bumps" Adams, David "Slim" Voorhees, Clara Lucas, Pearl Novci.

Lonesome Luke is a plumber's helper with a sure ignorance that will always get things just exactly wrong and make them so that they cannot be fixed. His boss, who rules by might rather than brain, does everything in the place except work. Mrs. Smith finds that the water in her bath-tub will not run and she calls the plumber. Luke and his boss get the job and Luke starts to work with his boss comfortably settled in a large chair superintending the eating of an apple by himself. In the meantime, Mrs. Jones, across the hall, also finds that the water is turned off in her apartment and comes across to borrow Mrs. Smith's plumber. As the plumbers try to run both jobs at the same time, two bears from a neighboring zoo escape and enter the house. After considerable chasing around, and an attempt by Luke to catch one of the bears by putting salt on its tail, the two bears chase the plumber until finally the boss escapes down a man-hole, and Luke leaves his bear up a tree. (Copyright description)

Harold helps himself while Bud Jamison is distracted in *Lonesome Luke, Plumber* (1917).

Two "special guest stars" in this short got all the attention in the reviews and trade magazine items:

> One of the best bits is where Harold Lloyd, as Luke, is carrying down a flight of stairs a bath tub inverted over his head. Two bears enter the house and make for him. He throws himself flat on the floor with the tub over him and then by crawling along like a giant turtle seeks to escape. The bears are pawing at the tub in their efforts to get at him.
>
> *Motion Picture News*, June 9, 1917.

The bears were said to have come from the Los Angeles Zoo, but it seems more likely that for safety's sake they were a couple of trained bruins who were busy working in pictures. At that time a bear named Bruno was a regular at the Mack Sennett Studio, as well as working with people like George Beban and Gale Henry. John Brown was another professional grizzly, who counted Buster Keaton, Stan Laurel and Charlie Chaplin among his co-stars. The movie bruins' acting choices were motivated by lunchables being stashed around a set or location – bananas in pockets, honey smeared on actor's faces, or bags of peanuts on tree limbs.

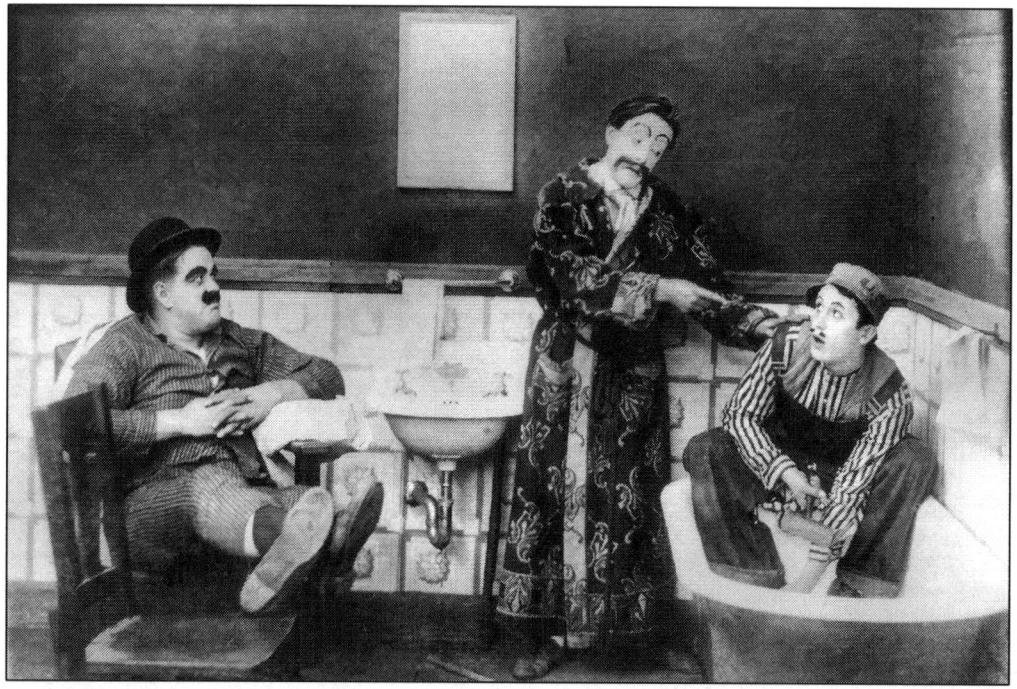

Bud Jamison and Snub supervising Harold's work in *Lonesome Luke, Plumber* (1917).

The need to now-and-then work with an animal was an occupational hazard for every silent comic. If they were lucky it was the more domestic kind like a dog, cow, or donkey, but often it was feral types like lions or tigers. Besides these two bears, during his comedy career Harold worked with dogs, chimps, mice, horses, ring-tailed monkeys, goats, alligators, camels, snakes, rabbits, a denatured skunk (which bit him), and in *The Sin of Harold Diddlebock* (1947) Jackie the lion (who tried to bite him). The Hal Roach lot had numerous animals over the years – frequent mules, usually named Dinah, Laurel & Hardy's little dog Laughing Gravy, and the *Dippy-Doo-Dads*, a surreal series of one-reelers with animal casts that spoofed love melodramas (*Lovey Dovey*, 1923), the evils of drink (*The Bar Fly*, 1924), and rousing Northwest Mountie sagas (*North of 50-50*, 1924).

Exhibitor's Trade Review (May 26, 1917): "This release is quite above the average for two reel slapstick comedies. In this case Luke is the plumber's assistant who is forced to do all the hard work. The arrival of two escaped bears from the Zoo provides the comedy bits. Quite to the contrary as to what may be expected from the title the old water gag has been entirely eliminated. The laughs can be found in abundance and the comedy brims with originality, making it all in all an exceptional offering as a mirth maker for any program."

Moving Picture World (June 16, 1917): "Lonesome Luke is a struggling young plumber and there is a laugh in every blow of his hammer.

Also prominent in the cast are two black bears from the Los Angeles zoo, who, in search of better fare than their keepers give them, enter the house where Lonesome Luke is engaged in first aid to bath-tubs."

Patterson Morning Call (August 24, 1917): "'Lonesome Luke, the Plumber' is one continuous reel of laughter and is a worthy presentation of the best comedy offerings."

The Kane Republican (November 12, 1917): "Positively the greatest two-act comedy ever produced. If you liked Chaplin, Saturday, see this one. It's positively a knockout."

Stop! Luke! Listen!

Released July 15, 1917. Produced by Hal Roach for the Rolin Film Company. Distributed by Pathé. Working titles: *Lonesome Luke in Stop! Luke! Listen!* and *Stop Look Listen*. Two reels. (Filmed from November 9-11 and 15-26, 1916). Copyrighted June 7, 1917 (LU10904) by Pathé Exchange, Inc. With Harold Lloyd, Bebe Daniels, Snub Pollard, Margaret Joslin, Gilbert Pratt, Gus Leonard, Charles Stevenson, Bud Jamison, Sammy Brooks, W.L. "Bumps" Adams, David "Slim" Voorhees, Arthur Harrison, Max D. Hamburger, Clara Drey, Elmer Ballard, Mable Ballard, Loretta Moreland, Billy Fay, Sandy Roth, Marie Mosquini, Della Mullady, Art Bass, Fred Newmeyer.

Lonesome Luke is asleep on a bench in the waiting room of a railroad station when a policeman bangs him on the feet and sets him on his way. He earns a quarter carrying two suitcases full of sample bricks for a man. Then trying to help a pretty young lady with her bag, he rouses the ire of the butler of a wealthy family. Finally he wanders to the park where he finds the valuable dog of the girl living in the house where the butler worked. The girl is so pleased at the recovery of her dog that she insists that he come to her house. In the meantime the girl's many suitors are still on the hunt for her dog and one of them offers a dollar to the boy of the gang who finds the dog. Luke is received cordially and tries to give a piano recital much to the disgust of the guests. The girl then orders a square meal for Luke but he must sneak out and get two pals first. They share the meal until near the end a fight starts and one of them with a gun chases Luke all over the house until Luke hits him on the head with a vase and knocks him out. This makes him the hero and the rich girl rushes to him. As they are standing on the front porch, the gang of boys see them and make for the one that offered them a dollar. Luke, mistaking their interest, turns tail and runs. The last that is seen of him, he is running as he never did before down the street with the kids after him. (Copyright description)

Bebe tries to pass Harold and Snub off to Elmer Ballard, Gus Leonard, W.H. "Bumps" Adams, Charles Stevenson, Gilbert Pratt and Margaret Joslin in *Stop! Luke! Listen!* (1917).

As always, Luke is the perennial sore thumb – always out of place in any society gathering. A bit of a re-working of *Luke's Society Mix-Up* (1916), again he impersonates a musical virtuoso for a high-toned gathering, and just as before it ends in comedic disaster.

Supporting player W.L. (Walter Lawrence) Adams was a heavy-set Roscoe Arbuckle clone, who started his career at Rolin in 1917 with shorts such as *Luke's Lost Liberty* and *Luke's Busy Day*. After appearing in the Lloyd films from 1917 into 1918, he took the nickname "Bumps" and began headlining in low-budget 1919 Romayne Super Film Co. comedy two-reelers like *Keyhole Reporter* and *Stale Eggs and Sweethearts* (both 1920). Working with

Dot Farley and fellow former Rolin player Dorothea Wolbert, the only one known to exist today is *Underground Romeo* (1920). This is a re-do of the second reel of Arbuckle's *The Butcher Boy* (1917) that has Dot Farley sent off to a girl's school so that her country lover "Bumps" can show up in drag as the "new student." Wolbert fills in for Agnes Neilson as head of the school, and Dot and "Bumps" end up evading Wolbert and Dot's father to get to the minister's home to tie the knot.

In 1920 the trade magazines announced that Adams would be starring in comedies for Screen Crafts, Inc.:

Featuring Bumps Adams

Work on the first two-reel athletic comedy featuring Bumps Adams started last week at the new studio of Screen Crafts, Inc. Maureen Chadwick is leading lady.

Adams and DeWitt Hagar are co-directing and Jack Figua is behind the camera. The Adams comedies are being produced by Screen Crafts, of which Capt. H.H. Lawson, owner of cinema playhouses in Arizona and Northern California is president and general manager.

Camera!, May 1, 1920

"Bumps" Adams' true gender is revealed by Dorothea Wolbert in 1920's *Underground Romeo*.

Screen Crafts, Inc. also announced that it would produce four Christian Science stories a year, but there are no known titles for the Adams shorts. After this there's dwindling mentions of "Bumps." *Camera!* reports in 1922 that Kenneth J. Bishop was directing Adams in a burlesque of the Northwest Mounted Police, and another issue states that he had set up Adams Productions, a company through which he was producing and directing animated shorts with puppets named Billy and Betty. At this point his starring career flatlined on the cinema's EKG monitors, and he later worked as a radio engineer until his death in 1943.

Moving Picture World (July 7, 1917): "In the picture Lonesome Luke indulges in some of the funniest antics even he has been guilty of. He impersonates Paderewski in a way that would make the great pianist's own mother unable to watch her son play without laughing at the thought of Lonesome Luke's burlesque.

  With the aid of a convenient mahogany table, he opens a little bar at the heiress's, at which he is both patron and bartender. When chased by an irate giant, he climbs the sides of the house, dashes in and out of the windows and clings to the roof with an agility that would go far to prove the correctness of Darwinian theory.

  All in all, 'Stop, Luke, Listen' is described as a thirty-minute laugh."

Motion Picture News (July 14, 1917): "Lonesome Luke (Harold Lloyd) is welcomed into the home of a fair debutante (Bebe Daniels) in this 'hit-me-and-I'll-hit-you' number, containing more action than incidental funny business. Kicking, slapping, drinking and running wildly about with no plot to speak of hardly constitutes all that could be desired in a comedy of this sort. When gags are few and originality at low tide the wild actions of the players don't get much in the way of laughter.

  There are some good stunts in the number and Luke and Snub Pollard are funny individually, but the various scenes don't hang together with even the small degree of continuity possessed by the majority of successful slapstick comedies."

Moving Picture World (July 14, 1917): "A one-reel[sic] Lonesome Luke knockabout farce. The expert method of the star and his support makes the picture amusing. It is up to standard for this brand."

Lonesome Luke, Messenger*

Released August 5, 1917. Produced by Hal Roach for the Rolin Film Company. Distributed by Pathé. Extant: CNC. Working title: *Luke in Messenger 19*. Two reels. (Filmed from February 16 – March 7, 1917). Copyrighted June 27, 1917 (LU10994) by Pathé Exchange, Inc. With Harold Lloyd, Bebe Daniels, Snub Pollard, Gilbert Pratt, Billy Fay, Gus Leonard, Slim Voorhees, Fred Newmeyer, Charles Stevenson, Margaret Joslin, Bud Jamison, Dorothea Wolbert, Harry Todd, Sammy Brooks, Marie Mosquini, Arthur Mumas, W.L. "Bumps" Adams, Sidney DeGray, Lottie Case, Mable Ballard, Nina Speight, Evelyn Paige, Max D. Hamburger, Harry Rindfleish, David "Slim" Voorhees, Vivian DeLadd, Mabel Gibson, Lois La Pearl, Zetta Robson, Alta Davis, Beth Darwin, Clara Drey, Loretta Drey, Lena Morris, Virginia Baynes, Lillian Sylvester.

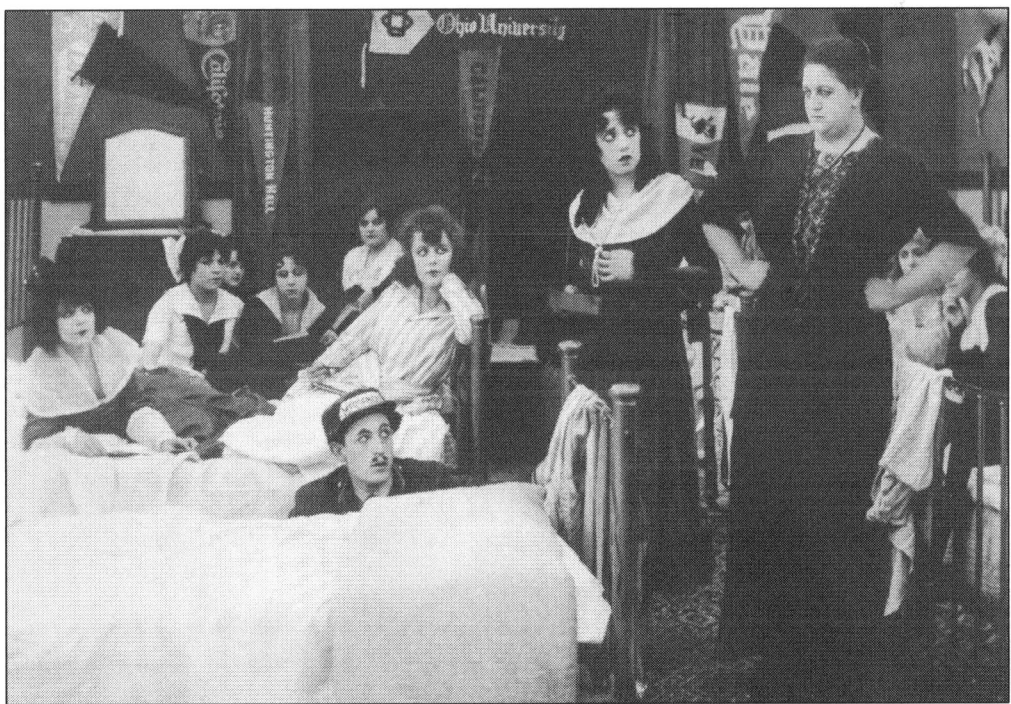

Thanks to Margaret Joslin, Harold's happiness is short-lived in
Lonesome Luke, Messenger (1917).

Lonesome Luke and Snub are having a quiet game of poker in a box out of sight of the rest of the messenger force. Luke is known as the "greyhound" of the squad so that when a young man came in wanting a speedy messenger, the boss had to look for Luke. The game being broken up, Snub was sent out too. Luke follows his man to a girl's seminary where he is sent in by way of a window to deliver a note. He is so impressed by the pretty girls that when he is caught by the matron and thrown out he wants to get back in, forgetting all about his man. He sees a telephone man on a nearby pole, seizes some of his instruments and makes for the school. In the meantime Snub happens along and finding out what Luke is doing decides to get in himself. He spies a paperhanger and gets a job as assistant. He and Luke have many scrapes with each other, and with the matron. Finally, another messenger comes along and tells who they really are. Luke is immediately chased and leads the crowd to a high stone wall where they can't reach him, so they pelt him with stones. He is knocked over the wall and lands besides two prisoners pounding rocks. A guard comes up and spying Luke tells him that he "needs a new infielder," and makes Luke grab a hammer. (Copyright description)

Over the last few years *Lonesome Luke, Messenger* has become one of the most accessible of the series – it's been shown on Turner Classic Movies, highlighted on the Criterion Channel, and is all over the internet. It's rapid-fire, non-stop knockabout, and it's easy to understand why Harold was frustrated with playing Luke. Although he, Roach, and their crew were becoming more and more proficient developing gags, routines, and comic timing, Luke as a character would always be one-dimensional, and never give Harold the opportunity for the originality and depth of which he was capable.

Being a speedy messenger is another profession that's a sure failure for Luke (he's more than ready to abandon his duties to make time with the girls at the school). Around the same time, Harry Watson Jr. was an equally poor bike messenger in *Blow Your Horn* and *Showing Some Speed* (both 1916) in the *Musty Suffer* series. Al St John was well-known for his bicycle skills, so in shorts like *The Big Secret* (1921), *Special Delivery* (1922), and *Service* (1925) ways were found to work in his trick riding as he maneuvered through busy traffic, chased bad guys, and balanced on the edge of tall buildings.

Universal even devoted an entire series to the subject with their *Messenger Boy Comedies*. Forgotten today, the shorts were written and directed by Scott Darling, and had Lewis Sargent as Jimmy Flannagan who was in delivery service for twelve one-reelers that included *The Speed Boy*, *A Dog Gone Day* (both 1922), *Whiskers*, and *Peanuts* (both 1923).

This is the surviving *Luke* short that gives the most extensive look at the Bradbury Mansion – both inside and out. Rolin first set up shop there in 1914, and while they would move around a bit they returned to the Mansion in 1916 and stayed there until Roach built his own studio in 1920.

Finished in 1887 at a cost of $80,000, the Mansion was owned by real estate developer Lewis L. Bradbury, who built the famous Bradbury Building in downtown Los Angeles (used as a location in many film noirs). Movie people began renting space in 1913, and there was plenty of space to be had – the Mansion had thirty-five rooms and five chimneys. Torn down in 1929, Harold gave a good description of it in his autobiography of the previous year:

> It is a place of many turrets, bay windows, word carvings and curlicues, a grand staircase, sixteen-foot ceilings, brocaded wall papers, stained glass, parqueted floors, hardwood finish, sliding doors and all the other elegancies of the 80s. In the yard a giant palm tree soars 110 feet and a rubber tree has grown so huge now that its roots are pushing up the cement walks. We called it Pneumonia Hall, from its wide and windy spaces.

The Bradbury Mansion was an early home to Rolin as well as to
many other small indie units.

There were plenty of cubbyhole spaces for small movie companies to rent, and among other units besides Rolin to use the facilities were Hobart Bosworth Productions, Zodiak Manufacturing co., Albuquerque Film Manufacturing Co., Pathé's Western Co., and J.A.C. Film Manufacturing (headed by James A. Crosby, who became Rolin's head of photography in 1916). Charlie Chaplin used it prominently in a number of his Essanay Comedies like *Work* and *A Woman* (both 1915), and even Famous-Players produced a number of Mary Pickford's early features there.

Motion Picture News (August 11, 1917): "Harold Lloyd, in his latest two reels of laughs, executes the "slapstick" variety with 'pep' aplenty and with a bunch of supporters who are capable of taking the fun where he leaves it and carrying it on to a laughing climax. He is ever in evidence and his unwillingness to overdo an act or rather his natural comedy instinct to 'let well-enough alone' places Mr. Lloyd in a rank with some of the best 'slapstick' comedians. In the role of a 'fleet-footed' messenger boy Mr. Lloyd creates some good comedy and when he is given the freedom (by right of conquest) of a girl's boarding school he keeps things moving in the realm of comedy.

'Lonesome Luke, Messenger,' is a good two-reel comedy."

Lonesome Luke, Mechanic

Released August 19, 1917. Produced by Hal Roach for the Rolin Film Company. Distributed by Pathé. Working title: *Luke's Mechanical Misfortune*. Two reels. (Filmed from September 13 – 29 and November 14, 1916). Copyrighted June 27, 1917 (LU10995) by Pathé Exchange, Inc. With Harold Lloyd, Bebe Daniels, Snub Pollard, Bud Jamison, Marie Mosquini, Charles Stevenson, Marguerite Nichols, Sammy Brooks, Estelle Harrison, Arthur Mumas, W.L. "Bumps" Adams, Sidney De Gray, Lottie Case, Mable Ballard, Elmer Ballard, Gus Leonard, Harry L. King, Dorothea Wolbert, Max D. Hamburger, David "Slim" Voorhees, Fred Jefferson, Ray Everhart, Frank Lake, Della Mullady, Joe Turner.

Lonesome Luke and Snub are mechanics at a garage and the boss gets a telephone call that a flivver is stuck on the road. They get out the emergency car and go out. They find that the engine has dropped out on the road. When found and restored to its proper place they start back to the garage and come upon a beautiful young lady stalled in her car. They rush to her aid and find that all the trouble she had was they forgot to put on the spark plug. A little farther on the way back to the garage they see a pretty Miss and jump out of the car, leaving it going, to talk to her. The car finally comes to a stop when it knocks an apple wagon over. When they come to get it again they are chased by the Italian but escape him and get back to the garage. In the meantime the flivver loses its engine again and they haul it to the garage, where an alarm clock is installed instead of the engine, and it goes fine. The young lady whose car was stalled on the road comes to the garage to get some gasoline and in the fight that followed in trying to serve her, she rescues Luke and takes him to her home. There he proceeds to get intoxicated and gets kicked out. He goes back to the garage to find it burning. He puts out the fire alone and is almost smothered by the smoke when his fair lady again rescues him. At this time the owner of the building enters and give Luke a large reward for saving his property. (Copyright description)

Sidney DeGrey (back) observes Bud Jamison, Harold, and Snub not working in *Lonesome Luke, Mechanic* (1917). *Courtesy of the Academy of Motion Picture Arts and Sciences.*

Auto-frustration and auto-destruction were regular themes in silent slapstick. At this point in time many families were getting cars, but they were still novelties and "new-fangled," and so extremely ripe as comedy material. Everyone from W.C. Fields to Al Alt had car problems, and notable examples include *Give 'Er Gas* (1919) with Lyons & Moran, Al St John in *His New Car* (1924), and Laurel & Hardy's *Perfect Day* (1929).

Out-and-out car destruction was on view in Roscoe Arbuckle's *The Garage* (1920), Buster Keaton's *The Blacksmith* (1922), and on a huge scale in Laurel & Hardy's *Two Tars* (1928). Besides his active garage work here, Harold would continue to have automobile misadventures in *Get Out and Get Under* (1920) and *Hot Water* (1924).

A young actress who had recently been hired in 1916 to appear with Dee Lampton in his *Skinny* one-reel series, also made a few appearances with *Lonesome Luke*. Marguerite Nichols was Los Angeles-born, and started her career as an extra with the Balboa Company, where she quickly worked her way up to lead roles. Not long after joining Rolin, she married the boss Hal Roach in September of 1916. Also appearing for the American Film Manufacturing Company, she co-starred with Henry King and Mary Miles

Marguerite Nichols worked at Balboa, American, and Pathé
before she became the second Mrs. Hal Roach.

Minter, and played Baby Marie Osborne's mother in the features *Little Mary Sunshine* (1916) and *When Baby Forgot* (1917). She retired to raise a family, and passed away in 1941.

A husband and wife that appeared in many of the later *Lukes* was Elmer and Mable Ballard. Teamed as Elmer Ballard ("juveniles, light character comedy") and Mable Alberta ("juveniles and ingenues") – they were billed as "experienced and reliable" and toured all over the California theatre and vaudeville circuits, starting around 1907:

> Elmer Ballard is undoubtedly one of the cleverest and most resourceful comedians that ever appeared here, while Miss Mable Alberta's pleasing performances in widely varying roles have placed her high in the merits of the company.
>
> *Morning Press, Santa Barbara*, July 14, 1907

Elmer Ballard with Ann Harding in *Her Private Affair* (1929).

They joined the Rolin family of performers in the Spring of 1916, and remained in the ensemble for about a year – making it to some of the new "glasses character" shorts. On the occasion of Hal Roach's marriage to Marguerite Nichols the pair wrote and performed a poem about the romance at a studio dinner. This was later printed in the November 18, 1916 issue of the short-lived, gossipy weekly film newspaper *The Screamer* (which became *Motion Picture Times*). They opened with a description of the company:

Now listen movie actors if you want to know
About a story of love in a studio.
It happened at the "Rolin" – the home of Lonesome Luke,
I'll not call this a comedy, for fear of rebuke.

You all know the studio up on the hill
Where they make Rolin comedies with a punch and a thrill.
There's no room for swell-heads or snobbishness there:
Not a chance for a haughty indifferent stare
From stars and directors to extras and crew,
Not a grouch in the bunch – not a chance for the blues.

It then goes on about how the new leading lady appeared at the studio, won the heart of the boss, they got married, and only had a weekend trip for a honeymoon.

When they left Rolin it appears that Mable retired, but Elmer remained very busy. In 1918 and 1919 he appeared in the New York Broadway productions of *The Walk-Offs* and *Cappy Ricks*. When talkies hit the film industry he was very much in demand – appearing in features such as *Alibi*, *Her Private Affair* (both 1929), *The Squealer* (1930), *Consolation Marriage* (1931), and *Les Miserables* (1935). Mable died in 1934, but Elmer worked into the 1940s before passing away in 1947.

Moving Picture World (August 18, 1917): "Lonesome Luke is seen in another two-reel laugh festival entitled 'Lonesome Luke – Mechanic,' produced by Rolin under the direction of Hal Roach. With only a hammer Luke can take the mote out of any motor, and as the handy man around a garage he shows himself to be some fixer, while Snub has to have a lot of tools to do his work too. We have with us also Miss Speedboy, played by Bebe Daniels, and Bud Jamison as the garage owner adds the finishing touch. The climax comes when the garage catches on fire, and Luke puts it out by pouring all over it the gasoline which he sells at $1 a drop. 'It is better to fight fire with than water itself,' says he."

Moving Picture World (August 18, 1917): "A knockabout comedy number, featuring Harold Lloyd as a mechanic in a garage. All sorts of fun is had with the automobiles, and there are several moments that bring laughter. Not much of a plot, but plenty of action and small business."

Lonesome Luke's Wild Women*

Released September 2, 1917. Produced by Hal Roach for the Rolin Film Company. Distributed by Pathé. Working title: *Luke's Wild Women*. Extant: MoMA. Two reels. (Filmed from November 27-29 & December 6-14, 1916). Copyrighted August 8, 1917 (LU11216) by Pathé Exchange, Inc. With Harold Lloyd, Bebe Daniels, Snub Pollard, Gilbert Pratt, Gus Leonard, Bud

Jamison, Marie Mosquini, Margaret Joslin, Harry Todd, Charles Stevenson, Fred Newmeyer, Sammy Brooks, Billy Fay, Estelle Harrison, W.L. "Bumps" Adams, David "Slim" Voorhees, Sandy Roth, Max D. Hamburger, Clara Drey, Elmer Ballard.

In *Lonesome Luke's Wild Women* (1917) Harold cuddles with Margaret Joslin until he. gets a good look at Bebe.

Luke and Snub have been shipwrecked and are sailing around on a raft where they have all the comforts of home except the eats. They discover the isle of Gek where the Shah holds his court and harem. They are captured and brought before him, and he has them put in jail. Then they overhear a plot to overthrow the Shah. They get audience before him and he frees them to help him. Luke and Snub capture the mutineers and the Shah gives them freedom of the palace, except for one of his girls. In the excitement, they forget the Shah's orders, and when he catches them with his favorite dancer, he gets his men to throw them out. They take the dancer with them and all escape on the raft they had come on just as they see a ship approach. (Copyright description)

With the move to two-reelers Rolin was able to spend more on extras and production values. This surviving short (at MoMA) is a re-do of 1916's *Lonesome Luke Lolls in Luxury*, but this time on a more elaborate scale:

Big Set Built for "Luke" Comedy

Hal Roach and Dwight Whiting of the Rolin Company, makers of Pathé's "Luke" comedies, breathed a sigh of relief last week and for the first in days were able to stick their heads outside of the studio. The cause of it all was a gigantic oriental set which towers far above the street and runs back nearly a full block.

In building it they were able to use some of the massive stone steps, the former entrance to a large private house, which burned down years ago. The set required carloads of lumber and now that it is built would make a good Billy Sunday tabernacle.

Motion Picture News, January 13, 1917

Gilbert Pratt is going to get even with Harold in *Lonesome Luke's Wild Women* (1917).

The massive steps mentioned above are the entrance to the Sultan's palace. They're very impressive and make a good setting for lots of physical business. According to film location historian John Bengston, the opening shipwreck exteriors were shot outdoors on Dead Man's Island near San

Pedro, CA. Of course these Rolin harem comedies are just an excuse for Harold and Snub to flirt with all the pretty ladies (as if they needed an excuse) while they avoid the amorous advances of hefty Margaret Joslin. Mid-way through the film there's a long sequence of Snub with his girl, which is another dry run for the future solo Snub Pollard comedies.

Moving Picture World (September 1, 1917): "A two-reel comedy number, with Harold Lloyd, Harry Pollard and Bebe Daniels. It is a good number. The exterior scenes are very beautiful in themselves and the interiors, which shows an Oriental palace, quite sumptuous. The release relies more on incident and the individual work of the players and director than the story. It tells of two sailors, who reach a shah's palace and harem."

Besides the fun that is in every scene the cast contains the usual Rolin beauty congress. The many exhibitors who play these comedies will find 'Luke's Wild Women' a very popular number."

Moving Picture World (August 25, 1917): "In 'Luke's Wild Women,' a two-reel comedy to be released by Pathé on September 2, Harold Lloyd, the inimitable Rolin comedian and his fellow fun-makers, 'Snub' Pollard and Bebe Daniels, appear in a typical 'Lonesome Luke' Comedy full of rough house and original stunts.

'Luke' and 'Snub' as shipwrecked sailors find their way via raft to the shore of an Oriental country. Here they are captured and brought before the Sultan. They find him surrounded by fair women whose charms are such as to make them forget completely their perilous plight. The Sultan claps them into jail from which with laughable simplicity they soon make their escape. In revenge they soon turn the tables on their captor and engineer a very complete little revolution.

Lonesome Luke Loses Patients

Released September 16, 1917. Produced by Hal Roach for the Rolin Film Company. Distributed by Pathé. Working title: *Luke in Love, Loot and Leisure*. Two reels. (Filmed January 8 – 16, 21 – 27, 1917). Copyrighted August 25, 1917 (LU11292) by Pathé Exchange, Inc. With Harold Lloyd, Bebe Daniels, Snub Pollard, Bud Jamison, Harry Todd, Marie Mosquini, Charles Stevenson, Fred Newmeyer, Sammy Brooks, Margaret Joslin, Billy Fay, Estelle Harrison, Gus Leonard, Gilbert Pratt, Elmer Ballard, David "Slim" Voorhees, Max D. Hamburger, Joseph Kelly, Lois La Pearl, Irene Tyner, Vivian DeLadd, Leila Jocelin, Floyce Brown, Naomi Tucker, Evelyn Paige, Clara Drey, Della Mullady, Joe Turner, S.P. Woods, Sam Becker, Nina Speight.

Lonesome Luke is running a sanitarium for the idle rich that needs the same kind of rest as the tired businessman. It is noted among its patrons for the pretty nurses so that they like to be sick. It has all the comforts of his club, but with the nurses. A certain rich man on learning of this throws a fit to get in, and when his wife takes him in he slips Luke a hundred to say that he is sick. He tells the wife that he has swallowed a buffalo nickel and it is kicking him. When assured that there are only men attendants, she consents to leave hubby. Everything is fine until wife brings a basket for hubby. That is all right, but she leaves her handbag when leaving, and when she goes back for it suddenly takes them by surprise. She cannot find her husband so she goes away and plans a way to get even. She comes back as a man, and when she tells who she is a riot is started, and most everybody in the place winds up in the swimming pool with Luke at the bottom. (Copyright description)

Lonesome Luke Loses Patients (1917) but he gets a lot of attention from nurses
Bebe and Evelyn Paige.

This is Luke's third go-round with the medical profession, although as "Doctor Killem" it's his first time as a medical professional (or at least pretending to be). The location of a sanitarium was most likely "inspired" by Chaplin's recent hit *The Cure* (1917), and the setting was generally used in silent comedies to present a variety of eccentric characters such as in *Good Night Nurse!* (1918) with Fatty Arbuckle, *Bug House* (1919), George Bunny's

Why Worry? (1921), and *Always a Gentleman* (1928) where Lloyd Hamilton, and a group of "nuts" from a booby hatch, cause problems on a golf course. The horror-comedy feature *The Monster* (1925) had a more ominous spin with supervising administrator Lon Chaney much crazier than his supposed inmates.

While this film is missing today, a selection of titles were quoted in the September 15, 1917 *Moving Picture World*; "I hope you get well – or something," "This part requires practice and sang froid – whatever that is," "My middle name is Cuddle," "He swallowed a buffalo nickel and it's kicking him," and "I feel like a camel on the eighth day." Not exactly hilarious out of context.

Rolin Film Co. photo postcard of ingénue Irene Tyner. *Author's collection.*

Since the bevy of beauties play a prominent part at Luke's sanitarium, this is a good opportunity to talk about pretty blonde ingénue Irene Tyner. According to the *Motion Picture News* the nineteen-year-old came from "the chorus of a traveling musical show." Her first film work appears to have been for Josh Binney's Pacific Pictures Productions Co., and then she spent two years at the Rolin Company. She appeared in late *Lonesome Lukes* and early glasses character shorts such as this, *Lonesome Luke on Tin Can Alley*, *The Lamb* (all 1917), and *Look Pleasant, Please* (1918). After leaving Roach she became a Mack Sennett bathing girl under the name Irene Tiver in shorts like *By Golly!* (1920), *She Sighed by the Seaside* (1921), and the feature *Married Life* (1920). She retired from films soon after, and passed away in 1950.

Moving Picture World (September 8, 1917): "In this comedy we find 'Luke' running a sanitarium which is a regular bonanza because of the big staff of hand-picked beauties whom he has secured as nurses. The sanitarium is very popular with men whose wives do not stack up in the pulchritude class. In this fact lies the undoing of the sanitarium. Wives visiting husbands who have suddenly claimed of being ill after seeing Luke's nurses find their hubbies need chaperones."

Motion Picture News (September 15, 1917): "Harold Lloyd is seen as the proprietor of a sanitarium in this number – a sanitarium where henpecked husbands repair to be attended by cohorts of pretty nurses. An extremely old flirt is brought on, tendered to the care of Bebe Daniels, while his frantic wife makes all sorts of attempts to discover whether he is playing possum or not. At length she learns the truth and after she possesses the knowledge Dr. Luke's place is very much of a wreck.

Lloyd appears in fine raiment in this comedy. Dressed in a cutaway and other accessories, and smoking cigarettes in a long holder, he affects a studied nonchalance that is thoroughly amusing throughout. The action is slower than in the last Rolin two-reeler and gives the principals more opportunity to register comical bits of business."

Birds of a Feather*

Released October 7, 1917. Produced by Hal Roach for the Rolin Film Company. Distributed by Pathé. Extant: BRUS. Working title: *Luke in Birds of a Feather*. Two reels. (Filmed March 26 – April 7, 1917). Copyrighted September 12, 1917 (LU11086) by Pathé Exchange, Inc. With Harold Lloyd, Bebe Daniels, Snub Pollard, Margaret Joslin, Harry Todd, Billy Fay, Bud

Jamison, Fred Newmeyer, Charles Stevenson, Sammy Brooks, Dorothea Wolbert, Lottie Case, Max D. Hamburger, W.L. "Bumps" Adams, David "Slim" Voorhees, Gilbert Pratt, Evelyn Paige, Nina Speight.

Bebe and Harry Todd watch Margaret Joslin give Harold the stink-eye in *Birds of a Feather* (1917).

Lonesome Luke and Snub run a lunch cart in Hottentot Village when a lawyer appears one day and tells Luke that he is heir to a million and a house on the Drive. He takes Snub with him and gives him a job in a monkey suit like all the other servants. Mr. and Mrs. Poindexter have been appointed by the lawyer to show Luke how to be a gentleman, etc. Immediately a mother and daughter appear to make a call and at the same time another does the same. After some difficulty Luke gets into new clothes and receives his guests. He soon gets the two girls fighting with each other. Mrs. Poindexter, however, invites them to dinner that night and they accept. At the appointed hour Luke appears in his "soup and fish" and starts to eat with the rest, but when he tries to serve the turkey it finally lands in one of the ladies' lap. Disgusted, he goes into the other room and gets into a scrap with Snub, whom he sends reeling back into the dining room table and upsetting it. The guests all leave in disgust, so Luke sends Snub to get the gang from Hottentot Hollow and they will have "a regular feed." (Copyright description)

Like *Great While It Lasted* (1915), *Luke's Society Mix-Up*, and *Luke, Rank Impersonator* (both 1916) before, *Birds of a Feather* sees Luke graduating to a high society setting where he sticks out like a sore thumb.

Joining the Roach organization around this time was Harley Marquis Walker, best known as H.M. Walker. This future dean of silent comedy title writers began his professional career as a telegrapher, where he tapped out the reports of boxing matches and sent them to newspapers. He became a sportswriter himself in 1903, and wrote the column *The Wisdom of Blinkey Ben* for the *Los Angeles Examiner*.

H.M. Walker (center) on the set of *Why Worry?* (1923) with Fred Newmeyer, Hal Roach, Harold, and Robert "Red" Golden.

The fall of 1917 saw Walker, on his time off from the *Examiner*, start as a part-time title and scenario writer for the *Luke* shorts. By 1920, he left sports writing to become the head of the Roach editorial department. For the next decade, his witty and pithy intertitles graced and added much to the studio's output. With the arrival of sound Walker proved less skillful with dialogue, but continued to title each film and write detailed critiques after previews until 1932. Later he worked on features such as the Zasu Pitts/Slim

Summerville comedies *They Just Had to Get Married* (1932), *Her First Mate* (1933), and *Love Birds* (1934), as well as W.C. Fields' *The Old Fashioned Way* (1934), and *The Affair of Susan* (1935). Walker passed away from a heart attack in 1937.

One of the more obscure among the regular Rolin supporting players was Lottie Case, a dark-haired, heavy-set older character lady. A long-time stage veteran as Lottie Somers, she grew up as part of the Somers Family Musical Company with her parents and sister Nellie. Married to theatre manager George Case, she entered pictures in 1915 and appeared with American, the Alhambra Film Manufacturing Company, and in some Baby Early comedies for Universal:

> Lottie Case, who has been with the American and Universal companies, has been added to the Rolin studios and will play characters under the direction of Gil Pratt.
>
> *Motography,* September 16, 1916

Having appeared in a number of Luke shorts, she stayed around for some of Harold's first glasses character shorts like *The Flirt* (1917) and *Here Comes the Girls* (1918), before dropping out of performing and becoming a film cutter.

Motion Picture News (October 13, 1917): "Harold Lloyd, better known as Lonesome Luke, and his large group of clever team mates strike their old stride in 'Birds of a Feather,' a fast and furious and funny stride that never abates in any of its departments. The comedy is typical Rolin stuff – there's a lot of kicking, falling and fighting, all done in such a nonchalant way that it registers as unusual, comic rough-house. In between the more conventional gags are interspersed a number of new ones that display the inventive genius of the producers to good advantage.

'Birds of a Feather' introduces Luke as the owner of a lunch counter. He comes into a million and thereupon makes his debut into 'smart society' to rather disastrous effect. He finally throws all his fashionable guests out of his house, and subsequently opens the doors to all his old friends."

From London to Laramie*

Released October 21, 1917. Produced by Hal Roach for the Rolin Film Company. Distributed by Pathé. Extant: OTT. Two reels. (Filmed March 8 – 24 & June 5, 1916). Copyrighted October 8, 1917 (LU11530) by Pathé Exchange, Inc. With Harold Lloyd, Bebe Daniels, Snub Pollard, Bud Jamison, Harry Todd, Marie Mosquini, Charles Stevenson, Fred Newmeyer,

Sammy Brooks, Billy Fay, Gus Leonard, Gilbert Pratt, Nina Speight, Dorothea Wolbert, Mabel Ballard, Evelyn Paige, W.L. (Bumps) Adams, Max D. Hamburger, John Christian, Bud Zelofer, Fred Jefferson, Della Mullady, Margaret Joslin.

Lord Algernon Snub and his valet, Luke, get off the train somewhere in Wyoming on their way to visit Snub's sister and her family at her husband's ranch. They are unable to find means of conveyance, except two old mules who have ideas of their own as to carrying freight, and soon lose their passengers. After some hard travel on foot, they strike the Bob-Cat Ranch stage and are taken on board. They are then held up by "Poison-Teeth" Brady and all their wealth is taken from them, but while Brady is trying to kiss a pretty little passenger Luke takes back everything. They finally arrive at the ranch and are cordially received by Mrs. Blair, but Betty, the daughter, and Brindle Blair, the owner of the ranch, do not take to them. Luke tries to be intimate with the cowboys but they will not stand for it. Snub has to sleep with Brindle and cannot because of such snoring, so both he and Luke sleep in the hay in the yard. The next day Brady comes into camp and demands food, which he gets at the point of a gun. When he finishes he takes Betty away with him and Luke chases after her and rescues her. Then Brady puts the Indians on the trail, and after Luke has beaten them off, Betty rushes to him with open arms, much to the disgust of Brindle Blair. (Copyright description)

Glass slide for *From London to Laramie* (1917).

The cleaned-up version of Luke continues to appear, this time as the effete valet of an equally effete British lord. This is a bit of a semi-western parody, with Luke and Snub as fish out of water in the wild and wooly surroundings.

From London to Laramie highlights a supporting player, like the previously mentioned W. L. "Bumps" Adams, who, after leaving the Rolin organization, would spend the rest of his career on the fringes of the film industry working for very extremely low-budget companies. After his days with Rolin, Fred Jefferson would go on to direct two of the most justly forgotten comedians of the silent era. Born in Australia, Jefferson came to the United States in 1899, with his film career starting at Universal in 1914. Around that time, he also appeared in some of the pre-Lonesome Luke Rolin endeavors. He can be spotted in photos for *Why the Boarders Left* and *The Fall of Lady Sampson*, and appeared as well in the drama *Into the Light* (1915).

Fred Jefferson (right) is a minister trying to bring calm to Martha Mattox, Mark Jones, Agnes Steele, Harold and Jane Novak in what may be *Why the Boarders Left* (1915).

Although not in the very first *Luke* shorts, Jefferson did eventually return to the fold. A September 9, 1916 item from the *Motion Picture News* describes a number of Rolin players that were hurt when a truck hit a studio car that was transporting them, adding "Fred Jefferson was the most unfortunate, sustaining a fracture of the collar bone in the fall." By December he'd been promoted to an assistant director, and worked behind and in front of the camera through 1917. After a 1918 break he returned for 1919 shorts like *Ask Father* and *The Marathon*, where he performed the famous "mirror routine" with Harold.

1920 saw Jefferson break out on his own and become director of two almost-off-the-radar series of independent comedy shorts. While overplaying his background at Rolin a bit –

> Mr. Jefferson is a comedy director of many years experience, having been with the Rolin company for many years directing Harold Lloyd, "Snub" Pollard and Bebe Daniels.
>
> *Moving Picture World*, February 26, 1921

his "stars" were George LeRoi Clarke and Denver Dixon. Clarke was an ordained Baptist minister who left his congregation to become a movie comic. Produced by an outfit named Paragon Pictures, the films were eventually released by Reelcraft Pictures, and survivors such as *The Lady Bug* and *Pussyfoot* (both 1920) prove that Reverend Clarke should have stuck with the pulpit.

The other poverty row series headlined Victor Adamson under the alliterative name of Denver Dixon. Produced by Plymouth Pictures, Inc., shorts like *The Goof* and *Snubbed* (1921) were underwhelming so Dixon moved on to producing low-budget silent and sound westerns, as well as playing bit parts in mainstream Hollywood films until 1966. Later his son Al Adamson carried on the grade-Z tradition with films such as *Psycho a Go Go* (1965) and *Dracula Vs. Frankenstein* (1971). Neither the Clarke nor Dixon series lasted very long, so Jefferson bounced around – directing a short or two for Schiller Productions in Yonkers, and a few non-theatrical biblical shorts for the Pictorial Club of New York. Getting further and further away from Hollywood the November 6, 1929 issue of *Variety* announced:

> Eska Wilson has taken Gladys McConnell and Hugh Allan to Honolulu to play leads in four productions for Jefferson-Hawaiian Films. First one "Aloha" from story by Carleton King. Some for distribution through national string of non-theatrical exchanges. No release yet obtained on the dramatic features.
>
> Wilson is president of Jefferson-Hawaiian Films and also of Standard M.P. Service.

Said Ms. Wilson was arrested in 1930 for abandoning the actors after the company ran out of funds, and it was even said that for a while Jefferson was "shooting" scenes without film in the camera to keep up the pretext of a viable company. From here the last mention of him is in the November 12, 1932 *Hollywood Filmograph*, where he's listed as the director of *Rose of Manila* starring LaMont Valencia for San Francisco's Manila Pictures Co. His last occupations were photographer and movie extra before his death from a heart attack in 1952.

Fred Jefferson (center in cap) directing Denver Dixon (in top hat being choked) and company somewhere in Long Beach, CA circa 1920. *Author's Collection.*

Moving Picture World (October 20, 1917): "With Harry Pollard as 'Lord Algernon,' Harold Lloyd as 'Lonesome Luke,' his valet, Bud Jamison as 'Brindle Pup' and Bebe Daniels as 'Betty Pup,' his daughter. When Lord Algernon arrives with his valet and about twenty trunks at Bob Cat Ranch things begin to happen. The boys put the Englishmen through their paces and at the end Lonesome Luke puts one over on them. Having adopted their own tactics, he tells them: 'I'll riddle the first man that follows us' and beats it for the tall timbers with the Belle of Bob Cat."

Moving Picture World (October 27, 1917): "The comedy will take its place among the very best of the rough and tumble playlets that Mr. Roach knows so well how to produce."

Intelligencer Journal (November 27, 1917): "The initial performance Monday afternoon of the show now running at the Colonial Theatre, was enjoyed by a big audience. As usual the entertainment opened with the moving pictures and they were capital, an interesting installment of the Pathé News being followed by a two-reel comedy, 'Lonesome Luke From London to Laramie.' It was one of the funniest of the Lonesome Luke series depicting Luke's trouble with a bunch of husky cowboys, and gave the screen favorite opportunity to display his remarkable ability as a horseman. The picture also affords excellent roles for Bebe Daniels and Harry Pollard, the comical 'Snubs.'"

Love, Laughs and Lather*

Released November 4, 1917. Produced by Hal Roach for the Rolin Film Company. Distributed by Pathé. Extant: BRUS, OTT. Working title: *Luke in Love, Laughs and Lather*. Two reels. (Filmed January 29 – February 14, 1917). Copyrighted October 19, 1917 (LU11588) by Pathé Exchange, Inc. With Harold Lloyd, Bebe Daniels, Snub Pollard, Harry Todd, Wallace Howe, Gilbert Pratt, Gus Leonard, Fred Newmeyer, Billy Fay, Nina Speight, Bud Jamison, Charles Stevenson, Dorothea Wolbert, Mabel Ballard, Evelyn Paige, W. L. "Bumps" Adams, Sammy Brooks, Max D. Hamburger, Harry Rindfleish, David "Slim" Voorhees, Chris Lynton, Wallace Howe.

Lonesome Luke lives in one of the worst – not the worst – boarding houses, and while dressing one morning he kicks a shoe out of the window. He cannot find it so he goes down to breakfast without it. The pretty waitress tells him that she found it and it is under his chair. After fishing around under the table he finally gets it but the party is broken up by one of the other boarders choking himself. The waitress loses her job for upsetting a tray and Luke takes pity on her gives her a dollar and his card for the barber shop where he works. Luke reports for duty by taking a taxi to a store that has two entrances, and leaves the cab and goes through the store and on to work. He has all sorts of customers and his manicurist gets sore and quits her job, but the pretty waitress shows up all dolled up on the dollar that Luke gave her. Then a husky westerner comes in and after nearly shooting up the place, Luke hits him over the head and leads him out. The waitress throws up her job as Luke hits the westerner when he was not looking. Then the taxi driver, getting tired of waiting for Luke, decides to get a shave and when he sees Luke, a fight starts in which they chase Luke all around the place. Finally, Luke gets out to the street and grabbing the first moving vehicle that he sees; he soon out-distances the rest. However before he has gone far two hands reach out and grab him and he finds that he is on a police wagon on the way to the station. (Copyright description)

Bebe, Chris Lynton, Snub, and Wallace Howe watch Harold give it to Harry Todd in the eye in *Love, Laughs and Lather* (1917).

Luke as a barber harks back to the early Rolin effort *A Barber for a Day / Close-Cropped Clippings* (1915). Since men frequently paid for shaves in those days, barber shops were a steady location for silent comedy shorts. Inept barbers ran rampant in shorts like *A Barber Cure* (1913) and the Hallroom Boys' *A Close Shave* (1920). When not shooting ducks Billy Bevan scrapes faces in *The Duck Hunter* (1922), while Andy Clyde gets a shave and a trim from Anna May the elephant in *Smith's Candy Shop* (1927). The Chaplin Brothers were very fond of spoofing men's toilette, and Syd started it off in his Keystone *Giddy, Gay and Ticklish* (1915) and the missing feature *King, Queen, Joker* (1921). Charlie experimented with a shaving sequence that he didn't keep in *Sunnyside* (1919), but ended up making one of the most memorable shaving routines ever for *The Great Dictator* (1940).

Possibly the funniest barbershop sequence is in the Roscoe Arbuckle-directed *Stupid But Brave* (1924). This five-minute segment is set in Tony Toenaili's Tonsorial Parlor. Al St John is led to believe that they give free shaves to men in need, but Al finds out that he's been tricked the moment he's strapped in the barber chair and gets a look at the tough pug-ugly barbers Jimmy Bryant, Steve Murphy, Johnny Sinclair, and Kewpie Morgan. Morgan begins to operate on Al, and a number of times twists his head completely backwards for better cutting access. This startling scene is close to an animated cartoon – when Morgan twists Al's head around it immediately spins back – and although it's easy to see how the trick was done, it's still initially a surprise and very impressive. This hilarious sequence is the culmination of shaving routines that Arbuckle had done previously in *His Wife's Mistake* (1916) and *The Bell Boy* (1918).

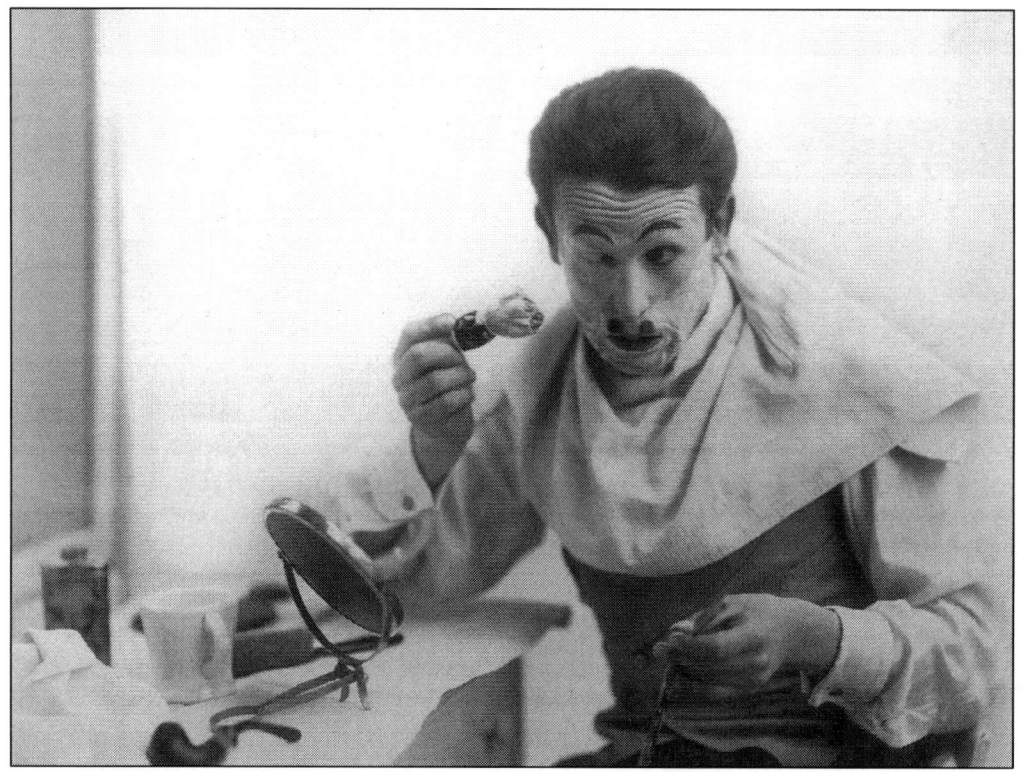

Harold practices his shaving technique on himself in *Love, Laughs, and Lather* (1917).

This late-run *Luke* features two new supporting players who would become mainstays in the new Harold Lloyd glasses character shorts (as well as the Hal Roach product in general). Chris Lynton was an older gentleman who was always on hand as professors, hotel guests, dock officials, and the leading lady's father. Having become a stage actor in the 1890s, he came to films in 1915, appearing in features such as *The Puppet Crown* and *A Yankee from the West*. In 1917, he settled on the Rolin lot, and besides the Lloyd films, he supported Eddie Boland, Paul Parrott, Our Gang, and Charley Chase into 1926. Having taught drama at Davis Musical College in Los Angeles in the 1920s, he appeared on and off on film until around 1932, and passed away in 1952.

Wallace Howe would become one of the most ubiquitous faces in silent comedy. So versatile that he was something of the genre's Lon Chaney, it's difficult to mention a specific, identifiable persona for him. Coming from West Coast vaudeville and theatre where he supported headliners like Lorraine Buchanan and Phillis Place, he acted in plays such as *The Girl Detective* and *The Slaves of Passion* before entering films in 1917. He took up residence at the Hal Roach Studio, and appeared in every Lloyd short and feature, as well as most of the Roach oeuvre from the late Teens through the 1920s.

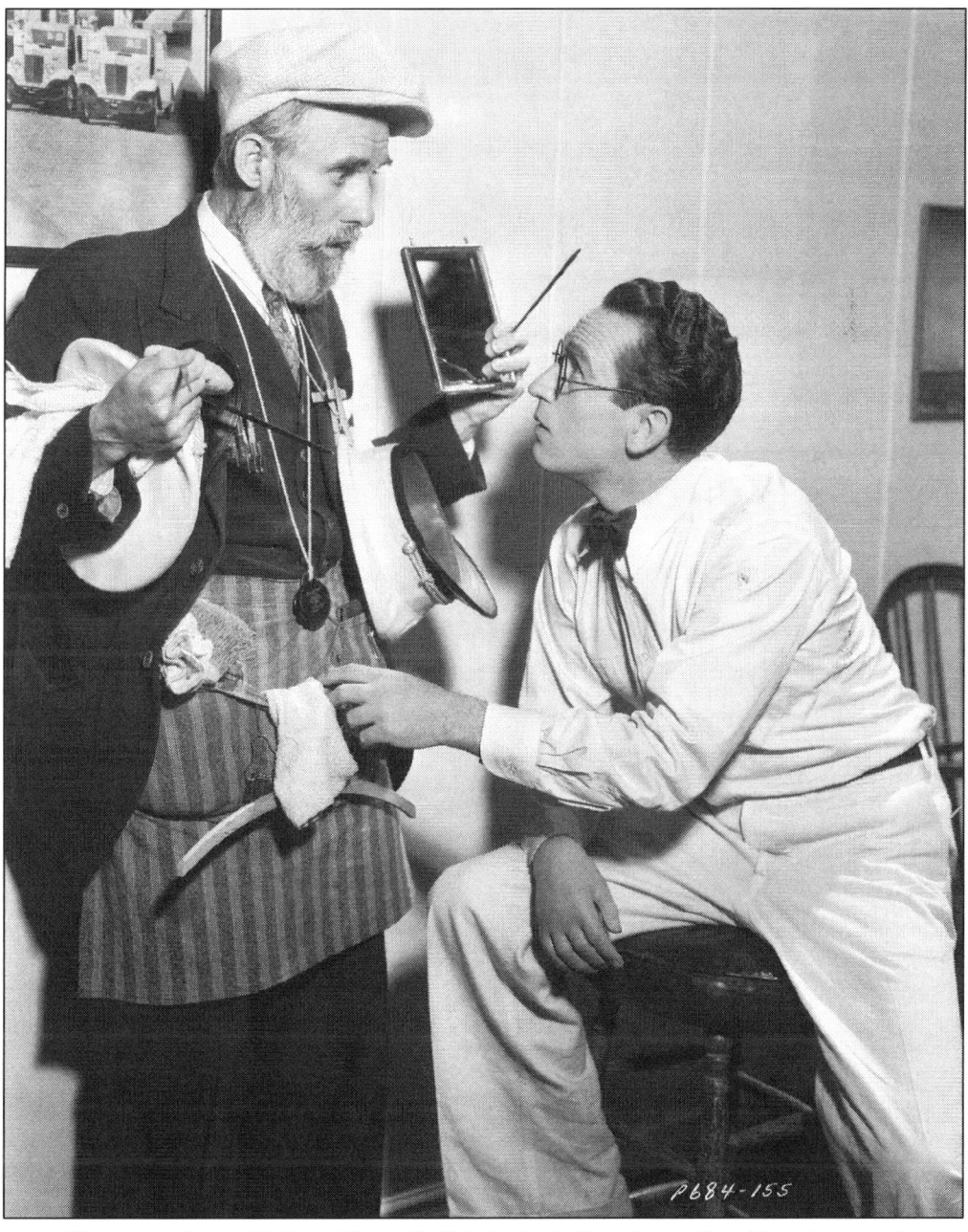

Character player Wallace Howe (left) is jack-of-all-trades to Harold on the set of *The Milky Way* (1936). *Courtesy of Jorge Finkielman.*

Turning up as shifty lawyers, crusty old men, seedy tramps, inept policemen, or feuding hillbillies, he was indispensable in the films of Lloyd, Snub Pollard, Our Gang, Eddie Boland, Stan Laurel and Will Rogers. He also did bits in the Lloyd-produced Edward Everett Horton shorts. Over the years, his bits got smaller, but he continued with an important position in the Lloyd organization:

> Bewhiskered little old Wallace Howe, valet and handyman, fussing over Harold Lloyd in the same capacity for over seventeen years. Somewhere in every Lloyd opus, Howes' face peeks out in a bit.
>
> *Photoplay*, October 1935

His last film appearance was in Harold's 1936 *The Milky Way*, and he died in 1957.

Moving Picture World (October 27, 1917): "'Lonesome Luke in Love, Laughs and Lather' shows our hero in the new and comical role of a barber. Every man, unless he cuts his own hair and shaves himself, will find this burlesque on a business with which he is in almost daily contact, laughable in the extreme. Harold Lloyd shines as the dandified barber who is less a slave to his profession than he is to the beauty of woman kind."

Moving Picture World (November 10, 1917): "An extremely laughable two-reel number featuring Harold Lloyd, Harry Pollard and Bebe Daniels. Both the scenes at the boarding house and in the barber shop are good: the latter, in fact are hilarious as anything recently shown. This is an exceptional comedy of the knock-about sort."

The Hutchinson News (February 2, 1918): "This is a 2-reel Lonesome Luke comedy and after you have seen one of these great fun producers you won't need to be told that there is a big time in store for you when a Lonesome Luke comedy is shown."

Clubs are Trump*

Released November 18, 1917. Produced by Hal Roach for the Rolin Film Company. Distributed by Pathé. Extant: BRUS, LOC, LOB. Working title: *Luke in Clubs are Trump*. Two reels. (Filmed April 10 – 25 & May 1 & 9, 1917). Copyrighted October 20, 1917 (LU11593) by Pathé Exchange, Inc. With Harold Lloyd, Bebe Daniels, Snub Pollard, Nina Speight, Evelyn Paige, Margaret Joslin, Marie Mosquini, Bud Jamison, Fred Newmeyer, Billy Fay, Gilbert Pratt, Sammy Brooks, David "Slim" Voorhees, William Blaisdell, Virginia Baynes, Ruth Rowan, Grace McLernon, Ruth Churchill.

Clubs are Trump (1917) finds Evelyn Paige, Margaret Joslin, Marie Mosquini and the other cavewomen jealous of Bebe and Harold.

Lonesome Luke and Snub are enjoying a pleasant afternoon in the park eating peanuts and they spy several loving couples. They decide to intrude and get one for themselves. They do not receive a cordial welcome and soon find themselves in the lake. Resigned to their own loneliness, they lay down on a bench to sleep. They dream of pre-historic days when men fought for their girls. They are strangers in the camp and Luke is put to work grinding corn while Snub has to make fire by rubbing sticks. They get out of this into more trouble, until they finally knock out all the men and grab two girls and start loving them. At this point they wake up and are chased by a cop, but they are corralled between the lovers and the cops and finally escape in a boat. (Copyright description)

This is another *Luke* comedy that's available to be viewed online – preserved and posted by Belgium's Brussels Cinematek. The framing story takes place in one of L.A.'s ubiquitous parks, but the bulk of the short is Luke and Snub's mutual dream of finding themselves in the Stone Age. While there are lots of pretty cave ladies, the pair doesn't fare very well with the hulking Neanderthal men. Oddly enough, the whole thing looks like a bit of a dry run for the later serious Hal Roach feature *One Million B.C.* (1940).

Long before *The Flintstones*, prehistoric times were fodder for film comedy – live-action and animation. After D.W. Griffith's drama *Man's Genesis* (1912) made a big impression, comedies quickly followed suit, and Charlie Chaplin's

Harold cracks a coconut with the help of a patient gator in *Clubs are Trump* (1917).

His Prehistoric Past (1914) led the way. Besides *Clubs are Trump*, other stone age comedy shorts included *Wooed by a Wild Man* (1915) from Kalem, Earl Montgomery and Joe Rock's *Caves and Coquettes* (1919), and the Century Comedy *Hit 'Em Hard* (1924), as well as the features *Fig Leaves* (1926), the British-made *The Prehistoric Man* (1924), and most famously *Three Ages* (1923) with Buster Keaton.

The Hal Roach people returned Snub Pollard to the dawn of time in his starring short *The Stone Age* (1922), and did the same for Laurel & Hardy with *Flying Elephants* (1927). Cartoon's prehistoric tour kicked off with *Gertie the Dinosaur* (1914), and moved on to various entries of *Tony Sarg's Almanac*, *Aesop's Fables*, *Oswald the Lucky Rabbit*, and finally Max Fleischer's 1940 series of *Stone Age Cartoons*. Among the later live-action features and TV shows are *It's About Time* (1966), *Caveman* (1981), *Encino Man* (1992), and *Year One* (2008).

Two young actresses who were regulars in the latter *Luke* shorts were Evelyn Paige and Nina Speight. Ms. Paige was a pretty, California-born blonde, who began her career in dramas for the Lubin Company such as *A Sister to Cain* and *The Rough Neck* (both 1916). In 1917 she switched her allegiance to comedy with Rolin, and besides appearing in *Lonesome Luke* outings like *Lonesome Luke Loses Patients* and *Lonesome Luke, Messenger*, she was in many of Harold's first glasses character one-reelers. Titles include *Pinched*, *Bashful* (both 1917), *The Tip*, *Look Pleasant, Please* and *Let's Go* (all 1918). Following the April 28, 1918 release *Hey There!* she left the screen.

> Nina Speight, who has appeared in several photoplays taken at Manly (Sidney) is leaving this month for the U.S.A., with a view to trying her luck in pictures. In addition to her appearances before the camera, Miss Speight has had stage experience with Pollard's Opera Company, and with a partner in a dancing turn in vaudeville.
>
> But it is as an artist's model that she has become known. She is the possessor of much beauty and charm, and was much sought after by prominent artists for face and neck studies.
>
> She gives great promise of a successful career in the pictures.
>
> *Moving Picture World*, April 22, 1916

The dark and exotic-looking Ms. Speight was born in Austria, but raised in Australia, where she appeared on stage performing a seduction "vampire" dance, posed as an artist's model, and had movie roles for the Australian Life Biograph and Frazer Films. Working with the Pollard Opera Company means she may have crossed professional paths with Snub Pollard, which led to her appearance in the *Lukes*.

Also known as Sapphire Speight, she joined the Rolin family in February of 1917, and usually stands out in shorts such as *Lonesome Luke Loses Patients* and *From London to Laramie* thanks to her unusual looks. In *Clubs are Trump* she does a bit of a dance for caveman Bud Jamison, whose reaction is to choke her and roll her off a cliff where she's caught below by Luke. Like Evelyn Paige, she moved on to many of Harold's glasses character shorts, as well as turning up with Toto, and in a couple of 1921 Eddie Boland shorts like *A Straight Crook* and *Stop Kidding*. Despite getting something of a build-up in many of the movie trade magazines, her career didn't seem to take off and ended by 1921.

Clubs are Trump also marks one of the first Hal Roach appearances of William Blaisdell.

> The Rolin Company announced two additions to their roster. William Blaisdell, formerly of the Balboa Company, has been engaged at the studios. Mr. Blaisdell was associated for some time with Edward Howard of Howard and North, and his experience on the speaking stage covers a period of seventeen years.
>
> *Motion Picture News*, May 26, 1917

Evelyn Paige and Nina Speight are on call as nurses in *Lonesome Luke Loses Patients* (1917), while in *Bride and Gloom* (1918) William Blaisdell (right) makes a trio with Harold and little Sammy Brooks.

Although his real first name was Charles, he was known as "Big Bill" and took the role of heavy (often Bebe's father or unwanted suitor) in the stock company of Harold's glasses character shorts. After three years and numerous one-reelers at Roach he moved on, menacing Monty Banks for a couple of years in his Warner Brothers and Grand-Asher shorts such as *A Bedroom Scandal* (1921), *Paging Love* (1923), and *The Golf Bug* (1924). Also appearing in Century Comedies, from 1925 on Blaisdell worked almost exclusively with Christie Comedies. Although there would be an occasional side trip to Educational and Roach for shorts such as *Waiting* (1925) and *Crazy Like a Fox* (1926), or a feature like *The Yankee Clipper* (1927), almost all of his screen time was spent as a foil for Christie headliners like Jimmie Adams, Neal Burns, Bobby Vernon, and Billy Dooley. Blaisdell disappeared with sound, and according to his *Variety* obituary died in 1930 at the age of fifty-six.

Moving Picture World (November 17, 1917): "'Clubs are Trumps' is one of those swift-moving, original burlesques which have given the Rolin people an enviable reputation as comedy producers. Lloyd and Pollard appear as cave-men of a particular funny type. Their endeavors to secure for themselves some of the many pretty girls, of whom the woods are full, are laughable in the extreme."

We Never Sleep

Released December 2, 1917. Produced by Hal Roach for the Rolin Film Company. Distributed by Pathé. Working title: *Luke in We Never Sleep*. Two reels. (Filmed May 4 -5, 10, June 2, 1917). Copyrighted October 20, 1917 (LU11600) by Pathé Exchange, Inc. With Harold Lloyd, Bebe Daniels, Snub Pollard, Charles Stevenson, Margaret Joslin, Bud Jamison, Sammy Brooks, Billy Fay, Gus Leonard, Harry Todd, Gilbert Pratt, Fred Newmeyer, Nina Speight, Dorothea Wolbert, Mabel Ballard, Evelyn Paige, W. L. "Bumps" Adams, Max D. Hamburger, Harry Rindfleish, David "Slim" Voorhees, Ruth Churchill, Golda Madden, Ray Braxton, Rudolph Black, Marie Mosquini, Della Mullady, Walter Stile.

Harold and Snub are supplicated by Sammy Brooks, Margaret Joslin, Bebe, Bud Jamison, Charles Stevenson, and Billy Fay in the final *Luke* opus *We Never Sleep* (1917).

Lonesome Luke and his associate Snub are put on the trail of Biff Bailey as they both admit that they are the greatest detectives living. They have his picture as a clue and start for the beach. At the station they encounter a man answering the description of the photograph and proceed to help his wife to the seashore. The supposed Biff follows on foot, as he had been sent to get milk for the baby before the train started. At the Ocean Mist Inn Luke announces that he is a great detective and tells all the girls that if they will help him catch the crook they will get their pictures in the paper. The plans are laid and just as Biff arrives, he is arrested. After a fight they get him cornered and caught but Luke receives a telegram telling him that the real Biff had been caught and he was discharged from the case. After the name that Luke had made for himself at the Inn, there was nothing for him to do but make all haste in his departure and his feet were better than any of those who tried to follow him. (Copyright description)

In the Harold Lloyd one-reel comedies the star is seen in a characterization entirely different from anything he had yet done. It is absolutely distinct from "Lonesome Luke."

Motion Picture News, September 1, 1917

Since the release of *Over the Fence* on September 9. 1917, audiences and exhibitors had been treated to two Harold Lloyds, as the *Luke* two-reelers alternated with the new glasses character one-reelers. Luke's popularity had built up steadily over the three years of his screen life, but it would be nothing compared to the ascent of Harold's new character, although that rise was still in the future. At the moment of change Pathé and Hal Roach were reluctant to let go of Luke as he had become a film comedy staple:

We wired Pathé, but they threw a fit. They said they'd spent thousands of dollars making Lonesome Luke well known. Nobody had ever heard of Harold Lloyd. I'd never had my name on the screen. They weren't going to throw Lonesome Luke over for an unknown.

Photoplay, June 1924

But, with the determination that carried him through his entire life and career, Harold had had enough of Luke and told Roach that if his new character wasn't approved he was quitting and going into dramatic films. Reluctantly Roach agreed to speak to Pathé:

Privately I believed that Pathé would conclude to hire another comedian and carry on with Lonesome Luke. Audiences would detect the substitution, but the picture was Luke, not Lloyd. Roach, however, argued my case better than I could have done, and won. He wired back that Pathé consented. Did I wish to make one or two-reel pictures in the new character?

An American Comedy, 1928

One-reelers were decided upon as the way to introduce audiences to the new persona. Also Pathé held back the release of the later Luke two-reelers to alternate with the new glasses character shorts as a sort of insurance policy in case the new character didn't fly. A key element for Harold was that the new series was branded "Harold Lloyd Comedies," putting his name above the title and production company. After his hardscrabble start in the film industry as an extra in 1913 Harold was really starting to arrive as a movie star.

> Until recently "Lonesome Luke" has been the mainstay of the Pathé farces. Unlike most comedians, this nimble person does not confine himself to one guise. I like him best with the big tortoise shell spectacles.
>
> *Photoplay*, February 1918

After *We Never Sleep* Harold was through with Luke, but his belief that someone else would take over the role would come to pass in a couple of years.

Motion Picture News (December 1, 1917): "This Rolin number features Harold Lloyd and Snub Pollard as detectives on the trail of a bank robber. They shadow a suspect and his pretty wife all the way to the seashore and capture him only after a great deal of effort, but all their work proves futile as immediately they receive word that the real robber has been caught. As a result, they are chased from the hotel in shame.

This makes an average comedy number – average for Rolin – considerably above it remembering the ordinary product of the day. Lloyd will certainly get a hearty laugh on his introduction and his subsequent activities on board the sleeper and at the beach are responsible for not a little comedy of the typical Lonesome Luke variety.

In addition, there are half a dozen pretty girls, without which apparently a comedy cannot be up-to-date, who lend complementary interest to the beach scenes. Bebe Daniels as the wife of the suspect and Bud Jamison as that gentleman himself, complete the quartette of principals."

Exhibitor ad for the concurrent Luke and new glasses character shorts.
It's already clear that Luke was on his way out.

CHAPTER THREE: LUKE'S LEGACY

Gaylord Lloyd ponders Lonesome Luke's extended life.

Lonesome Luke was laid to rest with *We Never Sleep* (1917), so Harold was free to happily focus on his new glasses character. At first his bespectacled young man showed a strong Luke streak – when material was needed their fallback was a reliance on hitting and kicking – but soon, as the character's everyman characteristics continued to develop, this would disappear. But it turned out that Luke was not totally dead – only dormant. A couple of years later another came along to give him a last gasp.

Luke had been a successful box office commodity, and Hal Roach, never one to let a proven asset die, passed the franchise on:

Lonesome Luke Comedies Prepared

Arrangements have been completed to launch Gaylord Lloyd, brother of Harold Lloyd, as a comedy star. He will impersonate the Luke character originated by his brother. Four pictures to be released soon will mark his debut.

Camera!, August 27, 1921

Exhibitor ad for Luke's short-lived revival.

In a November 1921 interview for *Picture-Play Magazine* Gaylord says that Roach and Harold wanted him to take over Luke right at the time that his brother had given it up, but the elder Lloyd had other ideas:

> Well, 'see, it came about this way. Hal Roach and my brother wanted to me to star when I came to California. Roach said he thought that I could revive my brother's character of *Lonesome Luke*, which had always been a favorite with him.
>
> But as I had just been operated on for appendicitis I didn't feel that it was a good time to begin. So I told them I'd rather wait. I said I'd like to start in and learn more about films, because all my experience had been on the stage.
>
> I began by doing some extra work in Harold's first two-reelers. I used to play Chinamen most of the time – because I happened to get a good make-up at the start. Then, after a bit I commenced doubling.
>
> I began doubling for Harold about two years ago, and for a while I did all the stunt stuff, like the riding in that burlesque on the Westerns, and driving the Ford car through fences and buildings in "Get Out and Get Under." I worked in most of the long shots, while Harold did the close-ups.

This last statement about his doubling for Harold created a bit of controversy at the time:

> Gaylord Lloyd once got himself into a hot box at the studio by confessing to an interviewer – who didn't know anymore than to go and print what he said – that he doubled for brother Harold, driving the Ford through fences and buildings for "Get Out and Get Under" and doing the railroad stunts for "Now or Never." Quickly hushed up, Gaylord has been most inconspicuous.
>
> *Picture-Play Magazine*, September 1923

As it was expected that slapstick comedians for the most part did their own stunts, the Roach studio did a little backpedaling on this, and re-interpreted Gaylord's comments.

A total of five updated *Luke* Comedies with Gaylord were released. The first shot was *Trolley Troubles*, which ended up being released last. The initial entry that the public saw was *Rough Seas*.

Gaylord strikes a familiar Luke pose.

Rough Seas*

Released September 25, 1921. Produced by Hal Roach for the Rolin Film Company. Distributed by Pathé. Directed by Alfred Goulding. Story by Hal Roach. Extant: UCLA. One reel. Copyrighted October 12, 1921 (LU17087) by Pathé Exchange, Inc. With Gaylord Lloyd, Beatrice La Plante, James T. Kelly, George Rowe, Vera White, Leo Willis, Chris Lynton, Mark Jones.

The story starts off with the comedian eloping with the girl. She has dressed in boy's clothes and they have successfully eluded the irate Papa. As they are making their escape, however, they are confronted by a pirate crew who promptly put them to work scrubbing decks. A terrific storm arises and the ship is wrecked. Gaylord and the girl find themselves on a desert isle. Eventually, the father arrives and rescues his daughter, but ignores his aspiring son-in-law. The comedian then brings the comedy to an uproarious finish. (*Exhibitors Trade Review*, October 1, 1921).

In spite of Hal Roach's conviction that the world needed a new Lonesome Luke, neither exhibitors or audiences welcomed him home. About *Rough Seas* and Gaylord the September 24, 1921 *Moving Picture World* disenthused:

> In this offering the new star does not exhibit any marked ability as a comedian, although his work is satisfactory.

The settings for the film are a bit more exotic than the usual Roach short – London and at sea. The shipboard intrigue led to the title, which was dusted off ten years later for Charley Chase. Gaylord's love interest is played by Beatrice La Plante, who would turn up again in *Trolley Troubles.*

Beatrice La Plante (right center) pleads for Gaylord as officer George Rowe (left), James T. Kelly, and Vera White (right) want him arrested in *Rough Seas* (1921).

Although Toto and Dee Lampton's series hadn't worked out, Hal Roach continued to look for new talent to fill out his production schedule. In 1920 he hit upon La Plante, a petite actress with dark eyes and hair, who resembled a mix of Mabel Normand and Fay Tincher, and starred her in a series of one-reelers. According to studio sources she was born in France, but other sources say that she had really come from Illinois. She broke into pictures in 1919, and after supporting roles in a couple of dramas she made an impression as leading lady to Sessue Hayakawa in his comedy feature *The Beggar Prince* (1920).

Her surviving Roach titles include *Merely a Maid*, *Little Miss Jazz*, and *Start the Show* (all 1920), where she's charming and vivacious. Not only adept at broader physical comedy, she also showed a knack for crisply timed little bits of character business. Sadly, the series wasn't warmly received and died after five entries before it could really get started. From here she had a nice supporting role in the Eddie Lyons and Lee Moran feature *Fixed By George* (1920), but after a couple more features she finished her Roach contract supporting Gaylord in *Rough Seas* and *Trolley Troubles* in this series. Having recently married, she retired from films and passed away in 1973.

Gaylord and Beatrice La Plante think that they dodged the cops in *Rough Seas* (1921).

By 1921 there was a new crop of supporting players that had joined the Hal Roach stock company. Some perennials like Sammy Brooks, Charles Stevenson, James T. Kelly, and Jack O'Brien remained, but others like Bud Jamison, Margaret Joslin, and Harry Todd had moved on. Dee Lampton had died, and Fred Newmeyer moved behind the camera. One of the "newbies" seen in *Rough Seas* was Leo Willis. Born in Oklahoma, he started life as a cowboy and as such he was recruited for motion pictures. His earliest known films were for William S. Hart, such as *The Bargain* (1914) and *A Knight of the Trails* (1915). Becoming a personal friend of Hart's, Leo appeared in a slew of his pictures – from the first Thomas Ince-produced shorts to later features like *O'Malley of the Mounted* (1921) and *Wild Bill Hickok* (1923). The tough-looking Willis also turned up in other Ince productions and in westerns with Roy Stewart.

He started a fifteen-year residency on the Hal Roach lot in 1920, and as the studio pug-ugly he played various hoods, railroad bulls, hard-bitten salts, and even cops and detectives, that made screen life difficult for Charley Chase, Snub Pollard, the Spat Family, Will Rogers, and Laurel & Hardy. Leo also supported Harold Lloyd in *A Sailor-Made Man* (1921), *For Heaven's Sake* (1926), *Welcome Danger* (1929), and had his all-time best role as Leo Hickory in *The Kid Brother* (1927). Having also worked for Mack Sennett and Larry Semon, Willis, with his tough-guy line delivery, was just as busy in sound films. Besides his regular Roach outings he was also in features such as *City Streets* (1931), *Monkey Business* (1931), and *Kid Millions* (1934). After leaving films in the late 1930s, he returned to ranching, and died in 1952.

Moving Picture World (September 24, 1921): "This single-reel serves as the introductory release of a new series which Pathé is distributing, in which Gaylord Lloyd, brother of Harold Lloyd, is the star. It is of the burlesque knockabout type of comedy, and is of only average quality, several of the situations having been used before. In this offering the new star does not exhibit any marked ability as a comedian, although his work is satisfactory. The fact should, however, be taken into consideration that he is handicapped by the comparison of his work with that of his very successful brother.

A clever piece of work in this film is done by an unnamed actor in the role of the intoxicated man."

Exhibitors Trade Review (September 24, 1921): "'Rough Seas' is the title of the first of the new series of comedies featuring Gaylord Lloyd, brother of bespectacled Harold Lloyd. Gaylord Lloyd assumes a role similar to Harold Lloyd's first screen characterization Lonesome Luke. He is extremely active, and performs acrobatic 'stunts' with skill and gusto. Beatrice La Plante is his leading lady and support are the Hal Roach comedians, including George Rowe."

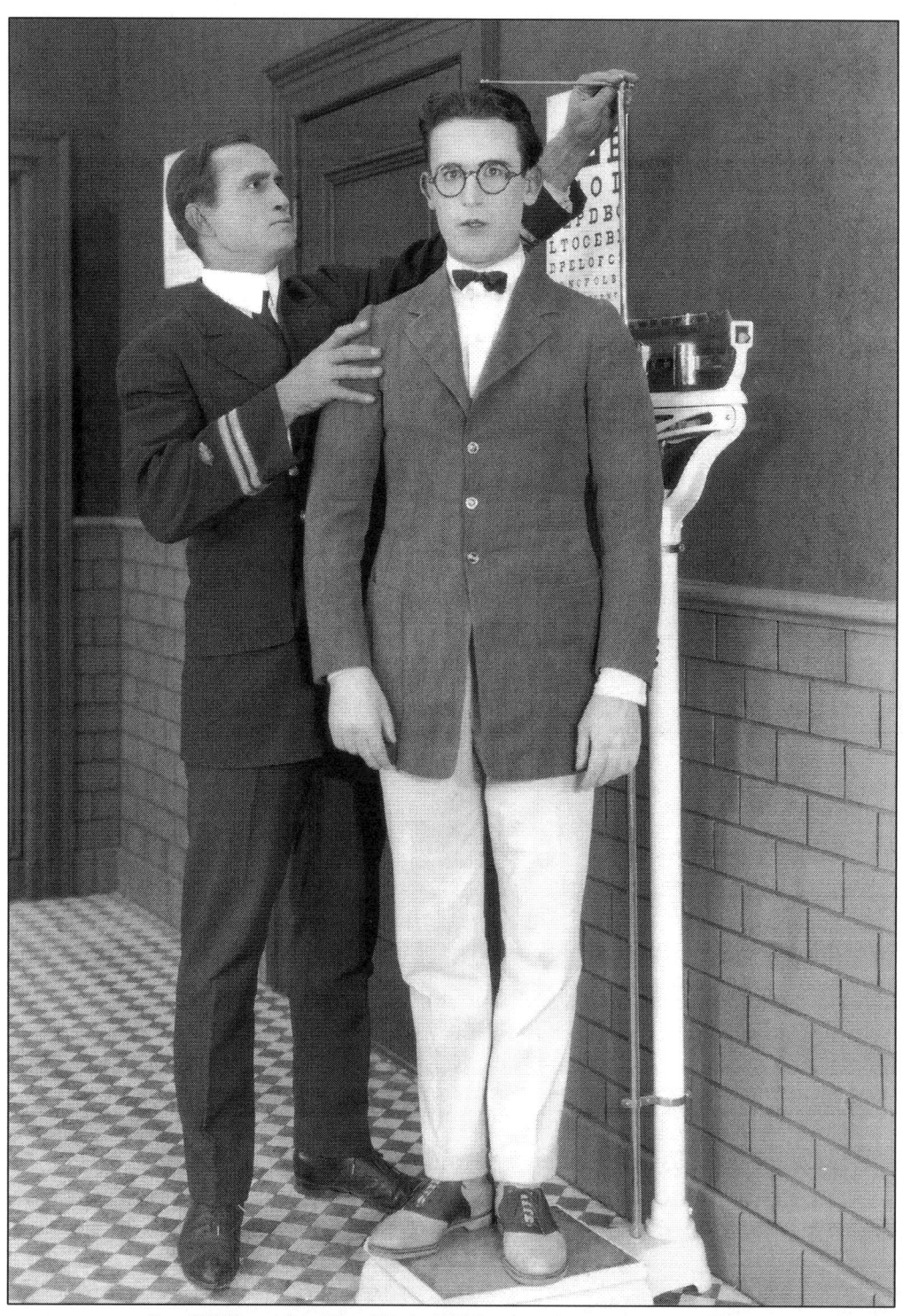

Leo Willis taking Harold's height in *A Sailor-Made Man* (1921).

The Lucky Number*

Released October 2, 1921. Produced by Hal Roach for the Rolin Film Company. Distributed by Pathé. Directed by Erle C. Kenton. Story by Hal Roach. Extant: LOB. One Reel. Copyrighted October 12, 1921 (LU17079) by Pathé Exchange, Inc. With Gaylord Lloyd, Estelle Harrison, Sammy Brooks, George Rowe, Mark Jones, Mollie Thompson, William Gillespie, Charles Stevenson, Vera White.

George Rowe, William Gillespie, Molly Thompson, Estelle Harrison and other guests watch Sammy Brooks and Gaylord clock in with *The Lucky Number* (1921).

Rich Lady Throttlemush finds that she must have some plumbing repairs made before her swell dinner takes place. The plumber and his assistant appear on the scene armed with blow-pipes, wrenches and time clock. After considerable effort the pipes are repaired and the assistant leaves the place. Then he hears the good news that he won a lottery that gives him the Throttlemush mansion. Just as he and the maid are about to claim it the whole thing blows up. But the hero is apparently not much concerned. He tells the maid he still has his health, and $7.50 in the bank. (Exhibitors Trade Review, October 1, 1921).

Perhaps the best of the Luke revival series, *The Lucky Number* is a straightforward action comedy with a rapid pace and plenty of gags. Gaylord seems much more at ease and comfortable in the role, and does some impressive stunt work – such as riding the end of a ladder that's protruding from the rear of his boss's auto. Something of a revisit of 1917's *Lonesome Luke, Plumber*, there's plenty of water leaks and people getting sprayed with hot jets of steam, and Luke's working of course causes a lot of problems for the swell dinner party that's trying to take place.

Stealing much of the focus as a drunken party guest is Mark Jones. Said to have been an acrobat on stage, Jones can be spotted in a few photos from the earliest Rolin films such as *Why the Boarders Left* (1915). Although he was with Rolin at the very beginning, he disappears and doesn't return until 1919 to become one of the most ubiquitous faces in the 1919 to 1923 Roach comedies. Usually seen beetle-browed with a big, black mustache, he played hotel managers, fathers, hoboes, and cops, but his specialty was a comic inebriate. As such he supported every star on the lot – Harold Lloyd, Snub Pollard, Paul Parrott, Our Gang, Eddie Boland, and even George Rowe in his only starring comedy *High Tide* (1922).

Mark Jones (left) and Sammy Brooks (right) don't have to work hard to steal
The Lucky Number (1921) from Gaylord.

The surviving footage of *The Lucky Number* has Jones turn up as a dinner party guest, but production photos suggest that he had an earlier traffic run-in with Luke and his boss Sammy Brooks. Jones left the Roach organization in 1923, and moved over to Jack White's Mermaid and Cameo Comedies to support Lige Conley and Cliff Bowes in shorts like *Exit Caesar* and *Hot Sparks* (both 1923). His only moment of stardom came in 1924's *Family Life*, a hilarious Jack White two-reeler. Jones' last screen appearances were in some early 1926 Roach shorts like *Don't Butt In* and *Pay the Cashier*. These were part of a crop of shorts held back and released later. After leaving movies he lived until 1965.

The poor society lady trying to throw the dinner party is played by Mollie Thompson, a plump character actress and Roach regular who specialized in mother-in-laws as well as society dames. Having worked with everyone on the lot from Harold Lloyd to Snub Pollard to Paul Parrott, one of her most memorable roles was in the premiere *Our Gang* comedy *One Terrible Day* (1922) where she was a wealthy lady who brings the Gang to her country home for fresh air and soon lives to regret it. She was also the casting director for the Roach Studio, a position she held at the time of her death in 1928.

The Lucky Number mostly circulates today in a cut-down version that was part of *The Laff-A-Bits*, a syndicated television package that sliced silent comedy shorts down to five minutes. Created and produced by Kay Arnold (aunt of Rosanne Barr's ex-husband Tom Arnold), the segments were used as filler between programs by TV stations in the 1980s.

Moving Picture World (October 1, 1921): "Not only has this single reeler, the second of the series featuring Gaylord Lloyd, a better story than the first one, but it shows Lloyd to much better advantage as a comedian, and he does good work. He has a style of work that is very promising and resembles very much that of his well-known brother Harold, whom he strongly resembles. Some of the business is not altogether new, but it is funny. The subject is also one offering good comedy possibilities as it deals largely with the attempt of a plumber to repair several leaks in a swell mansion. Lloyd has good opportunities and makes excellent use of them, as the plumber's helper."

Exhibitors Trade Review (October 1, 1921): "This is an improvement over the first Gaylord Lloyd effort. Perhaps it is more in his key. The comedy is a clever satire on the plumbing trade and full of humorous subtitles, which help it along."

A Zero Hero*

Released October 9, 1921 by the Rolin Film Company. Produced by Hal Roach for the Rolin Film Company. Distributed by Pathé. Directed by Erle C. Kenton. Story by Hal Roach. Extant: LOC, EYE. One reel. Copyrighted July 19, 1921 (LU17084) by Pathé Exchange, Inc. With Gaylord Lloyd, Estelle Harrison, Chris Lynton, Mark Jones, Vera White, William Gillespie, Charles Stevenson.

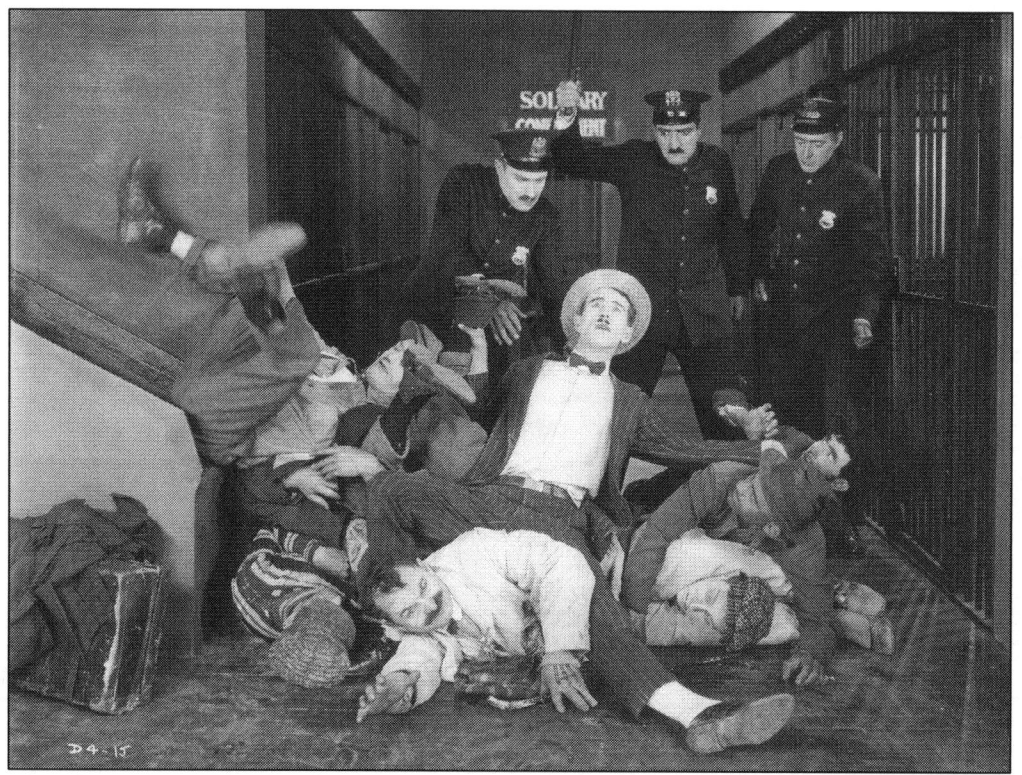

Gaylord and Mark Jones pile into the pokey in *A Zero Hero* (1921).

A bank clerk is in love with the banker's daughter. He wants a vacation but the boss can't see it. Then he stages a fake holdup in the outer office and after he has apparently beaten up the "robber" and recovered the cash he gets the expected reward from the banker, in the form of a vacation and substantial reward. He visits "Malaria Meadows," plays a queer game of golf and kicked up the dirt but not making a hole all day. (*Exhibitors Trade Review*, October 15, 1921).

A Zero Hero is an unusual one-reeler as it's split into two distinct halves – the first part where Luke is not working hard at the bank, and the second on a vacation golf course. This sort of split was done frequently with two-reel shorts, but usually comedy units had enough material for ten minutes of film. At the bank Luke is mostly irritating the girl's father (and the audience), but then pretends to be a crook so that he can play the hero as he "captures himself" in another room.

A comic making the illusion of fighting with himself was a popular routine, and was done most memorably by Max Linder in *Be My Wife* (1921) and Charley Chase in *Mighty Like a Moose* (1926). After a slight detour to jail, our hero arrives at the golfing resort Malaria Meadows to recycle the situation from 1915's *A Foozle at the Tee Party*. While Gaylord performs the fighting with himself routine well enough, the rest of his timing and gags are very weak, making this one of the lesser entries in the reincarnated Luke series.

Erle C. Kenton directed *A Zero Hero*, as well as *The Lucky Number,* and *Dodge Your Debts* in the series. A busy director of shorts and features for more than thirty years, he started his career as an actor, making his film debut at D.W. Griffith's Reliance-Majestic Company. After acting and assistant directing for Morosco and Lasky, he joined Keystone as a supporting player in 1915. Also filling in as a writer and assistant-director he graduated to full-director in 1919, and helmed shorts and features such as *Salome Vs. Shenandoah* (1919), *Fickle Fancy*, *Down on the Farm* (both 1920) and *A Small Town Idol* (1921) for Sennett.

While shooting *A Zero Hero* (1921) director Earle C. Kenton helps Estelle Harrison and Gaylord with their backswings.

He moved on to Roach, Punch Comedies, Fox Sunshine, and Universal, but after returning briefly to Sennett, he made the jump to features. Some of his best-known films include *Golf Widows* (1928), *Island of Lost Souls* (1932), W.C. Fields' *You're Telling Me* (1934), the Abbott & Costello vehicles *Pardon My Sarong* (1942) and *It Ain't Hay* (1943), and a number of Universal's horror franchise entries like *The Ghost of Frankenstein* (1942) and *The Houses of Frankenstein and Dracula* (1944 and 1945 respectively). In the 1950s he moved to television, and passed away in 1980.

Vera White eavesdropping on Gaylord and Beatrice La Plante in *Rough Seas* (1921).

Doing their best to support Gaylord are Estelle Harrison, Chris Lynton, Mark Jones, William Gillespie and Vera White. White was something of a female Lon Chaney. As the "woman of a thousand faces" of supporting comediennes, she was really as unknown to audiences of her day as she is today. Small and dark-haired, with features seemingly made of rubber, she played all types of characters. Although anonymous to moviegoers, the people making the films, particularly Stan Laurel and Hal Roach, were well aware of her skills and used her over and over.

Born in Australia, she married Joseph T. Everett in 1913, and they toured American vaudeville for many years as Joe and Vera White. Making their film debut in 1918 for the National Film Company, they wound up on the Roach lot in 1921. Joe made little impression and disappeared, but Vera became ubiquitous supporting Harold, Snub Pollard, Our Gang, Paul Parrott, Eddie Boland, Charley Chase, Laurel & Hardy, and this Lonesome Luke returned from the dead. Among her many turns her best remembered character was the spit-curled good time girl who's teamed with Kay Deslys to entertain Stan & Ollie in *We Faw Down* (1928).

In addition to working for Roach she made the rounds of all the various comedy units. She supported Brownie the Wonder Dog in *A Howling Success* (1923), played the innocent towns lady who's startled by Stan Laurel popping a blown-up paper bag in *Dr. Pyckle and Mr. Pride* (1925), and practically out cross-eyed Ben Turpin as his optically challenged wife in *The Cross-Eyed Family* (1927). She also turned up in features such as *Keep Smiling* (1925) with Monty Banks, and the drama *Is Your Daughter Safe?* (1927). The changeover to sound saw her appearances drop off. Although overlooked before and after she passed away in 1956, her films and performances are available on home video, shown theatrically, and still enjoyed today.

Motion Picture News (October 8, 1921): "Gaylord of the Lloyds certainly indicates in his mannerisms and style of comedy interpretation that he is a blood relative of Harold. Resembling his more famous brother in certain features he emphasizes this likeness by employing the same style of expression. And since Harold puts it over, there is no doubt that Gaylord will succeed. 'A Zero Hero' finds him making capital of his vacation. He is a bank employee when the comedy starts and is given the usual two weeks for putting over mock heroics which have to do with a fake robbery and rescue.

This bit of incident is familiar even when the fight with himself is exploited. The high spots arrive when he picks up his golf sticks and displays his novel system of the knocking the royal and ancient game for the goal. The small bit where he makes a deep excavation all around the tee-ball, which he never succeeds in hitting is certainly good for a laugh. And there is sufficient spontaneity of comedy action to make it an acceptable offering, Once in a while it lapses, but a title is brought to the rescue. And Gaylord Lloyd displays enough ability to establish a following, even though customers will think of Harold Lloyd and his clever offerings when they see him."

Exhibitors Herald (December 24, 1921): "Very good slapstick comedy. Look out Harold, or he will double cross you."

Dodge Your Debts*

Released October 16, 1921 by the Rolin Film Company. Distributed by Pathé. Directed by Erle C. Kenton. Extant: ACAD, FRIU. One reel. Copyrighted October 12, 1921 (LU17080) by Pathé Exchange, Inc. With Gaylord Lloyd, Estelle Harrison, Tiny Ward, George Rowe, William Gillespie, Jack O'Brien, Chai Hong.

Tiny Ward (center) throttles a bill collector as Gaylord and Estelle Harrison ponder how he should submit his bill in *Dodge Your Debts* (1921).

In England they don't stop at anything – that gang that hangs around Mike's Place in Bilgewater Lane. It's a tough neighborhood and it's here that Lloyd, as a bill collector, comes to present a bill to Mike himself. Incidentally, of course, Mike has a lovely daughter, Susie, and she sympathizes with the youthful collector, especially when he is shunted through the door by Big Mike. It ends with a free for all battle with the odds very much in favor of Mike's gang. The police look as if they'd been through a battle with the Sinn Fein. (Exhibitors Trade Review, October 22, 1921).

Like *Rough Seas*, this short has a British setting and shares some of the same background sets and locations. Many appear to be from Universal City's old Limehouse district. Big U maintained elaborate standing sets and would rent them out to different companies, which an independent producer like Joe Rock would use quite frequently in shorts such as *Dr. Pyckle and Mr. Pride* (1925) and *Alice Blues* (1926). *Dodge Your Debts* even has the pub with the swinging doors where Gaylord's brother Harold did a memorable chase with little Peggy Cartwright in 1919's *From Hand to Mouth*.

As to why a British setting for both this short and *Rough Seas* is a mystery. Perhaps the Roach staff thought that Gaylord looked funnier in an Eton collar, but outside of the novelty of having the supporting cast as Bobbies, and Cockney busker and coster types, the English setting doesn't add much, and creates a funny discrepancy during the climactic chase. Gaylord turns a corner and is suddenly in sunny California, where he jumps on the kind of double-decker bus that was used in tons of L.A.-made shorts. That Moose-Head Mike "just happens" to be sitting on the top level of the bus just adds to the dislocated fun. After Mike chases Gaylord off the bus and back to the British settings, the film ends with the mother of all cinematic brick throwing battles, which our hero survives since he is in England, by renting a suit of armor.

Playing Moose-Head Mike, Estelle Harrison's extremely tall father, is Roscoe "Tiny" Ward, who at over 6' 7" was always an extremely tall something. Since silent comedy thrived on exaggeration, Ward's tremendous height opposite the generally small star comedians made him a film comedy staple. More than just a sight gag gimmick, he was truly funny, and was capable of deft interplay with the likes of Chaplin and Harry Langdon. Born in Illinois, he attended Nebraska Military Academy, and at the University of Nebraska became the center rush for their football team (something he would relive with Harold Lloyd in 1925's *The Freshman*). He entered films in 1918, and stands out as a gigantic German soldier that's terrorized by Loyal Underwood's tiny commander in Chaplin's *Shoulder Arms*. Very soon he was making the rounds of all the comedy units – Fox Sunshine, Bulls Eye, and a gazillion films for Sennett and Roach such as *On Their Way* (1921), *When Summer Comes* (1922), and *The First 100 Years* (1924).

Tiny Ward bears down on Harold in *The Freshman* (1925).

Later in the 1920s he also worked for Century, Bray, and Weiss Brothers, and his feature appearances included *Spangles* (1926*), West of Zanzibar* (1928), and *City Lights* (1931). Remaining busy in sound shorts, he supported The Three Stooges, The Taxi Boys, El Brendel, and even Joe McDoakes. After the mid-1930s his appearances became more sporadic, but he remained in pictures until 1946. He was the regular Santa Claus in L.A.'s May Company department store before passing away in 1956.

One of Tiny Ward's minions is William Gillespie, who also appears with Gaylord's Luke as a party guest in *The Lucky Number*, and his rival in *A Zero Hero*. Gillespie was a silent comedy veteran who worked for the Selig Company, Essanay, and Charlie Chaplin's Mutual Comedy – he's *Easy Street's* drug addict and the café violinist in *The Immigrant* (both 1917) – before he took up residency at the Hal Roach Studios. There he was ubiquitous, supporting Harold Lloyd, Snub Pollard, Eddie Boland, Stan Laurel, and Our Gang, spending sixteen years playing everything from snooty department store managers to old tobacco-chewing farmers. His occasional features include *Grandma's Boy* (1922), *Safety Last* (1923), *Stop, Look and Listen*, and *Exit Smiling* (both 1926), and he remained a busy presence into the early 1930s.

An interesting moment early in the film is another bill collector who tries to collect on Moose-Head Mike, and is roundly beaten-up. Although not credited, the height, ability to stunt, and body language of this performer makes it apparent that it's Snub Pollard doing a cameo in a monocle and different style of mustache.

William Gillespie (left) and George Rowe (right) suffer through Frank Butler's (center) sour notes in *Tol'able Romeo* (1925). *Courtesy of Cole Johnson.*

Film Daily (October 30, 1921): "The scene of this comedy is planted among the Coster element in the East End of London. Gaylord Lloyd takes the part of the rent collector and presents his first bill to Mike, the celebrated man-killer of bill collectors. Both the police and Costers are mixed up in the rough house that follows and is kept up till the end of the reel. In the final brick fight between the police and Mike's army, the hero puts on a suit of armor and comes through the battle uninjured. When both armies are vanquished the collector enters the saloon and takes his money from the cash register. The comedy is swift in its action and contains a good number of laughs. It is built along 'Easy Street' lines, but has new atmosphere and additional business."

Trolley Troubles*

Released October 23, 1921 by the Rolin Film Company. Distributed by Pathé. Director Alf Goulding. Story by Hal Roach. Extant: LOB. One reel. Copyrighted October 12, 1921 (LU17081) by Pathé Exchange, Inc. With Gaylord Lloyd, Beatrice La Plante, George Rowe, Vera White, James T. Kelly.

A young man who gets in trouble with the police dons a motorman's uniform and gets on a trolley car to elude them. All kinds of curious things begin to happen, various strange types of people get aboard and finally a heavy man almost upsets the car. In trying to fix the trolley, the hero is shocked and cannot let go. The fat man and the girl come to his assistance and they get into the same predicament. The hero makes a hit with the girl, and a kind-hearted simp offers to run the car for him. He guides it up on the sidewalk and finally runs it into the drawing room of a palatial estate. (*Moving Picture World*, October 22, 1921).

Gaylord Lloyd on location in a candid shot from the making of *Trolley Troubles* (1921).

Trolley Troubles vies with *The Lucky Number* for being the funniest of the resuscitated Luke series. Harold had started the streetcar antics rolling with *Lonesome Luke's Trolley Troubles* (1916), which led to this remake with Gaylord, and then was redone again in 1922 with Paul Parrott as *Take Next Car.*

Paul Parrott is now engaged in a new comedy featuring the rivalry of two streetcar lines. The motor truck car, which first was used in Gaylord Lloyd's "Trolley Troubles" will be used in some of the action.

Close-Up, May 5, 1922

George Rowe in a publicity photo for the mid-1920s touring stage attraction
Movie Makers of Hollywood.

Other comics who had problems as motormen include Hank Mann in *The Nickel Snatcher* (1920) and Charley Chase in *Hasty Marriage* (1931), whereas Earl Montgomery and Joe Rock spent most of their time ogling their female passengers in 1919's *Fares and Fair Ones*. Riders on the trains have their own share of troubles, illustrated by Charlie Chaplin, Lloyd Hamilton, Ethelyn Gibson, and Mabel Normand as working stiffs trying to navigate wildly overcrowded cars in *Pay Day* (1922), *Nobody's Business*, *Working Winnie* (both 1926), and *Anything Once!* (1927). Harold has his own difficulties trying to escort a live turkey home via transit in *Hot Water* (1924), and even Oswald the Lucky Rabbit has animated streetcar issues in his own *Trolley Troubles* (1927).

A large part of Gaylord's *Trolley Troubles* comedy content is provided by the Roach company's mystery goof George Rowe. Mostly what's known about Rowe is that he appeared in a ton of Hal Roach shorts from 1920 to 1926. Referred to as the "wall-eyed gink" in Roach publicity, this walking sight gag looked like a visitor from another planet with his tiny head, jug-handle ears, moth-eaten mustache, and chicken neck that led to a scrawny and undernourished body. Of course, his most prominent feature was his eyes, whose pupils looked like magnets that were attracted to each other. At home in the early wild and crazy comedies of Paul Parrott, Snub Pollard, and Stan Laurel, Rowe no longer fit in once the Roach shorts became more sophisticated in the late 1920s, and after a few later appearances like *You're Darn Tootin'* (1928) he disappeared from the screen.

Alf Goulding directed *Trolley Troubles*, as well as *Rough Seas*. A well-seasoned comedy pro, and a valuable asset of the Roach organization, he was born in Melbourne, Australia and began working there as a child alongside Snub Pollard as a member of Pollard's Lilliputians. After years of touring in English and American vaudeville, he started at Roach in 1917, directing Harold's early glass character shorts. Although not knowing much about the camera, Harold said that Goulding "could pull gags out of the air, and thin air at that." Handling Lloyd shorts like *Look Pleasant, Please, On the Jump* (both 1918), and *From Hand to Mouth* (1919), when Snub Pollard was launched in his own pictures Goulding was in charge of initial entries like *Start Something*, *All at Sea*, and *Call for Mr. Caveman* (all 1919).

After continuing direction on the Pollard shorts, around 1921 he moved over to Century Comedies and put Harry Sweet, Brownie the Wonder Dog, and Baby Peggy through their paces. From there Goulding moved around directing the Smith Family Comedies for Mack Sennett, a couple of features for MGM, and even acting – playing with both Norma and Constance Talmadge in their pictures *A Lady* and *Learning to Love* (both 1925). The arrival of sound found him helping silent clowns like Lloyd Hamilton and Roscoe "Fatty" Arbuckle transition to talkies, and he directed numerous shorts for Warner Brothers, RKO, and Universal before he moved to England in 1936. He later returned to helm the Laurel & Hardy feature *A Chump at Oxford* (1940), but most of his later work was done in Europe (including uncredited work on Laurel & Hardy's *Atoll K* in 1950). His last film was in 1959, and he passed away in Hollywood in 1972.

Alf Goulding (right) directing Snub and Marie Mosquini with the new Roach Studio under construction. *Courtesy of The Museum of Modern Art.*

Film Daily (October 30, 1921): "Gaylord Lloyd and a trick trolley car that can run on and off the tracks are the stars of this laughable comedy. After an exciting chase, which starts the ball rolling in this picture, Lloyd climbs aboard a street car and plays motorman. He carries on a little flirtation with one of the pretty passengers, and the trolley leaves the tracks and runs up an alley. Passengers of varying type all help to contribute to the fun in the trolley. The picture is full of laughs and a few screams. The action is brisk and the ideas will amuse and satisfy almost any audience."

Exhibitors Trade Review (November 5, 1921: "The possibilities of the trick trolley car have been worked out to the limit and the comedy will probably please the majority of people who enjoy a good laugh."

Lonesome Luke's return didn't light any fires with exhibitors or audiences. The problem was that Gaylord just wasn't Harold:

> Gaylord Lloyd displays enough ability to establish a following, even though customers will think of Harold Lloyd and his clever offerings when they see him.
>
> *Motion Picture News*, October 8, 1921

> He's extremely active, and performs acrobatic "stunts" with skill and gusto.
>
> *Exhibitors Trade Review*, September 24, 1921

Gaylord sits with Estelle Harrison, director Earle C. Kenton (center with cigarette), Mark Jones (right), William Gillespie (left) and other cast and crew of 1921's *A Zero Hero*.

In all five shorts, Gaylord performs all the physical action and business efficiently and with crispness, but he was totally lacking in any kind of real screen charisma. It would be unfair to expect him to have anything like Harold's immense charm, but sadly, Gaylord didn't even match up to Snub Pollard or Paul Parrott. The Roach organization saw the handwriting on the wall and put the kibosh on the series.

The failure of this truncated Gaylord revival was the stake through Lonesome Luke's heart – he was truly cold. With the end of the series Gaylord went back to assisting on Harold's productions and working on other films (see *Luke's Double*, page 114). Hal Roach had bought Dwight Whiting out in 1918, and by 1919 he acquired sole ownership of the Rolin Film Company. It soon became the Hal Roach Studios, and a new production plant was built in Culver City at 8892 West Washington Boulevard.

Rolin Film to Celebrate New Studio's Opening

Producer Hal E. Roach soon will move the Harold Lloyd Comedy Company and the Rolin Comedy Troupers, headed by "Snub" Pollard, to the new home of the Rolin Company at Culver City, a suburb of Los Angeles.

It is promised to be some house warming. A Spanish barbeque, vaudeville show and athletic events are on the program. The Spanish feast is to be spread on the new stage. The famous Rolin Company band will then take a chunk out of the musical program. This band has a large repertoire and producer Roach says they play both pieces well.

Motion Picture News, January 31, 1920

Although there was a new incorporation, the shorts kept the old name until mid-1922, so the reconstituted Luke shorts were still released as Rolin Comedies. At the same time the studio was having tremendous success with Harold's glasses character shorts, moving from one to two reels, and then finally to features.

Their initial full-length films like *Grandma's Boy* (1922) and *Safety Last* (1923) made Harold one of the biggest stars of the 1920s. But, after working together for ten years, Hal and Harold went their separate ways after 1923's *Why Worry?* On the surface the split was amicable, but Harold had been planning the move for at least a year before, setting up the Harold Lloyd Corporation on April 24, 1922. Instead of being more or less in charge of his features, Harold became his own producer with distribution through Pathé.

Hal Roach later claimed that he insisted on the split, saying that Harold needed too much of his time and guidance to be funny, but the truth is the loss of Lloyd left his studio in the lurch. Harold had become a feature film star, and Hal had no one to take his place. While the studio was busy turning out popular shorts with Our Gang, Snub Pollard, Stan Laurel, and Will Rogers, as well as action-adventure serials with Edna Murphy and Ruth Roland, it wasn't the same as making money-making features.

Harold and Hal together in the 1920s, and later reminiscing in the 1930s.

Rolin lost a good deal of its prestige when Harold left, and really wouldn't regain it until Laurel & Hardy became feature stars in the 1930s. On top of that, key members of the studio staff left with Harold – Fred Newmeyer, Sam Taylor, T.J. Crizer, Tim Whelan, Wallace Howe, and Roy Brooks. Not an easy roster to replace, but eventually Roach filled in by giving Charles Parrott his own series (as Charley Chase), promoting Fred Guiol and James Parrott, and hiring James W. Horne, Stan Laurel (actually a rehire), F. Richard Jones, Clyde Bruckman, and especially Leo McCarey.

After the split the ex-partners always maintained a friendly front to their relationship, but it had always been fraught with ups and downs. Early on, this manifested itself in Harold's frequent walks for more salary and autonomy, as well as acknowledgment of his important contribution to the films. Although Roach's success was tied up with Harold's, or perhaps because of this, he had a tendency to take Harold for granted. It may be that Hal continued to think of Harold as the apprentice comedian he was when they started Rolin, but Harold had quickly become a seasoned practitioner, and as the hard-working breadwinner for the unit, it must have infuriated him when Hal started new "finds" like Dee Lampton and Toto at double his salary. Sometimes it would require the mediation of Pathé, who would step in, smooth the waters, and bring the team back together.

Going out on his own in 1923 proved that Harold had learned screen comedy inside and out. His films got better and better as he lavished more time and money on them, which led to an extremely high standard of comedy features that produced masterworks like *The Freshman* (1925), *The Kid Brother*

(1927), and *Speedy* (1928). Harold's success as a producer also encompassed eight excellent Edward Everett Horton two-reelers made under the aegis of his Hollywood Productions.

When sound swept the film industry Harold jumped on the bandwagon – redoing a completed silent feature, *Welcome Danger* (1929), as a talkie. It was his largest box office hit, but soon after middle age and the Depression made his screen character dated and he began to lose his audience – despite great sound comedies like *Movie Crazy* (1932) and *The Milky Way* (1936). By the end of the 1930s his film work tapered off, and after a disappointing experience starring in Preston Sturges' *The Sin of Harold Diddlebock* (1947) he retired. Besides devoting his boundless energy to charitable work and hobbies, Harold maintained strict control of his films and was his own archivist (purposely excluding Lonesome Luke). In the 1960s he released a couple of compilation features with success, and remained active to his death in 1971.

Hal with two of his late 1920s players – Martha Sleeper (left) and Viola Richard (right).

Although there was a slight dip for Roach when Harold moved off on his own, he soon restocked his talent pool, and quickly hit his stride again. In fact, with Leo McCarey as director-general of the studio the late 1920s saw the final peak of silent comedy take place at the Roach lot with the amazing comedies of Charley Chase, Our Gang, Max Davidson, and especially Laurel & Hardy.

When sound arrived, Roach was in an enviable position as his top stars made the transition easily, and actually became more popular talking. For a while he continued making his comedies in the loose way of the silent days, but by the mid-1930s with production costs rising, Roach decided he could make only features. Charley Chase was fired, and Our Gang sold to MGM, with only Laurel & Hardy left to continue the original Roach style of comedy until *Saps at Sea* in 1940. Roach branched out with all types of features such as *Topper* (1937), *Of Mice and Men* (1939), *One Million B.C.*, *Captain Caution*, and *Turnabout* (all 1940).

The 1940s need for

eatures led Hal to create what he called "Streamliners" – featurettes of about fifty minutes. They were essentially short and snappy little "B" pictures that starred William Bendix, Zasu Pitts, William Tracy, and Jimmy Rogers. They lasted through 1943, and through much of World War II the studio was leased out to the U.S. government to make army training and propaganda films. After the War "Fort Roach" returned to civilian filmmaking, and primarily produced television shows. Some of their popular items included *My Little Margie*, *Racket Squad*, and *Screen Directors Playhouse*.

By this time, Hal had turned production over to his son Hal Jr. Following some years of financial ups and downs the studio closed in 1959. Officially dissolved in 1962 with everything auctioned off, it was physically demolished in 1963. When interviewed Hal said the end of the studio wasn't a terrible blow to him as the army had wrecked most of the equipment when they occupied the facility, so most of the original items had already been replaced. An interesting sidebar about one good thing that came from the studio auction comes from film historian Sam Gill. Robert Knutson was head of the University of Southern California's Special Collections, and told Sam about his visit to the event:

> Bob explained that he just went to the auction to observe the goings-on, but when out there he was finding boxes and boxes of "stuff" strewn all over the studio, stuff meaning company records and I think photos as well. Bob asked a security guard what was going to happen to all that material, and the guard said, "Oh, those aren't part of the auction. Why? Do you want them?" Bob said yes, and according to what Bob told me, he gathered up all the boxes he could find, put them in the trunk of his car, and brought them all to USC. How's that for serendipity?

This is now USC's Hal Roach Production Files Collection, which includes production notes, payroll ledgers and other financial records, and scripts.

In later years Roach would get litigious, suing individuals like Charles Tarbox and organizations like NBC-TV for "pirating and mutilating" his silent shorts. He also maintained that he wasn't getting credit or recompense for some of the early films used in Harold's compilation features (although Harold had purchased the rights from Pathé). Hal also outlived Harold by twenty years (and practically everyone else who had ever worked for him), and developed a habit of taking credit for all innovations (such as creation of the glasses character). While he was alive Harold remained stoic on this, but a lot of it must have rankled. Living to one hundred and becoming notoriously hard of hearing, between receiving honors and awards, Hal spent much of his time kicking around ideas for numerous projects or playing cards at the Bel-Air Country Club up to his death in 1992.

1921 Pathé Bulletin ad for the Harold Lloyd one-reel reissues.

While Harold and Hal thrived on their own, Lonesome Luke didn't fare so well, and was treated critically very much as he had been on screen (slapped, punched, and kicked in the rear). Throughout the 1920s Harold's early glasses one and two-reelers were reissued by Pathé. Not so Luke. There was zero interest in him. In addition much of the original materials were thought to have been destroyed in a big 1919 Pathé fire. A few years ago the

Library of Congress estimated that 75% of silent films have been lost. The *Luke* series is a good example of this, with the majority of the titles missing, and those known to exist scattered around the world at various film archives and difficult to see.

In the 1920s and 1930s there should have been surviving release prints of the Lukes around, but Harold's attitude that they were inferior and not worth seeking out ruled the day. There was another large Pathé fire in 1938, but according to cinematic urban legend, most of the *Lonesome Lukes* were lost in a 1943 vault fire on Harold's Greenacres estate. The August 6, 1943 *New York Times* reported:

Harold surveying the damage from the 1943 fire at Greenacres.

Harold Lloyd Saved From Fire By Wife
It Destroys Star's Old Silent Films Valued at $2,000,000

Beverly Hills, Calif., Aug 5 – Harold Lloyd was overcome but rescued today in an explosion and fire at his Benedict Canyon Drive estate. Original films of the former film star's silent era comedies, which he valued at $2,000,000 were destroyed.

He was rescued by his wife Mrs. Mildred Davis Lloyd, who caught him as he collapsed in the doorway of his film vault, where the explosion occurred. Seven firemen and one employee at the Lloyd estate were overcome by chlorine and were taken to the hospital.

Mr. Lloyd's former secretary, Roy Brooks, now a Navy yeoman, was blown from his bed by the force of the explosion. He was sleeping next to the engine room, which is connected with film vault, swimming pool, gymnasium and other service buildings on the estate. These buildings are some distance from the mansion, which was undamaged.

This was in the "paper of record," but Harold's good friend Richard Simonton Jr. reports that the comedian gave a very different private version of the incident:

It's time to dispel the myths surrounding Harold Lloyd's 1943 film vault fire and it won't be an easy task. The newspaper photo of Harold surveying the aftermath, and its accompanying text, have been the proof necessary to making the story widely believed, but it is mostly Fake News! (You've heard of fake news?). Harold was not happy with the story and wasn't sure how much to blame his publicist, but someone got carried away, adding exciting details with no basis in fact, though they did sell papers.

According to Harold – and he told this many times – there was not much of value in that vault. In fact, it wasn't even a proper film vault, but more of a storage room that should not have had nitrate film in it. He said the door blew off with great force and might have severely injured the watchman, had he not just passed by. Harold was in the house, a long walk from the vault, but acknowledged there would have been nothing to save even immediately after the explosion. Nitrate film is fierce. There's no time for roasting marshmallows. That remark is no more silly than the published "facts."

Harold insisted he did not rush in to save what he could, he was not dragged out unconscious by his wife, and seven firemen were not overcome by chlorine gas fumes, as the newspapers had claimed.

As for films lost to the fire, Harold said it was only trims and odds and ends, and a couple of prints of later films produced by the Harold Lloyd Corporation. Nothing that mattered or was irreplaceable. Before Harold's death in 1971, people had already begun to assume that any film not in his real nitrate film vaults, must have been lost to that fire: the early Lonesome Luke films for example. But he believed the Lukes had burned up in a fire at Pathé in 1919 and he didn't want them anyway, so never had any.

Billy Fay (right) helps Harold have a damp smoke in *Bughouse Bellhops* (1915).

So, Harold attested that he didn't have any *Lukes* and didn't want them. Like most film buffs on first hearing about this fire I also assumed that the *Lukes* had been lost in it – although I went a bit further and suspected that Harold may have set the fire on purpose to get rid of them.

By the 1950s Harold's negativity about the films, combined with the lack of examples to be viewed, caused the standard critical consensus to solidify that the *Luke* shorts had no merits of their own and were only worth noting as a transition period for Harold. They certainly weren't worth pursuing or actively seeking out. Despite the efforts of a few historians such as Eileen Bowser, Sam Gill and Raymond Borde to the contrary, this is still the critical attitude today.

But during ten productive years, Harold Lloyd and Hal Roach became a formidable cinematic force, and Lonesome Luke was the lighting rod, the catalyst, for their success. Without him the world might never have heard of either man. Luke's popularity enabled them to lay the foundation for careers that developed and defined screen comedy.

BIBLIOGRAPHY

Luke Lugs Luggage (1916) and weighs in Bebe's chapeau.

Periodicals – Trade Publications and Newspapers

Altoona Times, 1915 - 1917

American Cinematographer, 1992

Camera!, 1919 – 1924

Close-Up, 1922

The Daily Advance, 1915 – 1917

Detroit Free Press, 1915 - 1917

Edison Kinetogram, 1911 - 1916

Exhibitors Herald, 1920 – 1927

Exhibitors Trade Review, 1922 – 1927

Film Daily, 1919 – 1933

Film Fun, 1916 – 1926

The Hollywood Reporter, 1934

The Hutchinson News, 1915 – 1917

Intelligence Journal, 1915 - 1917

Kalem Kalender, 1911 – 1915

The Kane Republican, 1915 - 1917

Mahoney City Record, 1915 - 1917

Modern Screen, 1934

Morning Press, Santa Barbara, 1915 - 1917

The Motion Picture Classic, 1928

Motion Picture News, 1913 – 1933

The Motion Picture Story Magazine, 1911 - 1914

Motography, 1913 – 1918

The Movie Magazine, 1916

Moving Picture World, 1910 – 1927

The New York Times, 1943 - 1992

Pathé Bulletins, 1910 – 1928

Pathex Catalog, 1927

Patterson Morning Call, 1915 - 1917

Photoplay, 1917 – 1940

Photoplayers Weekly, 1915 - 1916

The Photo-Play Journal, 1916 - 1921

Picture-Play, 1915 – 1938

The Salt Lake Tribune, 1915 - 1917

The Screamer, 1916

Screen Actor, 1987

Variety, 1910 – 1966

Periodicals –Articles

Caslavsky, Karel. *American Comedy Series: Filmographies 1914 – 1930.* Griffithiana # 51/52, October 1994.

Mitchell, Glenn. *Glenn Mitchell Interviews Hal Roach: Hal Roach in London, October 1986.* The Laurel & Hardy Magazine Vol. 2, No. 3, February, 1987.

Slide, Anthony. *Hal Roach.* The Silent Picture #6, Spring, 1970.

Books

Bengtson, John. *Silent Visions: Discovering Early Hollywood and New York Through the Films of Harold Lloyd.* Solana Beach, California: Santa Monica Press, 2011.

Braff, Richard E. *The Universal Silents.* Jefferson, North Carolina: McFarland & Co., 1999.

Brownlow, Kevin. *The Parade's Gone By.* New York: Alfred A. Knopf, 1968.

Blum, Daniel. *A Pictorial History of the Silent Screen.* New York: G.P. Putnam's & Sons, 1953.

Cahn, William. *Harold Lloyd's World of Comedy.* New York: Duell, Sloan and Pearce, 1964.

Calman, Craig. *100 Years of Brodies with Hal Roach.* Albany, Georgia: BearManor Media, 2014.

D'Agostino Lloyd, Annette. *The Harold Lloyd Encyclopedia.* Jefferson, North Carolina: McFarland & Company, Inc., 2004.

Dardis, Tom. *Harold Lloyd: The Man on the Clock.* New York: The Viking Press, 1983.

Everson, William K. *The Films of Hal Roach.* New York: The Museum of Modern Art, 1971.

Kiehn, David. *Broncho Billy and the Essanay Company.* Berkley, California: Farwell Books, 2003.

Kerr, Walter. *The Silent Clowns.* New York: Alfred A. Knopf, 1975.

Lahue, Kalton C. *World of Laughter: The Motion Picture Comedy Short.* Norman, Oklahoma: University of Oklahoma Press, 1966.

Lloyd, Harold, with Stout, Wesley W. *An American Comedy.* New York: Longman's, Greene and Co., 1928.

Magliozzi, Ronald S. *Treasures from the Film Archives.* Metuchen, New Jersey: Scarecrow Press, 1988.

Maltin, Leonard. *The Great Movie Comedians.* New York: Bell, 1978.

Massa, Steve. *Slapstick Divas: The Women of Silent Comedy.* Georgia: BearManor Media, 2017.

_____. *Rediscovering Roscoe: The Films of "Fatty" Arbuckle.* Orlando: BearManor Media, 2019.

Mast, Gerald. *The Comic Mind*. Indianapolis, Indiana: Bobbs-Merrill, 1973.

McCaffrey, Donald W. *4 Great Comedians: Chaplin-Lloyd-Keaton-Langdon*. New York: A.S. Barnes & Co., 1968.

_____. *Three Classic Silent Comedies Starring Harold Lloyd*. Rutherford: Farleigh Dickinson University Press, 1976.

Mitchell, Glenn. *A-Z of Silent Film Comedy*. London: Batsford, 1998.

Montgomery, John. *Comedy Films*. London: George Allen and Unwin, 1954.

Moore, Joseph, Farr, Robert, and Roberts, Richard M. *Hal Roach Studios Filmography 1914 – 1948*. Phoenix, Arizona: Practical Press, 2013.

Roberts, Richard M. *Smileage Guaranteed: Past Humor, Present Laughter*. Phoenix, Arizona: Practical Press, 2013.

Reilly, Adam. *Harold Lloyd: The King of Daredevil Comedy*. New York: Collier Books, 1977.

Robinson, David. *The Great Funnies*. London: Studio Vista/Dutton, 1969.

Schickel, Richard. *Harold Lloyd: The Shape of Laughter*. Boston, Mass. New York Graphic Society, 1974.

Skretvedt, Randy. *Laurel & Hardy: The Magic Behind the Movies*. California: Bonaventure Press, 2016.

Slide, Anthony. *The New Historical Dictionary of the American Film Industry*. London: Fitzroy Dear Publisher, 1998.

Stone, Rob. *Story by Grover Jones*. Culpeper, Virginia: Split Reel, 2024.

Vance, Jeffrey, and Lloyd, Suzanne. *Harold Lloyd: Master Comedian*. New York: Abrams, 2002.

Walker, Brent E. *Mack Sennett's Fun Factory*. Jefferson, North Carolina: McFarland & Co., 2010.

Ward, Richard Lewis. *A History of the Hal Roach Studios*. Illinois: Southern Illinois University Press, 2005.

Online Sources

Another Nice Mess – Hal Roach Studios 1914 – 1948
   lordheath.com

Library of Congress Copyright Descriptions Collection
   loc.gov/collections/motion-picture-copyright-descriptions

Media History Digital Library and Lantern Search
   mediahistoryproject.org

Other Sources

Robinson Locke Collection of Theatrical Clippings 1870 – 1920. New York Public Library for the Performing Arts.

ABOUT THE AUTHOR

Steve Massa is the author of *Lame Brains and Lunatics 2, Victor Moore and his Klever Komedies* (with Rob Stone), *Rediscovering Roscoe: The Films of "Fatty" Arbuckle, Slapstick Divas: The Women of Silent Comedy, Marcel Perez: The International Mirth-Maker,* and *Lame Brains and Lunatics.* Co-host with Ben Model of the live-streamed *Silent Comedy Watch Party,* he has organized and curated comedy film programs for the Museum of Modern Art, Library of Congress, the Museum of the Moving Image, the Smithsonian Institution, the Pordenone Silent Film Festival, AFI Silver Theatre, London's Cinema Museum, Niles Essanay Silent Film Museum, Bristol's Slapstick Festival, and Japan's Kobe Classic Film Festival.

In addition to consulting with EYE Filmmuseum, Netherlands, the Cineteca di Bologna, the Royal Belgian Cinematheque, and other archives, Steve has contributed notes to the National Film Registry, the National Film Preservation Foundation, the Criterion Collection, and the San Francisco Silent Film Festival. He is a founding member of Silent Cinema Presentations, which produces NYC's *Silent Clowns* Film Series.

Steve has also provided essays and commentary tracks to many comedy DVD and Blu-Ray collections such as *The Forgotten Films of Roscoe "Fatty" Arbuckle, Harry Langdon: Lost and Found, Becoming Charley Chase,* Kino Video's *Buster Keaton: The Short Film Collection,* and *The Mack Sennett Collection,* Vol 1. He has co-curated Undercrank Productions' *The Mishaps of Musty Suffer,* Volumes 1 &2, the *Alice Howell Collection,* as well as the award-winning *Marcel Perez Collection,* Volumes 1 & 2, *Edward Everett Horton: 8 Silent Comedies,* and *Raymond Griffith: The Silk Hat Comedian,* and the upcoming *Rediscovering Roscoe* Blu-Ray/DVD.

INDEX

ALSO AVAILABLE . . .

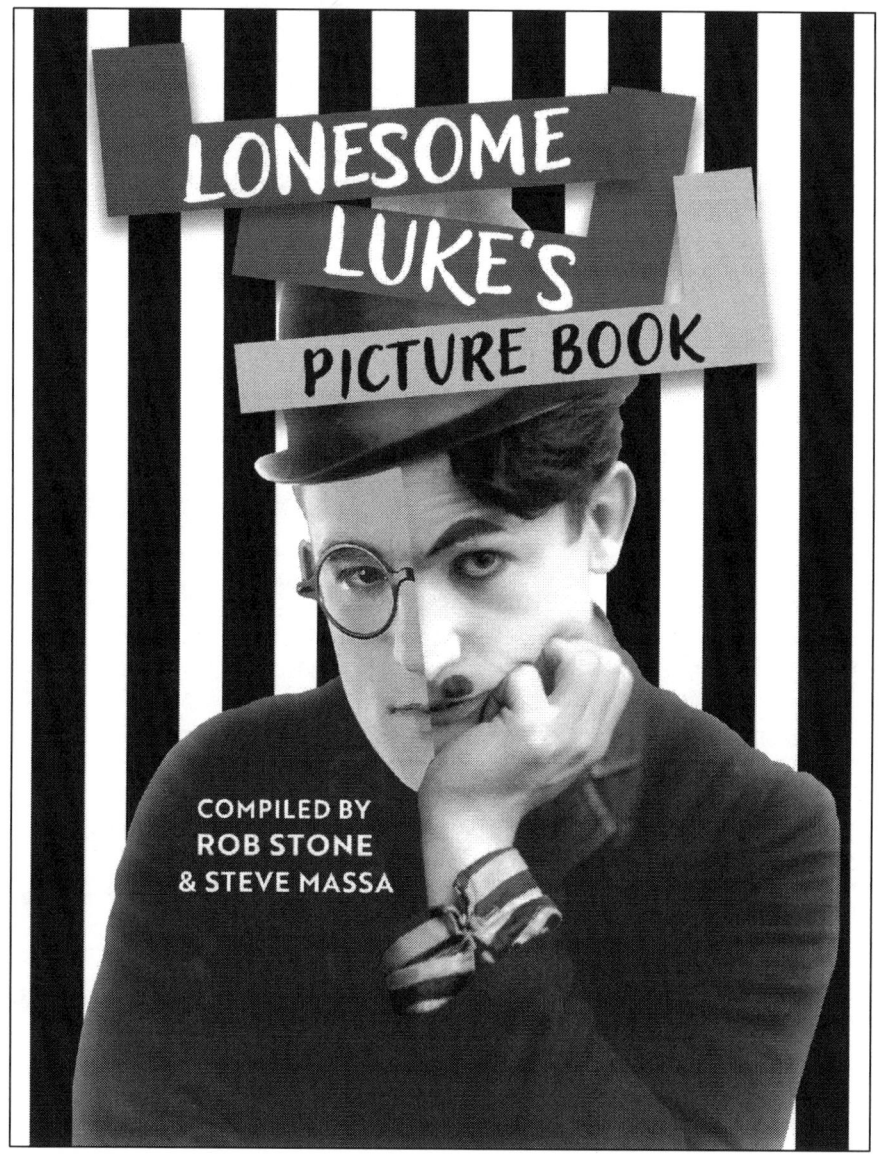

Dozens and dozens of additional photographs
highlighting Hal Roach, Harold Lloyd
and the Rolin Film Company.
8 ½ x11, 100 pages.

SPLIT REEL
www.split-reel.com